Praise for
Building Better Plots

Building Better Plots

Robert Kernen

WRITER'S DIGEST BOOKS
CINCINNATI, OHIO

www.writersdigest.com

Other fine Writer's Digest Books are available from your local bookstore or direct from the publisher.

Visit our Web site at www.writersdigest.com for information on more resources for writers.

To receive a free E-mail newsletter delivering tips and updates about writing and about Writer's Digest products, send an E-mail with "Subscribe Newsletter" in the body of the message to newsletter-request@writersdigest.com, or register directly at our Web site at www.writersdigest.com.

03   02   01   00   99   5   4   3   2   1

Library of Congress Cataloging-in-Publication Data

Kernen, Robert.
    Building better plots / by Robert Kernen.—1st ed.
        p.   cm.
    Includes index.
    ISBN 0-89879-903-1 (alk. paper)
    1. Authorship. 2. Fiction—Technique. 3. Plots (Drama, novel, etc.) I. Title.
PN218.K47   1999
808.3—dc21   98-55333
                                                  CIP

Editor: David Borcherding
Production editors: Nicole R. Klungle and Michelle Howry
Designer: Wendy Dunning
Cover designer: Brian Roeth
Cover photography by © Digital Vision
Production coordinator: John Peavler

ABOUT THE AUTHOR

Robert Kernen has written for just about every imaginable medium. He began his career as a copywriter and producer, creating radio programs that have aired worldwide. He wrote and produced the first English language radio show ever aired in the People's Republic of China.

A graduate of the University of Southern California Film School, he has written numerous screenplays. Proving the age-old Hollywood adage, "What I really want to do is direct," Robert co-wrote, produced and directed the 16mm film *Driven to You*.

He moved into children's entertainment when he began working with the late legendary entertainer Shari Lewis. He won an Emmy Award for his writing on "Lamb Chop's Play-Along." Always interested in finding new ways to tell a story, Robert has most recently worked in new media as a writer and producer of programming for WebTV and Women.com's Crayola Family Play.

He lives in the San Francisco Bay Area with his wife P.J. McCormick, a writer and food critic.

TABLE OF CONTENTS

Introduction

Think about every book you ever read that had you turning pages until well past bedtime, every film that kept you glued to your seat, every play that ever held you breathless in the dark. What kept you there? Characters may win your sympathy, the atmosphere may draw you in, but it's the plot that rivets you to the story and keeps you on edge until the final page, the credit roll or the curtain call. Without a compelling story, even the best writing is missing something, and the audience's experience is diminished. The plot is the engine that propels drama—whether on page, stage or screen.

One must approach the act of storytelling with the deliberation of an architect building a skyscraper. The foundation may be constructed first, but it can't be built properly without knowing exactly where the pinnacle of the structure ultimately will be. The author must know her story thoroughly, from beginning to end, before the actual construction can begin. The secret to this craft is knowing the basic building blocks of drama and how to manipulate them. A skyscraper may be just a magnificent pile of bricks to the layperson, but the architect knows intimately the foundation, the steel skeleton, everything from cornerstone to cornice.

This book will introduce you to the tried-and-true elements that make up all good plots. We'll examine them in depth and see what makes them work and how they work together. Good stories don't happen by accident. Good plots come about through great planning and craftsmanship. A gasp-producing twist, such as Queequeg's life-saving coffin appearing at the end of *Moby Dick*, wouldn't be very effective if the seeds of that twist hadn't been planted much earlier as Ishmael watched him build the strange wooden box.

Writing good plots is more about skill and craftsmanship than talent. It helps to have an active, fertile imagination—a flair for asking "what if?"—but executing your scenario takes skill and practice. This book will provide examples, exercises and inspiration to help you form your plots effectively.

Building good plots requires the writer to look at the story's overall construction while zooming in on the most minute plot detail. You'll be introduced to a technique for constructing your story that will make these transitions from big picture to fine detail easier to conceive and manage.

You'll learn to become an inveterate planner, making outlines and sub-outlines, graphs, charts, whatever tools you need to lay your plot framework. Then you'll learn ways to approach the fine art of tinkering. Once your story has become a first draft, you must be able to go back to it and fine-tune it, trying new ideas and moving the pieces of the plot around to find the perfect fit. The cliché "writing is rewriting" is most assuredly true.

I will use examples from popular novels and films wherever possible to illustrate the various concepts. The end of each section of the book has lists and exercises to help you apply what you've learned. Some ask you to compare or dissect sample plots. Others will give you practice at applying the discussion principles to your own work. The book is arranged to help you take your own story from concept to reality, building it as you go. It provides lists of questions for you to ask yourself at each phase of story development. These questions will help keep you focused on your objective and spark insight into the strengths and weaknesses of your story. I encourage you to try these exercises as you read the book, and also to come back to them each time you are working on a rewrite or a new story.

You will learn a technique for outlining your plot using 3×5 cards, a simple way to organize and keep track of your story. This tool may not work for everyone, but take some time to try it; then modify it to your own needs. Use it as a basis for developing your own tools for use in your work.

Try not to look on these principles, guidelines and tools as limiting. They aren't there to inhibit your creativity, but rather to set it free. Many writers, particularly beginners, find the intangible quality of writing makes it difficult to get started or to overcome blocks or problems. The craft of writing can help you to get over artistic hurdles. The principles of effective plotting then become tools. They provide structure, guidance and clues to help when the going gets rough. Just as the same stars can guide different travelers to different places, the principles of storytelling, while consistent, enable the telling of infinite tales.

Once you have mastered these principles and can apply them effectively, you can challenge or break them as you see fit. Once they are second nature to you, they will disappear into your story, leaving only the fruits of your imagination built upon your strong, but invisible, framework.

The Building
Materials of Plot

CHAPTER ONE

The Narrative

I t is important to understand what we mean when we talk about the plot of a book. Often if you ask someone to recount a story from a book or film, what you'll hear is a series of events that made up the action. Frequently, the teller will describe these events in chronological order, even if that isn't how they occurred in the book or film.

The plot of a book is not just the events of that story. It is the way those events are recounted to the audience.

There isn't much craft involved in telling an audience a sequence of events as they happened. The art of the plot is in how those events are described to the audience. Think of a historical event, such as World War II. Hundreds of books, movies and plays have been written about the single biggest event of the twentieth century. And while they all tell of the same basic events—Germany's aggressive expansion throughout Europe, the fall of Paris, the Blitzkrieg, the concentration camps, the eventual involvement of the United States, D-day, the liberation of Paris and the eventual surrender of the Nazis—each story takes a different perspective on the war.

The plot of a book is not just the events of that story. It is the way those events are recounted to the audience.

The stories that were successful, those that held their audiences' attention, are ones in which the author found a compelling way to present the events. The events told in these stories are influenced by the way the author interpreted and told them. They were given a spin, a perspective unique to that plot. Out of that manipulation of events (however minor) grew the plot's compelling nature.

A plot isn't merely a string of occurrences; it is a carefully orchestrated telling of events that might include breaking up their temporal order, taking out certain pieces or emphasizing other pieces. It is in that manipulation that a simple story becomes a plot.

Choosing a Subject

People tend to read authors who tell great stories, and the first step toward telling a great story is picking a great subject. Choosing the subject of your story will be the first challenge you face when you begin writing. When you have a story in mind, ask yourself the questions about subject matter (see the quiz on p. 8).

After you've answered the first of each of these pairs of questions, make a list of the specific elements requested in the second question. Having these elements written down will give you a good source of ideas to draw on later.

If you were able to come up with satisfactory answers to most of the questions, you have a strong subject for your plot. If there are certain questions where your answers felt weak or inadequate, you know that those are areas you will have to work on, and areas that you may want to change altogether. If you feel like your answers to *all* of the questions aren't satisfactory, you may want to completely overhaul or disregard your idea and look for something else.

Chances are, some element of your idea was the kernel of inspiration that made you think it would be a great story to tell. If that kernel stood out to you, it's likely that there is something of merit in it. Go

---

A plot isn't merely a string of occurrences; it is a carefully orchestrated telling of events that might include breaking up their temporal order, taking out certain pieces or emphasizing other pieces. It is in that manipulation that a simple story becomes a plot.

EXERCISE

Take a favorite book or movie and arrange the information in it (including back story and exposition—see glossary) in chronological order. See how this affects the dramatic impact of the story.

I have used the Stanley Donen film *Two for the Road* as an example. You can see how the author used the geographical journey as his basis for the narrative, jumping about in time. The left column shows the rather dull chronological series of events in a disintegrating marriage.

Use the two columns on the right to try this exercise with your own story.

Story: *Two for the Road*		Your Story	
CHRONOLOGICAL ORDER	**ORDER STORY IS TOLD**	**CHRONOLOGICAL ORDER**	**ORDER STORY IS TOLD**
Two single people take a trip from London to the south of France	Two single people cross English Channel		
Newlywed couple takes trip to France	Newlyweds cross English Channel		
Couple married several years takes trip to France	Couple married several years crosses English Channel		
Couple having marital difficulties travels to France	Couple having marital difficulties crosses English Channel		
Couple on verge of divorce travels to France	Couple on verge of divorce crosses English Channel		
	Two single people travel toward Paris		
	Newlyweds travel toward Paris		
	Couple married several years travels toward Paris		
	Couple having marital difficulties travels to Paris		
	Couple on verge of divorce travels toward Paris		

There are several prisms through which any set of events, whether real or fictional, must pass on the way to becoming a story. The two most basic prisms are the subject and the point of view.

QUICK QUIZ
SUBJECT MATTER

Does my concept create obstacles that effectively challenge the characters?
☐ **YES**   ☐ **NO**

If so, which specific elements will be the source of that challenge?

_____

_____

_____

Does my concept provide a strong backdrop for exploring the strengths, limitations and psychology of my characters?   ☐ **YES**   ☐ **NO**

What specific elements does the plot have that provide vivid comparisons and contrasts that will delineate my character in intriguing ways?

_____

_____

_____

Does my concept provide a strong environment for the messages and themes I want to explore?   ☐ **YES**   ☐ **NO**

What metaphors and motifs grown naturally out of that environment will illuminate those themes and messages?

_____

_____

_____

Does my concept provide any realistic hooks that will make it easy for the audience to relate to?   ☐ **YES**   ☐ **NO**

What elements will they relate to? Even if you are writing fantasy or science fiction, you will want to give your audience some element to which they can connect their sympathy.

_____

_____

_____

Does my concept provide enough tension to hold the audience's interest?
☐ **YES**   ☐ **NO**

What are those sources of tension?

_____

_____

_____

_____

back to what originally drew you to your subject and try to build on that strength. In the arduous process of conceiving a story, it is very easy to get derailed or sidetracked on a weaker element. If this happens, stop what you are doing and go back to that strong element and begin working again from there.

A narrative is a series of events told from a unique perspective.

WRITER'S BLOCK RX

If you feel like your answers in the Subject Matter Quiz (p.8) are insufficient to start writing your story, try these techniques for shaking loose your preconceived notions.

- Consider your subject from a different, unique perspective—maybe through the point of view of another character.
- What element in your basic idea is the most unique and interesting?
- Invert an idea altogether. Try turning your idea upside down, or going at it from the exact opposite perspective. This radical change may inspire something exciting.

Point of View

Every story is filtered through its author's eyes. That author decides how to approach the story, which events stand out to her, and which ones make some sort of emotional connection. Those are the events upon which the author will focus her tale. Since every author will look at a given situation a little bit differently, you'll find that the plot of the story will change according to that writer's unique *perspective*.

An audience turns to a certain plot because they are looking for an *interpretation* of events (fictional or real). Anyone can look at a set of events and gather some understanding of them. An audience is looking for the author to filter those events and put a particular spin on them. They want the author to point them toward the events that are important or relevant and tell them why. People choose to read certain authors or to see certain films for the same reason people tend to read the same newspaper every day—they are looking for a perspective on events that they like, one to which they can relate.

The reason many people read the same authors and see films by

---

A narrative is a series of events told from a unique perspective.

---

the same directors over and over again is because they develop a level of trust with the author. They know that the author has a perspective on events they can relate to, as well as a way of communicating those events that is interesting and enjoyable.

EXERCISE
WHAT'S YOUR PERSPECTIVE?

1. Think about what makes your approach to your subject matter unique.
2. If the narrator of your story is a player in the story, what makes that character the one who is most appropriate as storyteller?
3. What elements make up the prism of your perspective?
   - Narrator's voice?
   - Temporal structure of the story?
   - Narrator or protagonist's attitude toward events?
   - Narrative style or structure?

Targeting the Story's Focus

The process of determining your perspective involves a number of other important factors.

First comes the decision about what to tell. Any given set of events will have a lot more happening in it than can be told in any one story. Trying to tell everything that happens would result in a meandering, unwieldy story. An audience being told a story is looking for the author's perspective, and the first thing that shapes that perspective is which events the author decides to tell the audience about. Going back to our World War II analogy, let's look at four films about the war that had *very* different perspectives.

FILM TITLE	WHAT IT FOCUSES ON	WHAT IT DOESN'T FOCUS ON
Saving Private Ryan	One small platoon on D-day	Large, complex political issues of the war
Patton	One key leader in the war and his perspective from above	The individual soldier, the psychology of the enemy or the war at home
Europa Europa	One young Jew's struggle to survive by passing as a member of the Aryan youth	The Allies' perspective, the Jews in concentration camps
Schindler's List	One group of Jews who survive due to the efforts of an ambiguously heroic man	The actual fighting of the war or the Allies

Whichever perspective the author chooses, the audience will be told a certain story. That story will still be about World War II and its effects, but the perspective will be specific and the point of view will guide the story.

What to Leave Out or Withhold

Decide which aspects fall outside the purview of the story. When you look at the events that make up your story, you have to cast a critical, disciplined eye on things and determine exactly which events are essential to the construction of your plot. You will surely be tempted to put time and energy (both yours and the audience's) into interesting details of the story. Some of those details will lend a useful perspective or create a richer texture for your story, but some will be mere diversions, and the author has to be disciplined about avoiding those sorts of detours. Remember that your readers are relying on you to give them what they need to know, and by the simple act of including something in your plot, you are saying to your readers that this is an important piece of information that is worthy of their time and consideration. While the occasional red herring (a misdirection or an element that deliberately fools an audience) can be a useful device, if you cry wolf too often, your audience will quickly lose faith in your perspective.

Decide what information to withhold. The art of withholding certain information is one that we will discuss in detail later, but for now, suffice it to say that deciding what to leave out is often much more difficult than deciding what to leave in. This will often be determined by the perspective of the narrator. An omniscient narrator won't have to worry about this as much since he is an all-knowing storyteller. First person and limited narrators, however, will only be able to let the audience in on their experience. They won't know every point of view, and there may be things going on within the events of the story that they don't know about. Using this type of narrator will give you the ability to withhold certain information and surprise the audience with revelations or leave certain events or motivations mysterious to the audience. Examine the chart at the top of p. 12. Each of these facts was withheld from the audience until the proper moment, then unleashed for maximum dramatic effect.

STORY	FACT TOLD	FACT WITHHELD
Angel Heart	Villain is a criminal named Lou Cypher	Lou Cypher (Lucifer) is the devil incarnate
Macbeth	Macbeth is invincible to any man "of woman born"	Macduff was ripped from his mother's womb and therefore not "of woman born"
Star Wars	Luke must defeat Darth Vader	Darth Vader is Luke's biological father

When and How to Tell

The third element that you'll have to address in taking a series of events and turning them into a plot is deciding when to give the audience certain pieces of information. This is one of the two most important elements separating good plots from bad plots (the other is choosing the subject matter). It is also what separates simple storytelling from great plotting. Alfred Hitchcock was a master at knowing when to reveal the crucial information. Whether it was the identity of Norman Bates's "mother" in *Psycho* or Scottie's fear of heights in *Vertigo*, Hitchcock always knew what to tell the audience and when to tell it. As a writer, you needn't be constrained from manipulating events to create the greatest impact for those events that you have chosen to include in your plot. It is entirely possible to present events out of order, or to withhold certain facts in order to make the impact of those events stronger. As you write, think about how you can reveal information or change the order of your plot in order to gain the maximum impact. In doing this, you will create the most effective plots. Throw off your own preconceived notions about sticking to certain tenets of realism. Remember that all writing is about heightened realism. If your audience wanted to read about reality as it exists, they could read a newspaper (well, maybe not certain newspapers!).

In creating your plot, challenge yourself to find new ways to look at events. How a story is told is crucial to its effectiveness. Writers throughout history have taken ordinary stories and turned them into outstanding plots by looking at ordinary events in new ways. Historical novelist James Michener took the settling of Chesapeake Bay in *Chesapeake* and the pioneers in *Alaska* and chose a specific perspective to make these large historical progressions into compelling drama. The rather mundane plight of the migrant worker was made dramatically poignant by John Steinbeck in *The Grapes of Wrath*.

Another example of this use of perspective is the modern comedy of manners. Stand-up comics have turned observational humor into an art form. What these performers do is look at the most mundane aspects of ordinary life and dissect them, putting them under a microscope. They've taken ordinary events that most people don't think twice about and made them enormously funny by playing with how the events are viewed. Literary and film movements from the Oulpians (see page 207) to the postmodernists to the Dadaists have changed the way we view things by altering the manner in which we look at everyday life.

Attempt to do this in your own work as well. This isn't to say you should start your own artistic movement, but challenge yourself to see the world in a new way, or find interesting ways to express your own unique worldview.

Once you have considered your subject, what you will and will not focus on, and how and when you will reveal certain information, you will begin to see your plot taking shape. You will probably have begun to stir your own creative processes and will want to focus on the ideas that work best.

EXERCISE

Write your story idea on a single 3 × 5 card, paring it down to its most basic elements. Write only the words or phrases that are absolutely critical to your story. This will help you find the essential pieces and make choices about what to tell, what not to tell, when and how to recount those events.

Use the result of this exercise as a starting place. You may feel a bit underqualified to answer those questions—that's probably why you're reading this book. But this exercise is a good one to give yourself an understanding of your starting point. The exercise is a good way to take an accounting of your knowledge of building plots. You probably came to your decisions using a combination of your existing knowledge of storytelling and plain old instinct. Do not underestimate the power of instinct.

CHAPTER TWO

Plot Structure

All plots, no matter how diverse, are made up of similar parts. Different authors and literary theorists may have different names for those parts, but all stories can be broken down into a consistent set of components. The parts are simply movements of the action—all plot is about action of some kind, either physical, emotional, or mental—that form the **arc** of a story. No matter how different two stories are they can usually be dissected into analogous parts. You will learn quickly to chart the different actions involved in your story and to see which ones are working and which aren't. You can also use this understanding to find the pacing for your work that will make the story most interesting and compelling.

The Arc

The basic outline of most plots follows a common structure that can be best described as an arc. A well-developed arc accurately describes several interwoven features of the plot (tension, character development, **conflict, goal**), as well as the emotional path the audience should follow. Simply put, the arc should describe the dramatic course of your story. From page one, the elements of tension in the story, emotional investment of the characters (*and* the audience), character development, and pacing should follow an upward trajectory as the story unfolds. All the major action of the story builds toward the apex of the arc—the climax. After the climax, the resolution is represented by a short, but important, downward piece of the arc.

Finding the arc of your story is one of the first and most critical steps you will take in the writing process. Once you have firmly nailed down the story's basic arc, you will have a guide to help you make all the other decisions related to your story. So how do you find the arc? Without sounding flippant—you'll know it when you see it! That is, if you have the essence of a strong plot, the basics of the arc should be apparent to you. As you outline the elements of the story, you should naturally feel the level of tension, anticipation, and your characters' stakes rising until you reach the "point of no return," the climax where your characters' lives are forever changed. To find the arc, trace your story's path event by event. If you don't feel the story's **rising action**, you probably don't have a clearly defined story arc. If this is the case, you need to go back to the basic elements of your story and look closely at what might be missing. Try asking yourself these questions.

 ## QUICK QUIZ
TESTING THE ARC

What is your protagonist's goal?
What obstacles keep him from that goal?
Who is the antagonist?
What does the protagonist have at stake?
What sacrifices must he make?
If the answers to these questions are unclear or not compelling, you need
    to reexamine your story.

The simplest way to find the initial arc of your story is by drawing a "line" between two simple events in your story (see illustration "Plot Arc"). First find the **inciting incident** (more on this later); this is the event that establishes the conflict your protagonist will face during your story. This is the beginning point of your story arc. Then find the **climax** (more on that later, too), the dramatic high point of your story. Once you have these two points, most of the significant events of your story will take place between these two events. Only your story's **resolution** will occur after the climax.

Many writers mistake **back story** (the history of your characters and the situation from which the plot grew) or **exposition** for the arc of the story. These elements, while important to the story, are not the essence of the arc. Simple events that describe your characters or their situation are not enough to give any story a sufficient arc. The elements of the arc of your story are those that give it forward motion, that propel the characters and drive them on.

One way to develop the arc of your story is to actually *draw an arc of your story*. Take the key events you have in mind and write them in along the actual arc. Start with the first significant thing that happens in the story. Then write in the other major events along your arc. If you have trouble, a good way to start is by placing the climax on your arc. Then find events between the beginning of the story and the climax. Estimate at which point along the arc they come and space them accordingly. This will help you to see where you are missing pieces or where you may have items in conflict.

Plot Arc

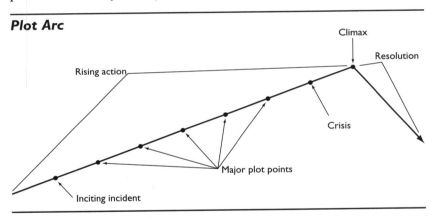

This step, while it may seem elementary, will save you many problems later. One of the leading causes of writer's block—story dead ends—can be prevented or cured by following this simple exercise. By holding your story to the strict demands of the story arc, you will avoid those frustrating detours and blind alleys that can take all the fun out of writing. By knowing how each element of the arc functions, and its place relative to the other elements, you can always be sure where you are in your story. The arc becomes a road map that, even when you consciously choose to take a detour, can lead you back to your plot.

The exercise of plotting your story against this arc will give you a consistent gauge by which to evaluate the possible impact of different story turns. By knowing where on the arc an event is located, you can judge whether or not a certain subplot or tangent is appropriate. Each time you develop a new event for your story, determine where it will fall on the upward trajectory of your story arc. The climax of your story, the irretrievable turning point, is your aim; this is where all the major plot events should lead. Hold each new scene in your story up to this template and see if it drives the story forward toward the climax. If a scene doesn't contribute to this goal, reevaluate it.

QUICK QUIZ
SCENE EVALUATION

Is the scene absolutely necessary to the central plot line of the story?
If not, does it constitute a meaningful, necessary subplot or tangent?
If it is a worthwhile subplot or tangent, is this a good place to put it? Would it be more effective somewhere else?

QUICK QUIZ
SCENES AND PACING

By following the story arc, you will also be able to judge the pacing of your story. Ask yourself the following questions after plotting your scenes against the story arc:

- Are you moving toward the climax at a pace to keep your audience's attention? Are you saving too many crucial scenes for the end?
- Are there long gaps between the significant events that move your story forward?
- Are you building (enough) tension into your story?

Graphing your story arc will also help you decide the best placement for new elements that will drive your story. You can figure out just where a certain clever plot twist should happen, when a secondary character should be introduced for maximum effect or where to plant that crucial clue that will make everything clear later in the story. Graphing the story will enable you to back-time elements (see the sidebar on page 18) so that these various characters and events will dovetail at the proper moment for optimal dramatic effect.

Back-timing is simply looking at where you want a certain element or event to end and then working backwards from that point along the arc to find the point in the story where it needs to begin in order to reach its culmination at the proper moment. It is a crucial technique in building effective drama. Think of it like cooking a meal: You know what time you want everything to be finished, but since the potatoes take an hour to cook and the fish only takes fifteen minutes, you decide when to put these things in the oven by measuring time backwards (hence back-time) from the time when you want everything to come out.

One of the most difficult things about writing longer works like novels, plays or screenplays is keeping track of exactly where in the story you are. This is particularly true if you like to write your stories out of sequence as many authors do. This exercise of actually drawing an arc and noting your various scenes on it will help you enormously in managing longer projects and in maintaining the tension and pacing that make for effective storytelling. Later in this book, I will describe several other tools and methods for structuring and managing longer, more involved works.

Once you've established a rough, but solid arc for your story, the rest of your plotting can begin. This arc will serve as the spine of your story and is the basis of your plot. As you write, refer back to the arc any time you feel lost or off track. I suggest keeping your graph of the arc of your story somewhere highly visible. Pin it to the wall or tape it to the edge of your computer monitor. It will help you in everything from choosing and constructing scenes to controlling the mood and tone of your writing. Mostly it will act as a constant reminder of where you are on the path of your story.

Three-Act Structure

The three-act structure is one of the most common in drama, so it merits some discussion here. It is certainly the prevailing format in screenwriting and is a good model for short stories. Three-act structure is less important in longer literary forms, which require a more complex treatment. Shakespeare, for example, wrote his plays (as did many of his contemporaries) in five acts.

What makes three-act structure so relevant to our discussion is that it is a good way to divide your story arc. Some theorists and writing instructors suggest that the three acts divide the story's length roughly in thirds, but others, including me, find this symmetry confining. I recommend looking at your play, screenplay or short story in the following way.

Act one. Act one should be a short, opening section of your plot leading to the first major event in the story, the inciting incident (we'll discuss this plot element in detail later). This first movement of the story should introduce the characters, set up the situation, provide some background or back story about the characters, and acclimate the audience to the environment of the story. It ends after the conflict is introduced and the characters proceed to face that conflict. The key to writing a good first act is to keep things short.

All of your writing should be crisp and economical, but it is particularly important in the opening act since you want to grab your audience quickly and immerse them in the world of your story.

While the length of act one is, of course, flexible, I recommend keeping it to no more than one-sixth of the entire length of your story. This may seem very brief and out of proportion to the following two acts, but you should compress your story's opening act so that the audience has all the information it needs but can get quickly into the major thrust of the drama.

Act two. Act two is the meat of your plot. Here the characters will be involved with the rising action (we'll discuss this element of the plot in detail later) of your plot. Here the conflict of your story will play itself out and the audience will learn more about the characters. While this act is the longest in a work, it is divided into several smaller sections (**major plot points**—which we'll look at in detail later). These smaller sections all move both the characters and the audience toward the climax. The crisis point of your story will be the final event of act two. It is the point of no return and the moment of highest drama in your story. Act two will probably comprise between one-half and three-quarters of the length of your story and will contain most of the major action.

Act three. Act three is the final movement of your story, and corresponds roughly to the climax and resolution of your plot. The final act of your story will, like act one, be fairly brief, but it will wrap up the plot and cement all of your themes, ideas and messages. This section of your story should comprise no more than one-quarter of its length, and I recommend keeping it somewhat shorter than that.

If you look at the story arc, you will see that acts one and two occur congruently with the upward arc of the story, while act three matches the apex and downward portion of the arc.

Fact: Most agents, editors and producers read only the first quarter of the screenplays and manuscripts they receive.

The most important element to consider in the three-act structure is how the "breaks" between the acts are handled. The break between acts one and two is important because it is the moment at which the story really takes off. At this point the conflict has been established and the action of the story commences in earnest. When you reach this crucial scene in your plot, you want the reader to have the feeling that "the die has been cast"—that there is nothing the protagonist can do but meet the challenge that has been laid out for him. You want to achieve this first "point of no return" at the end of act one. The first scene in act two is equally crucial, as it is at this point that the character's difficult journey through the conflict actually begins. These two scenes should be remarkable in their own right and also have a natural flow and continuity to them. Think of it like shifting gears smoothly when driving a car. The momentum you've built in act one needs to be preserved as act two begins; otherwise, your plot will stall.

The transition from act two to act three is even more critical. Act two will end with the moment of crisis in your story. If well planned, this should lead to the natural, exciting high point in your drama. The key is to carry this energy into act three. The first scene in act three should be the climax. After that, the audience should feel the dust beginning to settle. Since there will be considerably less action and suspense from this point on, it will be necessary for the energy and momentum of the climax to carry the story through to the end of the third act. Therefore, a smooth transition between acts two and three is essential to maintain the story's forward motion.

Fact: Most agents, editors and producers read only the first quarter of the screenplays and manuscripts they receive.

Much has been written about three-act structure and how to execute it properly. Though it is not the focus of this book, these ideas are implicit in what comes later. What you will notice as you continue through this book, however, is that the art and craft of constructing a good plot is filled with "threes," many of which relate closely to the concept of the three-act structure.

THREE-ACT STRUCTURE	CASABLANCA DIRECTED BY MICHAEL CURTIZ	RUM PUNCH BY ELMORE LEONARD	ZEN AND THE ART OF MOTORCYCLE MAINTENANCE BY ROBERT PIRSIG
Act I	Rick is running the café; Ilsa arrives	Characters in normal life—writing bail bonds, flying, dealing guns—whose lives converge	Phaedrus and son take off on bike toward Montana
Act II	Nazis close in on Rick, Ilsa and her husband	Stewardess helps cops nail gun dealer	Phaedrus and son take hike up mountain
Act III	Rick helps Ilsa and her husband escape	Stewardess rips off money, tricks cops	Phaedrus and son continue to California

Conflict, Crisis and Resolution

Let's dissect the plot arc further by looking at it on a deeper, more emotional level. If you take the three major pieces of the arc—rising action, climax and the resolution—you can intuitively link them to the emotional arc you want your protagonist, and your audience, to follow. Writer Janet Burroway described these same arc pieces as conflict, crisis and resolution, and it follows that all good drama must contain these three elements. These three states are an excellent description of the emotional journey that the characters in your story need to follow if they are to hold the audience's sympathy and interest. This is also the path down which the audience must be led in order to have a satisfying experience with your story. In most stories, it is easy to identify these three pieces, but even when conflicts and crises are more subtle, the author must be aware of them at all times. These terms are not meant to be limiting. Conflict and crisis don't have to mean that the protagonist is faced with a life and death struggle, but without resistance and a moment of truth, no protagonist will be sufficiently interesting to hold an audience's attention or sympathy.

You can think about this triad of conflict, crisis and resolution in relation to the story arc: The first part of the journey, the rising action, is all about conflict. (We'll discuss the nature and the many types of conflict in the next section.) It is during this initial phase of the narrative that the character's situation is defined and he begins to pursue his goal. This is the part of the story where you will win the reader's sympathy for the protagonist, and where the reader's emotional investment in the characters and your story will be made. The conflict (also the rising action) is the largest part of the story, and most of the characters' time will be spent engaged in the conflict, so the writer must be sure that all the elements of this part of the story are properly developed and accurately aimed at the second piece of the arc—the crisis.

The crisis of your story will occur immediately after the conflict. While the climax is the precise scene where the protagonist's fortunes are made or lost, the crisis is the slightly larger section that culminates with that key climactic scene. Think of the crisis as the final sequence of events where the outcome of the story is decided, the time at which control of the characters' situation slips into the hands of fate. The first key to a successful crisis sequence in any story is the events, exposition and back story that the author has built into the conflict. If you arrive at your crisis and it seems flat or dull, you probably haven't set it up sufficiently. While the crisis makes up the smallest part of the story, in terms of dramatic time or pages, it is the moment at which the rest of your work pays off. A well-constructed crisis will be devastating for the characters and gripping for the audience. It should also have an element of inevitability ("we knew this moment would come"), while still providing the audience some element of surprise ("but I didn't expect *that*").

The other key element of your story's crisis is that it be concise and to the point. The careful building of suspense that the author has achieved must, in this small window of narrative time, come to fruition, but many writers, even experienced, accomplished ones, damage the suspense in their stories by dragging out the crisis, dissipating the impact of the climax. In constructing the arc of your story, the crisis portion is the target at which all events have pointed, and if they have accomplished their goal, the crisis should occur naturally, and the suspense should result in a gripping, exciting payoff to your hard work.

But the work isn't over. One of the most difficult portions of the story is the resolution. Unfortunately, resolutions are often the neglected part of the plot. Many beginning writers rely on them to take care of themselves, and squander hard work by truncating the story and its dramatic structure. After the dramatic, noisy and colorful explosion of the climax, the resolution functions as the dramatic "ahhh" in the story. It is during this moment that the drama is etched indelibly and your story's message is impressed on your reader's mind.

Planning your resolution is perhaps the most difficult part of constructing the plot. It must flow naturally out of the crisis and the climax. It must also reinforce all the themes and subtexts of the conflict. In this final section of your story, all the threads of your work that have surfaced during the crisis must now be tied together. Some writers damage the impact of their story in these final moments either through neglect or overreaching. Some writers will abruptly end the story, leaving the audience searching for clues to its meaning. While this ambiguity can sometimes be effective, it is more often frustrating. Even ambiguous endings should leave the reader with some clue, some idea about the author's message, or at least with something tantalizing to chew on. Other writers will dig into their resolution and extract all sorts of messages and jump to wild conclusions that were never alluded to in their story. Or they will try to draw out large, universal meanings from the simplest story, essentially telling the audience what to think. This sort of ending denies the audience the afterglow of a good story when the reader gets to draw his own conclusions.

Therefore, approach the resolution to your story with great care. Think of it as you would the follow-through to a tennis stroke. While it occurs after the moment of impact, it is no less important and, in fact, is pivotal to the success of what comes before it. Review your previous work before you begin writing the resolution and follow the natural trajectory you've set up to its logical conclusion.

Also, you can use this third piece of the story arc to give your audience one last surprise. The best resolutions will tie in some forgotten element from the story or draw together any previously unrelated themes or subtexts. When you can achieve that "oh, yeah" reaction in your readers, you've given them something extra and, hopefully, added resonance to your work.

So take the elements of conflict, crisis and resolution and use them just as you use the graphic drawing of the plot arc—as signposts or milestones. By keeping them in the back of your mind as you construct your story, you will have a clear set of goals to guide your work. They will also provide good measuring tools for evaluating your work. Just as you measure your plot points against the arc, you can measure these basic elements in your story.

QUICK QUIZ
CONFLICT, CRISIS AND RESOLUTION

Is the story's conflict clear to you as the author?
Is the conflict communicated clearly to the audience?
Does the conflict challenge the protagonist?
Does the conflict engender enough sympathy for the protagonist?
Does the conflict lead to a crisis?
Will the crisis have a strong impact on the characters and the audience?
Does the crisis put the protagonist in an all-or-nothing situation?
Does the resolution provide a satisfying, meaningful end to your story?
Does the resolution answer the audience's questions about the protagonist
    and his journey?
Will the resolution leave your audience sated, but thoughtful?

If the story arc is the foundation of your "building," then conflict, crisis and resolution are the cornerstones. Take your story, at whatever stage, and try distilling it down to these three simple elements. If you've written quite a bit, a first draft or more, this will be challenging. But to assure that your story is well plotted, you should strip away everything, until you have just the central conflict, the crisis and the resolution. You should be able to describe each element in one sentence, even in a few words.

STORY	CONFLICT	CRISIS	RESOLUTION
The Yearling	Child wants to keep wild deer as a pet	Child is ordered by parents to kill deer	Child learns about cycle of life
The Velveteen Rabbit	Rabbit wants to be alive	Rabbit is sent to incinerator after child gets sick	Rabbit learns that to be loved is to be alive

Once you've considered these questions and distilled your story down to just these three simple elements, post these statements where you can refer to them often. It will help if you can see them and read them each time you sit down to write. If you begin to lose focus, just refer to them and your story arc to remind you of the work you've done planning your story. It will save you numerous detours and frustrating trips down blind alleys. These visual reminders will give you a clear awareness of your plan and will free your mind to think about other aspects of your work.

Goal and Obstacle

You can think of your protagonist's goal as the irresistible force of your story and the **obstacle** as the immovable object he or she must confront. When these two elements come together, you are certain to have a powerful reaction. In *Gone With the Wind*, think of Scarlett and Rhett's love as the irresistible force and the Civil War as the plot's immovable object. The result is a deeply passionate story where the characters lose everything only to gain it back and lose it once again. Mitchell plots her story in such a way that these two tremendous forces are placed in direct opposition to one another. The reader (or viewer) is compelled through the story by the vastness of what is at stake for the characters. In *Moby Dick*, Ahab's quest for revenge is opposed not only by the wily whale, but even by nature itself. The enormity of his quest and his determination make for one of the greatest epics ever written.

Without these diametrically opposed forces that make up the conflict of your story, there is no drama. And without drama, there is little reason for the reader to turn the page. Even the most beautiful, most lyrical writing is only a prose poem without the clashing forces of goal and obstacle. Just as an electromagnet drives a motor by the pull of alternating poles, similarly, the motor of a plot is driven by the alternating forces of goal and obstacle. More elemental than protagonist and antagonist, goal and obstacle can be just about any force—physical, emotional or psychological. Examine any good story and you'll find these two forces.

STORY	GOAL	OBSTACLE
The Wizard Of Oz	Use ruby slippers to get back to Kansas	Wicked witch wants ruby slippers back
Huckleberry Finn	Help Jim escape from slave owner	Hazards of the river and the people Jim & Huck encounter

Equal but Opposite

These two elements, like a seesaw, function best if they are equal in weight and on opposite sides of the pivot point (the conflict); so remember that goal and obstacle must be:

- opposed
- equal (or close to equal) in strength

If either is too strong or too weak, the outcome of your story will never really be in doubt, so why should the reader continue?

Plots are most effective when the conflict is clear to the audience, so beware of scenarios that lead to overly ambiguous conflicts. You might end up with a goal and obstacle that are unrelated and which will pass by each other rather than create the collision necessary to produce good drama. Many writers, in search of depth or greater meaning, will introduce elements of ambiguity. I am not recommending against this. Toward the end of this book we will discuss how to deepen the impact of your plot in several ways, including the introduction of ambiguity. But while ambiguity can certainly increase the resonance of your story, be careful not to let it muddle your plot.

Elements of tension and suspense are directly reliant on the alignment of the protagonist's goal and the obstacles to it. Proper opposition of these two elements will also provide excellent opportunities for subplots and character delineation.

STORY STARTER

What if the protagonist's rival turns out to be his own best friend? What if the hero is reluctant to confront his domineering father, but challenging his dad is the only way he can become his own man? Look for ways to make these two elements function on multiple levels.

What if the protagonist's goal is in opposition to his morals?

What if the achievement of his goal would result in the loss of something dear?

Proper design of these elements will open the door to a deeper, richer experience, allowing you to introduce more complex elements like irony and ambiguity. By setting up this clash of forces from the beginning, you will have less trouble creating suspense or building to a dramatic crisis.

Setting the Goal

Setting the goal isn't usually a task the writer has to engage in consciously. Unless you are writing a serial and are trying to determine your protagonist's next adventure, you probably conceived of your character's goal in the earliest stages of your process. That goal may have occurred to you even before you identified the character who would endeavor to achieve it. But having determined who your protagonist is and what he desires is only the beginning. Just as in laying the other parts of your foundation, you need to distill your ideas into a simple, one-line description of your character's goal in order to write a clear, compelling story.

First, describe the actual *physical* goal. What is it that the character *does* in the story? In *Moby Dick*, Ahab's physical goal is to kill the white whale—one simple sentence. On that small kernel the rest of the story can be constructed. Yet, for your story to have meaning and power, you also need to determine, and then describe, the character's deeper *psychological* goal. Ahab's psychological goal is to take revenge on the creature that took his leg—again, a sentence that is simple and to the point. It is not sufficient to know that your character wishes to be president of the United States. You must also have a clear understanding of *why*. Without this deeper understanding, your story will be thin, a simple string of events.

STORY	PHYSICAL GOAL	PSYCHOLOGICAL GOAL
The Client	Protect boy "client"	Resolve guilt over losing custody of own kids
The Rainmaker	Win lawsuit against insurance company	Establish own identity and reputation
The Pelican Brief	Expose corrupt oil company	Avenge murdered lover and establish independent reputation
Your character		
Your character		
Your character		
Your character		

Your reader probably won't understand the character's motivation initially—that's the fun part of reading the story—but the author must know it from the beginning. Usually, as you begin to develop your character, you will begin to understand his motivation and the psychological or emotional basis for his goal. Even if you never fully reveal your character's motivation, it still must be clear to you as the author. Otherwise, your story's forward motion, its thrust, will be dissipated and unfocused. Remember, part of the fun of being an author is knowing more than your reader!

Once you think you have a strong understanding of your character's goal, both the physical and the psychological parts of it, analyze these parts to and see if they match up—if they complement each other. Sometimes a writer will create a terrific character who has a wonderful, sympathetic goal. Also, he has in mind a fascinating, compelling story to tell. Unfortunately, the two don't match up! For instance, a character who is trying for the first time to be true to himself probably doesn't synch up well with a revenge tale. So look at these elements and determine if the story you have in mind makes sense for the type of character you have in mind.

You must also make sure that your character's goal is sufficiently challenging. A writer may run into trouble when she creates a goal that is too easily attainable and doesn't require her protagonist to make a long enough and difficult enough journey. The power of your story will be realized through the distance (physical, emotional, psychological or spiritual) that your protagonist must travel. When the goal isn't sufficiently challenging, you will often end up a short distance into your story and realize that you don't have anywhere left to go. It may be early in your story, well before you are ready to reach the crisis or the climax, and you may find that your character has achieved his goal already. The contrast between where your protagonist begins and where he ends up is one of the key elements of good drama.

Finally, it's important to make sure that the goal of your protagonist is clear to the audience on at least one level, either physical or psychological, fairly early in your story. If the character's goal remains unclear for too long, the reader won't stay with the story. This goal is the carrot that will keep the reader reading, and it is also what will lure your character along through the story. You may elect to make your character's goal obvious from the beginning—he is trying to get from New York to Los Angeles. His emotional goal may be to reunite with his long lost love. Or, you may decide to keep the physical goal a mystery, sharing with your reader the emotional engine driving the character. The character wants to make peace with the memory of his dead father. What the readers don't find out until later is that he intends to do this by killing his uncle.

Placing the Obstacle

Giving your characters obstacles that will challenge them and test them will make it easy for you to develop strong momentum, and thus an exciting climax to your plot. While your character's goal may grow directly and easily out of your protagonist's situation, identifying an obstacle that will allow you to squeeze all you can out of that character is a little more difficult. However, choosing the appropriate obstacle will make your conflict complete and define the central drama in your story. It also gives you the opportunity to plant the seeds for the subplots, character delineation and ideas you want to draw out in your story. These things can be grown from the seeds of this conflict.

While we like to think of a central obstacle to the hero's goal, in actuality, he will overcome numerous obstacles on the journey from your story's beginning to end. Each plot point in your story will involve the overcoming of an obstacle, but, like a mountaineer, while we may scale several peaks, we need to have our eyes on the summit at all times. If your character's central and minor obstacles are a significant challenge, then all the richness of character and your writing will come out.

One way to identify and establish the obstacles in a story is by looking at the protagonist and his or her goal and asking a series of questions (see the Quick Quiz, p. 30).

Balance the elements of goal and obstacle against each other carefully and assure yourself that they are each strong enough to put the outcome of your story in question. A hero's win over a less-than-worthy foe doesn't make very good drama. In fact, the obstacle should appear stronger than your hero, and the odds should be stacked against him. David vs. Goliath is a short, boring story if Goliath wins.

It is, however, equally hazardous to stack the odds too highly against your hero. If you do this, it may become impossible to make

QUICK QUIZ
PLACING THE OBSTACLE

"What would make the attainment of my character's goal the most difficult?" Once this has been identified, the central obstacle in the story will become much clearer.

In *Casablanca* seeing Ilsa safe means that Rick must let her go.

"What is my character's greatest weakness?" Exploiting this vulnerability will provide a rich source of drama.

Hamlet's course of action is clear—expose his uncle. His weakness is his indecisiveness.

"What is my character's greatest fear?" To draw the most depth from your protagonists, they must face their greatest fears.

In *Vertigo*, Scottie's greatest fear is high places, yet he must go into the bell tower to expose the murderer.

"What is my character's greatest strength?" This will give you a clue as to how your protagonist will eventually overcome the obstacle.

In *The Fountainhead*, Howard Roarke is able to succeed only through the tremendous force and conviction of his principles.

Answering these questions should point you right at the obstacle that will give your story the greatest drama and create the utmost tension.

---

your story believable. The underdog almost always inspires a good plot, but the writer needs to be clever in making his eventual triumph believable. The hero needs some secret reservoir of strength, or the obstacle must have some hidden, but discoverable, weakness. Only then will the audience accept, and cheer, your hero's ultimate triumph. (See the exercise, p. 31.)

After you've written this formula down, post it with your other reminders. Slowly, you should begin to see a preliminary sketch of your plot developing.

Types of Conflict

Conflict is the fulcrum, the crux, of your plot. It is the balancing point upon which the rest of the story turns. There are four basic types of conflict that exist in drama. While these designations are quite broad, they help us to understand more about the nature of conflict and how it works within our story. While every story has at least one of these

EXERCISE

Think about the elements of goal and obstacle in their raw state early in the writing process, before they are integrated into the story. Just as we did with conflict, crisis and resolution, try to sum up each of these two elements in one sentence. Just as a sporting event is billed as Wildcats vs. Spartans, try to boil down your protagonist's goal and obstacle to an X vs. Y equation. For example, "desire for independence vs. father's need for an heir."

Goal = _____

Obstacle = _____

My plot boils down to:

_____ vs. _____

Once again, after you've written this formula down, post it with your other reminders. Slowly, you should begin to see a preliminary sketch of your plot developing.

types of conflict, most good stories can be looked at through the prism of two or even three. There are four basic types of conflict:

Protagonist vs. Antagonist

This is the simplest and most straightforward type of conflict. It is essentially person against person. Your protagonist has a goal or a desire to be fulfilled, and there is another person who is standing in the way. This type of conflict, while simple, is also one of the most interesting because it gives the writer the opportunity to dig into the depths of two characters. "This time, it's personal," has great resonance with most audiences, since most people have confronted at one time or another a person whose goals were in opposition to their own. It's also full of opportunities because it provides a chance to not only plumb the psyches of two individuals, but also to do one of the most enjoyable things in writing: create a great villain. Villains are some of the most interesting and memorable characters ever created. From Iago to Long John Silver, these characters have provided authors with opportunities to dig into the dark side of human nature. Creating a good villain is also the most direct way to create an adversary who will bring out the best (and worst) in your protagonist. If your story fits this protagonist vs. antagonist category in any way, the conflict you are dealing with should be relatively straightforward. It is one person against another, so the key to your conflict is pitting these two characters against one another in the most dramatic, interesting way.

STORY	PROTAGONIST VS. ANTAGONIST	
Othello	Othello	Iago
Treasure Island	Jim Hawkins	Long John Silver
The Untouchables	Elliot Ness	Al Capone
A Streetcar Named Desire	Blanche Dubois	Stanley Kowalski

Protagonist vs. Nature

This type of conflict is a little more difficult to pin down than the simple person vs. person type. These stories fall into a couple of categories; often they are rather straightforward adventure stories that pit the protagonist against the natural elements in some sort of quest or journey. Jack London wrote many stories that set his protagonists against the very forces of nature. In *The Call of the Wild*, the domesticated wolf-dog Buck fights against and eventually gives in to his own wild nature. The second type of protagonist vs. nature story is a bit more obscure and involves characters struggling to overcome the natural elements around them. In the movie *The River*, the farm family headed by Mel Gibson fights to save its land from the irresistible force of the swollen river. These types of conflicts have several features which can make for excellent drama. First of all, the forces against that the characters struggle are larger than life; they are all-encompassing natural phenomena that can't be described by a mere human being. These massive forces make the odds against the character very steep, so his eventual victory is richly won. It also gives the writer the opportunity to have the character *not* conquer nature, but be forced to come to terms with it and find harmony within nature. The themes that can be explored in such stories are rich.

The difficulty with these types of conflicts is that, unlike the person vs. person conflict, there is no sentient being against which the characters struggle. This can make the confrontations with the obstacle elusive and sometimes difficult to illuminate. The writer has to work harder to make the conflict draw out the depth and nature of the protagonist's character. Nevertheless, under the right circumstances, protagonist vs. nature can make for exciting, compelling drama.

STORY	PROTAGONIST VS. NATURE	
The Call of the Wild	Buck, the wolf-dog	Urge to return to instinctive roots
The River	The Garvey family	Force of the river
Jurassic Park	Paleontologists	Dinosaurs
The Stand	Survivor group	Disease

Protagonist vs. Society

This is a well-worn type of conflict that pits the protagonist against a larger, collective body. This body could be his social circle, his community or the traditions and values against which he rebels. There are many examples of this type of conflict, from Marlon Brando's *The Wild One* to Hester Prynne in *The Scarlet Letter* to Romeo and Juliet. All these protagonists in some way rebelled against their societies. This sort of conflict gives the author an excellent opportunity to deepen the resonance of a story by introducing overarching and possibly timely issues. Hawthorne used his character Hester to question the Puritan ethics prevalent at the time he wrote his novel. *The Wild One* was a comment on the repressed emotional state of society in 1950s America. Brando's character rebelled against that repression.

This sort of conflict can allow the author to comment on grand social issues, public mores or secret hypocrisies. The risk in this sort of conflict is that it can often leave the protagonist with a rather amorphous foe, making it difficult for the author to create the kinds of active, concrete scenes that will engender audience sympathy for the character. It is usually necessary to distill the societal forces at work down to a specific character or characters who represent them. This allows the writer to work on a scene-by-scene level using protagonist vs. antagonist confrontations that will crystallize the larger conflict at work (see the chart on p. 34).

Protagonist vs. Self

Like protagonist vs. society, this type of conflict can be hard to pin down, which makes it difficult to create a compelling plot with which an audience can connect. As a general rule, it can be hard (nearly

STORY		PROTAGONIST VS. SOCIETY	ANTAGONISTIC CHARACTER
Romeo and Juliet	Romeo (and Juliet)	Families have long-running feud	Capulet family/Montague family
On The Waterfront	Terry	Corruption of local union	Charlie
The Scarlet Letter	Hester	Societal taboo against adultery	Governor Bellingham
The Fountainhead	Roarke	Tyranny of classical architecture and polite society's embrace of it	Keating

impossible in cinema) to communicate a character's interior thoughts in an interesting way if there is insufficient external activity. Therefore, if your story is one in which the central conflict is a character's internal battle with herself, be sure that you populate your story with lots of other characters and events (facilitators) that will give your protagonist plenty to react to. Create these characters and events so that they will draw out and illustrate the protagonist's inner conflict. The Pat Conroy novel *The Prince of Tides* is a good example of an inner conflict illustrated by lots of external events. In this novel the inner conflict is broached by the protagonist's relationship with the psychiatrist. This external character, while not the antagonist, is the cipher through which we travel into the protagonist's mind and history. Through the use of this third party the author informs the audience of the man's troubled childhood and brings the scars of that childhood into dramatic relief. If the character's troubles were revealed only through his interior thoughts, we would be stripped of the palpable drama that we experience during his conflicts with the psychiatrist. Without understanding the compelling fact of his sister's suicide attempt, we would see no compelling reason for him to make this inner journey and there would appear to be no tangible goal. While self-discovery can be a worthy goal, it alone doesn't make for good drama.

When determining which type of conflict you are dealing with in your story, keep in mind that you may have elements of all of them and consider how they can work together to raise the level of drama in your story. You may even want to see how they could work against each other—drawing your protagonist in different directions and forcing her to make difficult choices.

Most good stories will have some element of protagonist vs. self in

STORY	PROTAGONIST VS. SELF		FACILITATOR
My Left Foot	Christy	His physical disability	Mrs. Brown, Dr. Eileen Cole
The Sheltering Sky	Port	His mental deterioration	Kit
The Catcher in the Rye	Holden	His angst, alienation and lack of self-esteem	The unobserved psychiatrist to whom he is telling his tale
Leaving Las Vegas	Ben	His alcoholism	Sera

them. One thing that makes for compelling drama is a character's internal struggle against her history, her psyche or her nature. Look for these elements in your story and for natural synergies with other, possibly more overt, conflicts you are dealing with. The essence of protagonist vs. self is the notion of personal growth, which is one of the most intense experiences an audience can share with a character. To root for that growth and to see the character struggle and then achieve it makes for a very strong bond between the protagonist and the audience.

It's also possible that you will find the elements of protagonist vs. nature and protagonist vs. society in many of your stories as well. These elements of nature and society may be present as subtexts or themes in your work, particularly if your story pits protagonist vs. antagonist. Don't resist them; they will give your work a depth and resonance that it wouldn't otherwise have. In fact, without the inclusion of one of these three other types of conflict, most protagonist vs. antagonist stories will often have no more meaningfulness than a simple revenge plot.

Knowing the sort of conflict with which you are dealing will help you to understand how that particular brand of conflict affects your work. You need to identify these elements to make them work most effectively in lending meaning and gravity to your story. If you know you are dealing with an inner conflict, you can expose it for your audience and draw in the other elements of your plot to support and delineate it.

Now that we've looked at the arc of the story and examined the major dramatic components and the various forces that drive the plot, let's dig into the details of how the typical three-act plot is built. This next section will examine the building blocks necessary for any workable plot. Each of these pieces serves a very specific purpose, and while they are mostly invisible in good plots, it's necessary to have a clear understanding of how they function. Once you've identified, created and analyzed these pieces, you can easily learn to smooth them into the flow of your story, allowing the structural points of your plot to submerge into the background.

This section will help you develop and arrange your major plot points so that your story builds through the conflict toward the crisis and finally results in a satisfying, meaningful resolution to your plot. As we discuss each building block of your plot, we'll also examine how each fits into the arc of your story, and we'll flesh out the plot arc to include these pieces and the specific events in your story that correspond to them. When we've finished this section, you'll have seen many classic stories plotted on the story arc, and you'll also be ready to create the map for your own project by plotting your story points onto the graph of the arc.

 ## QUICK QUIZ
TYPES OF CONFLICT

To determine the type of conflict in your story ask yourself these questions:

- Which person or people oppose your protagonist in pursuit of his goals?
- What natural forces (if any) does the protagonist confront?
- What societal forces (if any) does the protagonist confront?
- What personal obstacles does the protagonist confront?
- Which of these opposing forces is most primary in the protagonist's efforts to reach his goal?

The answer to this last question will give you the type of central conflict your are dealing with.

EXERCISE

Chart your own story's conflict below:

PROTAGONIST	ANTAGONIST	TYPE OF CONFLICT	FACILITATOR OR REPRESENTATIVE FOE

In order to cement your understanding of the various pieces of the plot, let's use the next few chapters to compare plot pieces as they manifest themselves in a number of classic plots. I've chosen four classics: a movie, a short story, a novel and a play. We will discuss and compare *Casablanca* as directed by Michael Curtiz, "The Fall of the House of Usher" by Edgar Allen Poe, *Moby Dick* by Herman Melville, and *Hamlet* by William Shakespeare.

CHAPTER THREE

Inciting Incident

J ust as the name suggests, this is the event that gets the story rolling. It is the event that sparks the conflict and sends the protagonist on her quest. Be careful not to confuse this crucial event in the story with the beginning of your plot. The inciting incident rarely occurs on page one. In fact, the most effective inciting incidents happen a short way into the story. This gives the audience time to settle in, get acquainted with the writer's style, meet the characters in a neutral setting and generally get the lay of the land.

Once this introductory phase has occurred, it is time to start the ball rolling. The best inciting incidents make a strong, vivid impression. It is usually best if the inciting incident is a specific action or event—one that definitively changes the course of events in the characters' lives. In some cases, you might decide to try a subtler inciting incident, which I call the "time bomb" effect, but this can be tricky. This is when the event occurs without any of the characters or even the reader really realizing that something has changed, like the setting of a time bomb. Only as the story unfolds do we realize something special happened that has changed life's course.

Writers typically fall into the trap of waiting too long to present their inciting incident. A reader will only read for so long without encountering a specific event that then drives the story. If you wait

DRAMATIC COMPARISON
INCITING INCIDENTS

STORY	INCITING INCIDENT
Casablanca	Mr. Ugate (Peter Lorre) gives Rick (Humphrey Bogart) the stolen letters of passage.
"The Fall of the House of Usher"	The Narrator is greeted by Usher.
Moby Dick	Ishmael enlists to be a crew member on the *Pequod*.
Hamlet	Horatio describes the Ghost to Hamlet, which further arouses his suspicion about his father's demise.

too long before really giving your story any significant forward momentum, you will lose many readers. Remember that impulse to turn the page that we spoke about in the first sentence of this book? The inciting incident is what first applies this force to your plot, and without it, your story will meander and fail to start the inexorable rise toward the climax.

The reason most writers wait too long to reveal the inciting incident is that they become bogged down in character development and exposition. They mistakenly believe that the audience needs a lot of information about the character and a lot of background about the story before they will commit to an emotional investment. While exposition and character development are necessary components of any work, the reader's emotional investment in the story can't be front loaded or forced. Your story will ultimately be stronger if those elements occur naturally as the story unfolds. If you try to force-feed your audience a lot of information early on, your writing will probably sound manipulative, and your exposition will seem long-winded and boring. Such wanton recruitment of an audience's sympathy will usually turn them against the character in the end.

So how do you create a good inciting incident? There are four key elements:
- timing
- duration
- magnitude
- conjunction (of characters, themes and setting)

Each of these considerations must be taken into account when creating your story's inciting incident.

Timing

The timing of your inciting incident is the first consideration. As mentioned earlier, placing it at the proper moment within the opening section of your story will do much to determine the event's effectiveness. Placing the event too early will not allow you to establish setting, characters or mood. Before a reader or viewer can comprehend an event as unusual, which the inciting incident must be, he must understand the accepted norms of your story's world. You have to give your audience at least a little time to get acclimated, to establish themselves in the rhythm of that universe. Inciting incidents that occur too early in the story may not even be noticed by the audience, or they may throw the characters into the conflict, with its heightened sensitivities, so early as to be disorienting to the audience.

An equally serious mistake, however, is waiting too long to establish the conflict and get your story rolling. As mentioned earlier, this phenomenon usually occurs when the author uses too much exposition and character development too early in the plot. Unless some tension is added to the mix, the audience will desert you. Try to avoid long descriptions and copious back story in the opening pages of your work. These elements will be far more effective if sprinkled throughout the story.

Before starting your writing, look at your characters and the back story, and determine which elements contain information necessary for the reader to understand the characters and the conflict you are going to establish with your inciting incident. Be rigorous in saving noncritical information for later. You will even find that less information will make your inciting incident more intriguing and the mystery of the conflict more compelling. Give your audience the necessary elements of character, setting, history and mood as you carry them into the first movement of the plot.

The timing of the inciting incident will vary depending on the length and scope of the story you are writing. Short stories and screenplays will require the inciting incident very close to the beginning. Screenplays are particularly sensitive to delayed inciting incidents, because the visual nature of the medium makes action so much more critical. Movies can be pretty dull if the characters just sit around talking or, worse, thinking. Written works, however, have a much greater capacity to get into the interior workings of their characters' minds. So if you're writing a novel, you have more leeway in placing your inciting incident.

DRAMATIC COMPARISON

STORY	TIMING OF INCITING INCIDENT
Casablanca	Ugate gives Rick the papers about seven minutes or so into the story, after the atmosphere of Casablanca and the Café American have been established as an outlaw haven in upheaval.
"The Fall of the House of Usher"	Narrator is greeted by his old friend Usher very early (approx. pg. 3) because as a short story, the action must start quickly. Nevertheless, the narrator has set the scene and created the necessary sense of dread before revealing the essence of the conflict.
Moby Dick	By the time Ishmael joins the crew of the *Pequod*, Melville has given us some background on the port town, the nature of the whaling trade, and just enough of a glimpse of Ahab to pique the reader's interest and give a sense of anticipation.
Hamlet	When Hamlet sees the Ghost, we've had a little background on the political situation in Denmark and a taste of Hamlet's mental state.

In each case the author gave the audience just enough information to set the tone and communicate necessary information. Each author started his story's engine with the inciting incident as soon as possible.

Duration

How long the inciting incident lasts is just as important as when it occurs. Beginning writers will very often create complex, diffused inciting incidents that make it difficult for the audience to realize that a change has occurred. You want your story to begin with a "bang," so this first major plot point must have impact and will be greatly enhanced if this event occurs swiftly and decisively.

Try to create your inciting incident as a single, discreet event. If you are writing a screenplay, make it a single scene. The event can be a surprise or it can be inevitable, but try to create it as a definable event.

If the change that defines your inciting incident occurs over several scenes or through several events, it may not be obvious to your audience, and you'll lose the impact of the shift in momentum that comes with establishing your conflict. The inciting incident may come *as the result* of several events, but you should try to create an obvious single

STORY STARTER
INCITING INCIDENT

Here are some events around which you could build your inciting incident:

- a confrontation between two characters
- the delivery of some piece of news
- a diagnosis
- a natural disaster
- a coincidence

moment where the protagonist makes a definitive decision.

While several things may happen to your protagonist, you should choose a single instance that is the actual catalyst for the change. There may be a gradual buildup, but the character should reach a "straw that broke the camel's back" moment. This approach can be very effective, as it gives the author time to create sympathy for the character before introducing the central conflict.

DRAMATIC COMPARISON

STORY	DURATION OF INCITING INCIDENT
Casablanca	The moment when Ugate gives Rick the papers is a short piece of a larger scene. It is a short, discreet conversation.
"The Fall of the House of Usher"	Since this is a short work, the inciting incident is literally one exchange between Usher and the Narrator when Usher describes his growing fear and sense of dread.
Moby Dick	The incident begins at the moment of decision by Ishmael and continues as he walks to the ship and signs up.
Hamlet	Hamlet's vision of the ghost lasts only a few seconds, maybe half a minute of stage time. His contemplation of it is brief and concise as well.

Magnitude

The third consideration is that your inciting incident be strong enough and of enough consequence to adequately send your protagonist on her journey. The event must firmly and dramatically establish the conflict that is going to carry your story through to its exciting climax. Therefore, you must be sure that it has enough impact and creates a significant enough change for your characters and your audience to really feel that impact. If the climax of the story is the explosion of fireworks, then the inciting incident is the spark that lights the fuse.

Just as in timing the incident we had to be concerned with too soon and too late, in setting the magnitude of the event, we must be concerned with too much or too little. Some writers, concerned about shooting their wad too early in the story, will hold back, making their inciting incident so subtle that it barely registers on the audience's dramatic Richter scale. A character's simple decision to get in a car and drive across the country doesn't give you a powerful enough incident to set the conflict. On the other hand, if the character has an argument with a parent or spouse and decides to leave—this will adequately establish the conflict and set the rest of the story in motion, since the character will not only be dealing with the travails of the road, but also resolving the conflict with the parent or spouse.

Making the inciting incident too dramatic can also cause problems for the rest of the story. Many action films these days start with huge first act set pieces that involve mortal danger for the hero. These big opening movements can become a tough act to follow, and the drama of the actual event may overshadow the conflict to come. For instance, the action film *Speed* begins with the bomber sabotaging an elevator. This thrilling "will they fall or won't they fall" scene sets a very high bar for the action to come. The film's continual raising of the emotional bar, as the story moves to the booby-trapped bus, makes it difficult for the film's final sequence on the subway to live up to this level of tension. While many people may think it succeeded, the film's climax is more of an anticlimax, in my opinion. So beware of inciting incidents

 ## DRAMATIC COMPARISON

STORY	MAGNITUDE OF INCITING INCIDENT*
Casablanca	Rick is faced with both the danger of having the stolen papers and the temptation to use them to get out of Casablanca.
"The Fall of the House of Usher"	Usher reveals his fear that he is dying and the Narrator feels the urge to save him.
Moby Dick	Ishmael has decided to leave everything in his life behind to go to sea—he also has a hint that his captain is not entirely sane.
Hamlet	Hamlet sees a ghost who may be his father.

*As you can see, each of these inciting incidents has a life-changing magnitude to it.

that will overshadow the rest of your story. Try to keep the incident in proportion to what will follow.

Conjunction

What do we mean by conjunction? The most compelling inciting incidents are ones in which all of the factors in the drama—characters, settings and circumstances—are present at the moment the conflict is set. Often, these elements won't merge again until the climax, but to properly establish the context and the conflict, it is most effective to bring all these elements together—face to face. If your story is about the conflict between two people, the inciting incident is a great place to bring them together.

By merging these central elements early in the story, not only will you create a memorable beginning to the conflict, but you'll also set the foundation for the twists and turns, subplots and strange bedfellows that will make the journey toward the climax interesting and compelling to your audience. It is as if by bringing these elements together you are setting up the chemical reactions that will fuel the conflict.

 DRAMATIC COMPARISON

STORY	CONJUNCTION OF INCITING INCIDENT
Casablanca	Rick, Ugate and the Nazis are present, as is the background of the war, and the theme of escape. Ilsa and Laszlo enter shortly after the inciting incident.
"The Fall of the House of Usher"	Both Narrator and Usher are present, and the sister's presence becomes evident. The theme of death is prevalent.
Moby Dick	The mystery of Ahab is present, as are many of the other crew members, though they are on the periphery.
Hamlet	The themes of madness and betrayal are very present; however, with so many characters it is difficult to bring them all together.

EXERCISE

IDENTIFY AND DEVELOP YOUR INCITING INCIDENT

Start by writing a short description of the inciting incident of your story on a 3 × 5 card.

Evaluate the timing of the incident.

How close to the beginning of the story is it?

_____

What information must you communicate to the audience before it occurs? _____

_____

_____

_____

Evaluate the duration of the incident.

Does it occur in a single scene? _____

How many pages/minutes does it last? _____

Evaluate the magnitude of the incident.

Does it change the course of the story? _____

Does it change the protagonist's life? _____

How? _____

_____

Evaluate the conjunction of the incident.

Which themes are present? _____

Which characters are present? _____

Which motifs and metaphors are present? _____

_____

CHAPTER FOUR

Rising Action

Rising action makes up the largest part of any story in terms of screen time or pages. Here your audience will spend most of their time, and this is the section of your story that requires the most careful attention to the details of plotting. The rising action of your story commences immediately after the inciting incident and lasts through to the climax. As the word "rising" suggests, it is a steady escalation in the drama. Here the elements of suspense and tension are added to the plot. On page 53 you can see the large section that is composed of rising action on the graph of the plot arc.

In plotting this particular section of your story, it is important that you break down its vast size into several smaller pieces. Each of these pieces will revolve around a major plot point. Think of these plot points as the milestones on your story's journey to the climax. As you lay out these milestones, you'll be able to double back and weave in the other elements of your story like character development, subplots and exposition. It is these key elements that will make up the backbone of your story and will keep it moving forward toward the climax.

Keep in mind that everything you do in this section of the story should somehow contribute to the *coup de grace* that you will deliver with the climax and create the resonance that will come from the resolution. The rising action of any plot is like an arrow that points to a single moment in space and time—the climax. While some of your plot points or subplots may not be part of the linear journey to the climax, they will broaden and deepen the overall impact of the movement toward that climax.

In designing the rising action of your plot, try to think of it as a gently rising slope that gains gradually in pitch and altitude as it reaches the summit. After your inciting incident, place your plot points so that the tension is created gradually. Each plot point should build upon the one before it to create a gradually growing cumulative effect. This is not to say that each plot point must be mathematically calculated to be a certain percentage larger in impact than the one before it. On the contrary, the tension should build as the story gently undulates, varying the pace as it proceeds. One danger to avoid during this point in the story is making the plot too linear. While you shouldn't destroy the forward momentum in the plot, if your story proceeds directly, inexorably toward its climax, it will certainly be less interesting and entertaining and the audience may lose interest. Even the most gripping novel by a Grisham or a Clancy has moments in which the plot takes a break from its dramatic escalation. Subplots, character development and exposition can all provide these "breaks."

Beats

To best construct the rising action of your plot, you should break it down into pieces even smaller than the major plot points. Divide the whole rising action of your story into **beats**. Beats are distinct movements of the plot, or individual sequences that make up discreet pieces of the story. A beat can also serve as a subplot or other digression in your story. As you begin the process of outlining your plot (which we'll discuss in detail later), divide the various sections into beats.

These beats should be apparent to you as fully developed units, almost small stories unto themselves. As you plan them, try to identify each beat's individual arc. Just as your story as a whole has an arc, so too do the individual beats that make it up, each possessing a rising action, a climactic moment and a resolution. These movements will be smaller, but should be distinct and fully developed dramatic moments. Look for these patterns as you write. Develop each beat in your story so that it has a recognizable arc.

PURPOSE OF BEATS

Beats make it easier to tackle larger works like novels by breaking them into bite-sized pieces for both the author and, later, the audience.

Each beat gives the audience a small bit of gratification, a reward, a resolution to some bit of business in the story.

Beats allow the author to regulate the rising action and the tension in the story by allowing the stakes for the characters to be raised a step at a time.

The beats of the plot that make up the rising action can be of several types. Some beats are major plot points; others are exposition; still others delineate subplots or enhance character development. Let's look at each of these elements in depth.

Major Plot Points

Some of the major plot points in your story should be self-evident from the early stages of story conception. When you first decided on your topic, the first narrative elements that came to you were probably major plot points. These are the *events,* the pieces of your plot that really drive the story. When you look at your plot, from the inciting incident to the climax, these are the stepping stones that will get the characters from point A to point B. However, many writers construct stories without ever clearly identifying these pieces and without looking closely at how they propel the audience forward. Often, when a story seems flat, or when a climax seems to come out of the blue, it is because one or more major plot points is either missing or not properly delineated in the story.

Once you've identified each plot point in the rising action of your story (see Dramatic Comparisons, p. 49), you will need to evaluate it further to see how it measures up in two areas: First, what is the objective of the plot point, and second, how does it fit into the pacing of the story?

In their initial conception, major plot points should be kept distinct from subplots or other story beats that don't directly involve the linear forward motion of the story. These beats should all be part of the main movement of the plot. Later in the process, when incorporating subplots, and when blending the various elements of your story, you

EXERCISE
IDENTIFYING MAJOR PLOT POINTS

Just as we've done with the other parts of the plot, identify each major plot point in your story. If you are writing a novel or screenplay, you should have in the neighborhood of six to ten major plot points. If you are writing a short story, you will probably only have two to five.

Once you've identified these major turning points, write each one onto a single 3 × 5 card. Describe the action of the plot point completely, but concisely, keeping just to the simple facts of the sequence.

We'll use these cards later to construct an in-depth outline of each plot point in your story.

DRAMATIC COMPARISON
RISING ACTION

Here are examples of some, but not all, of the major plot points in the rising action of our classic stories:

STORY	MAJOR PLOT POINTS
Casablanca	Rick's drink with the Nazis and Renault; entrance of Laszlo and Ilsa. Ilsa's return to café to find Rick drunk. Renault closing café.
". . . Usher"	Introduction of sister, Madeline, as she passes in hallway. Entombment of Madeline. Storm and appearance of mysterious light.
Moby Dick	First pursuit and capture of a whale aboard the *Pequod*. Ishmael falls overboard and is rescued by Queequeg.
Hamlet	Hamlet's conversation with the Ghost. Polonius tells King and Queen of Hamlet's madness. The performance of the players. Hamlet kills Polonius and confronts Gertrude.

can more tightly weave subplots into your major plot point events.

Ideally, your plot points are devised in such a way as to accomplish multiple objectives and to bring together several threads in your story. The strongest plot points will be those where there is a convergence of forces. To merge these forces, design your major plot points to maximize the effect of:

- the setting
- the characters present
- the current subplots
- the timing

QUICK QUIZ
OBJECTIVE OF MAJOR PLOT POINTS

Determine the objective of each major plot point by looking at several different criteria:

How does this event advance the story?

Does it lead the protagonist and the audience toward the climax?

How does this event increase the tension and suspense of the story?

How does this event affect the development of the characters?

Where does this event need to lead the protagonist emotionally/mentally for the plot point to be successful?

Early major plot points might involve:

- the protagonist questioning the status quo
- the protagonist making a stand
- the protagonist having an initial confrontation with the antagonist and possibly failing or backing down
- the antagonist plotting against the hero

Middle plot points might involve:

- the protagonist doubting himself
- a secondary (and previously neutral) character revealing herself as an enemy
- betrayal by an ally
- the antagonist inadvertently revealing a weakness
- new evidence coming to light about the nature of the conflict

Late plot points (just before the climax) might include:

- a second confrontation with the antagonist
- the protagonist finding a secret, hidden or previously unrealized strength
- the protagonist reconsidering his reluctance and redoubling his effort

Setting

Choose a setting that highlights what is happening at that moment. In *Hamlet*, when the young Danish prince confronts his mother about her relationship with Hamlet's uncle Claudius, it is in her chamber where the busybody Polonius is hiding. This scene could have been played anywhere in the palace, but Hamlet's feelings are amplified by setting the scene in this most intimate of places. When he questions his mother's fidelity (or, more accurately, her rush to marriage), it is in the very room where she had slept with Hamlet's father. In *Vertigo*, Jimmy Stewart's character, who is afraid of heights, witnesses the apparent suicide of the heroine high in a bell tower. Stewart's fear may or may not have influenced his perception of events. These settings illuminate aspects of the characters' dilemmas and challenge their sensibilities.

Characters

Bring the different characters in your story together during major plot points for the maximum impact. The narrator in *Zen and the Art of Motorcycle Maintenance* recalls his nervous breakdown while traveling with his son who shows signs of having mental illness himself. Michael Douglas's character in *Fatal Attraction* is confronted on the telephone by his illicit lover while his wife is nearby in the next room and could walk in at any moment. These convergences of character not only add to the drama of the story, but can act as punctuation, highlighting your important themes. Think not only of the convergence of protagonist and antagonist, or protagonist and supporter, but also of the third and fourth parties who can be present in a scene and witnesses to it, lending added emotional force.

Subplots

Work the subplots into your major plot points to give them resonance, and also provide the opportunity to smoothly move from a subplot back into the main story. This is tricky business, however, and the better your plan is for building the rising action of your story, the easier it will be to weave these threads together. Just as a subplot can delineate and enhance the main plot, so too can a major plot point enhance a subplot.

For an example, let's turn again to a master plotter—Alfred Hitchcock. In *Rear Window* the main story involves photographer Jeff's suspicions about the disappearance of his neighbor's wife. A subplot involves Jeff's rocky romance with fashion editor Lisa. Near the climax of the story, Lisa tries to get evidence that the neighbor has murdered his wife by surreptitiously going into the neighbor's apartment. Jeff sees the neighbor returning home. While the audience is caught up in the excitement of whether or not she will be caught

---

COMPARE THE POTENTIAL IMPACT OF THESE TWO SCENES

Background
A recently widowed, hard-charging entrepreneur is in the middle of making the deal of her career. If it succeeds, she will be wealthy and able to sell her company to raise her young son. However, the deal could cause an environmental disaster.

Scene one
The woman presents her proposal in a boardroom filled with other executives who grill her on her facts and challenge her every point.

Scene two
The woman presents her proposal to the chairman in her office, while her young son, for whom she couldn't find a baby-sitter, plays in the next room.

Scene one may create a charged environment, with lots of hard-looking executives staring her down. But scene two allows you to put the themes of the child's future and the environment right on the page or screen, making the entrepreneur's choice that much harder: Should she pursue her objective for the sake of her son and possibly risk his future, or should she walk away from the deal and forego the opportunity to give her son an abundant childhood?

While the first scene would certainly confront her with a potentially tougher adversary (the whole board), the second scene would bring together more of the author's themes, thus creating a deeper, more layered scene.

---

by the murderer, Hitchcock skillfully shows us the depth of Jeff's love for Lisa, as he worries about her escape. The subplot of Jeff and Lisa's romance is furthered by the major plot point of Lisa's foray into the apartment. You can see how the convergence of these events deepens both the main story and the subplot.

Timing
The final consideration in creating your major plot points is timing. There are several different factors to keep in mind:
- The timing of the elements within the plot point. Things should happen quickly and concisely, making your points all the more

forceful by the speed with which they occur.

- The timing of the major plot points along the arc of the story. You want to place your plot points so that they naturally push the story up the arc. They are, in essence, the pillars that hold up the arc of your plot. Therefore, you need to be sure that each succeeding plot point does the job of propelling the story forward to the next plot point.

- The placement of the plot points relative to each other. While they should each support one another and draw the reader from point to point, they should also have a rhythm to them. If each major plot point increases suspense and drives drama by the same, ever-increasing magnitude, your story's rhythm will be lifeless, uninteresting and predictable. You want your plot points to push the story forward, but you also want to vary their scope and impact in such a way that you keep the audience guessing.

Pillars of the Plot

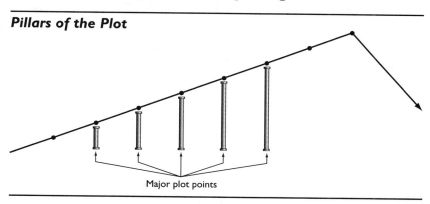

Major plot points

It's okay to have major plot points that allow tension to ease. These moments of comic or other relief are crucial to keeping your readers interested and, frankly, not wearing them out! Many of today's Hollywood movies are like high-speed freight trains, careening violently from one explosive plot point to another, never giving the audience a chance to relax, reflect or recover. This sledgehammer approach to storytelling often leaves audiences feeling assaulted rather than entertained or enriched. Unfortunately, many of today's best-selling authors have adopted this *more is more* attitude as well. It's true that many authors, from Tom Clancy to Dean Koontz, have created gripping novels that sometimes seem like runaway trains, but even they introduce elements that allow the story's pace to ebb. For Clancy this may mean putting in an exposition scene in an office or conference room somewhere (the Pentagon, maybe?) where the story's tension is preserved, but there is a diminished sense of imminent danger. For Koontz, it may be the addition of a scene that takes place in broad daylight, during which the audience can get a short breather. The point is that even the authors of these thrilling novels know that the audience will become numb to the tension if they aren't given an occasional chance to recover a bit.

Try to create a rhythm to your work, a natural ebb and flow of the major plot points, but one that nonetheless moves steadily toward the climax. Many writing teachers go so far as to assign page numbers where major plot points should be placed. I don't recommend adhering to anything this rigid; just space your major plot points so that they occur naturally in the flow of the story. This said, it is still necessary for you to make sure that they occur at intervals that keep the story moving without overwhelming the audience with too much information too quickly.

There are several ways to regulate the placement of your plot points depending on the type of story you are writing and the effect you are seeking.

Build

If you are writing a suspenseful mystery or thriller, the effect you may want to achieve with the pacing of your rising action could be called a *build*. In these stories your major plot points start out relatively far apart, then begin to occur in more and more rapid succession as the story moves toward the climax like a snowball rolling downhill. The goal is to build suspense by creating the impression that events are picking up speed and gradually spinning out of the protagonist's control. Each major plot point builds on the one before it, steadily raising the stakes and increasing suspense. This sort of relationship between major plot points *is* rather linear and is best used when the desired effect is the "die has been cast" and the story is now moving inexorably toward its climax.

An example of a plot that works on a build is a film like *Titanic*. The story moves forward in a brisk, but not urgent, way as Jack and Rose's affair unfolds. Once the ship hits the iceberg, the build begins.

As the ship gradually sinks and more and more things go wrong, the story builds. At first, everyone is fairly calm, then people start to worry. The ship begins to list and the tension builds, and when the lifeboats begin to run out, it builds more. Chaos breaks out on deck, and the steerage passengers are locked below. Finally, the ship stands on end as the story reaches its climax.

Diversion

A diversion is another technique that can be used to propel your audience through various parts of your plot's rising action. A diversion, as the term suggests, is a major plot point that doesn't *seem* to have anything to do with the main thrust of the story. However, later in the story or during the diversion itself, the scene's purpose and its relevance to the plot become clear. Diversionary plot points require cleverness, but they will help your plot avoid becoming overly linear. Diversions are also great ways to deepen the meaning of your story or delineate characters. Because diversions appear to veer off course, they afford a chance to throw your audience off guard and to reveal deeper themes or as yet undiscovered traits.

The writers of the television sitcom *Seinfeld* were masters of the diversion, continually introducing strange, out of context elements that seemed to have nothing to do with the main story, but that played an important and usually hilarious part later. One example is the episode when Kramer is making small sculptures out of dry pasta. He creates "fusilli Jerry" and gives it to Jerry as a gift. It seems to be a silly throwaway, but when George's father has an "accident" with it later, it precipitates the visit to the doctor that reveals the owner of Kramer's mistakenly received license plate.

Pause

Some plot points create a pause in the progress of the rising action. These scenes impart more information than action. A pause is a scene that reveals critical information surrounding the conflict and the protagonist's relationship to that information. While most plot points should have a lot of "punch," this type is like the blow that misses. Did you ever climb a flight of stairs in the dark and make that last step up only to find it wasn't there? Or attempt to force open a sticky door only to have it open easily? If you remember the surprise you felt, then you will understand the impact that these "pauses" can have in your plot.

If your audience is expecting a confrontation or battle and doesn't receive one, this can be as significant as the most explosive scene. Horror stories use this type of plot point most effectively. Think of the myriad scenes in horror books and movies where the hero approaches the door at the end of the dark hallway and with trepidation pulls it open only to find—nothing. The result of these plot points, ironically, is an increase in tension. Since what was expected didn't occur, the likelihood of it occurring in the near future increases. Simultaneously, the audience will feel less certain of when to expect something horrific, since it didn't occur when they thought it would. They'll think, "I know it's coming, but now I'm not so sure when." As you can see, this type of plot point can do wonders for increasing tension and avoiding the inexorable, linear progression of some stories.

Hitchcock used such a pause in *Rear Window*. Jeff becomes convinced his neighbor has killed his wife. He sees Thorwald taking out a suitcase and calls his friend, the cop. The cops stop Thorwald and inspect his suitcase, but it is empty. The audience expects them to find the murdered wife, but when they don't, the tension is escalated, because we, too, are convinced he did it, and now he knows someone is onto him, so Jeff is in greater jeopardy.

Another use of the pause is to *relieve* tension. Sometimes a story is on such a roll, with one shocking event happening after another, that the audience, the characters and even the author need a moment to reflect and rest. It's even possible that they just need a break from the central action of the story. These major plot points are great opportunities to take stock of or sum up your themes and the ramifications of what has happened so far. These scenes tend to be thoughtful and, as pauses when the protagonist decides on his ultimate action and girds for the final conflict that looms just ahead, are effective preludes to the climax. They function as a place to collect the momentum before releasing the tension in the next forward movement of the plot. The key to placing these scenes is being confident that the forward momentum will carry through this moment of "coasting." So, it's just as important to understand these pauses as it is to know how to propel your story forward.

In Elmore Leonard's book *Out of Sight*, the protagonists—a bank robber and a female agent—pursue one another as he commits his crimes and she tries to catch him. They are obviously attracted to each other, so when they finally agree to meet—as lovers, no law and order involved—it is a pause in the main action of the story. It gives the characters a chance to consummate their desire, and when it's over, the stakes have been raised.

Exposition

The second major function of the rising action is to provide a place for the exposition that is necessary in every story. Exposition is the revealing of facts, information, background, back story and character development information that is relevant to the main thrust of the plot. Exposition can be one of the most effective ways of creating and increasing the drama in your story. It can also be the quickest way to kill a plot's momentum and get your story bogged down in detail. Too much exposition, or too much at one time, can seriously derail a story and be frustrating to a reader or viewer eager for a story to either get moving or move on. As mentioned in the earlier section on inciting incidents, many authors are tempted to put all of the exposition at the beginning of their stories. Perhaps they are hoping to get it out of the way, or to give the audience all the information up front, but the real impact is to delay the start of the story, essentially asking your audience to proceed through many pages or many minutes without the least bit of forward momentum. You may have an audience dying of curiosity about the story that is soon to unfold—the trick is making sure they don't die (!) and put down your book or walk out of the theater. Exposition comes in many different forms.

Character Development

In our everyday lives we learn about people a little at a time. You may know all about a co-worker's professional life and history, but very little about what she does at home. On the other hand, you know all about your parents, but as a kid, didn't you wonder what they did at work all day? As you get to know your co-worker and perhaps become friends, or as you grow up and learn more about your parents' jobs, you gain a new insight into each of these people and what makes them tick. And, as you learn about multiple parts of a person's life, you can begin to make correlations and draw conclusions about them. But it takes a long time.

It is the same with the characters in your stories. Your audience should get to know them a little at a time. Too much information about a character too soon can be confusing to an audience and leave them trying to remember what was said about that character as they encounter events later in the story. Too much exposition about a character too early in the story also leaves the reader without the crucial element of context in which to judge the character.

The best way to give information about your characters is to use the "time release" method. Sprinkle facts about the character, revelations and other information throughout the story. Give your audience a little bit at a time and try to make the revelations relevant to the action that is occurring at that time. For instance, if you divulge that a character is afraid of heights just as he ascends a tall building, that piece of information is not only instantly relevant, it has impact beyond the simple fact and will be conferred to the audience naturally. On the other hand, if you had said at the beginning of your story, "Sid was afraid of heights," it would have less impact during the ascent.

One exception is when a fact about a character can be used as a ticking time bomb to add tension. For instance, "Sid was recovering from surgery on his defective heart." Such a fact will lie dormant in the readers' minds until that moment when Sid is under strenuous circumstances, and they will remember that fact you revealed earlier.

Background and Relevant Facts

These are pieces of exposition that lend meaning to the story as it progresses. In real life we might ordinarily know this information about a situation, but in the world of drama, it can be revealed in such a way as to lend real impact to the plot. As with character-based exposition, it is most effective to sprinkle these facts throughout the story. Try to place your expository points in places where they make the most sense contextually. Avoid going off on long expository tangents at moments when action and forward movement is occurring.

Back Story

This type of exposition often gets authors in trouble. Back story is what happened before the beginning of the segment of time that is encompassed by the book or film. Frequently, the temptation is to incorporate all the important parts of the back story into the very earliest stages of the work. However, so much information too early can overwhelm an audience. Just as too much character information can be difficult for readers to remember, it is likely that they will forget the back story by the time it becomes useful later. Avoid the urge to get all the cards on the table early.

Some facts concerning the past can be much more relevant later in a story when they directly relate to the action that is occurring. Back story can also provide much of the mystery that will keep your audience moving forward. Just as the unfolding of information can provide momentum, so too can mystery. The hero with the dark past is a classic archetype of literature, and the revelation of that dark past through back story is what really makes those stories so compelling.

In some stories the author may treat the exposition of the back story as almost a story in itself, revealing it in parallel to the main plot. In *Zen and the Art of Motorcycle Maintenance*, Phaedrus, the narrator, tells of his cross-country journey on a motorcycle with his son, while simultaneously describing his descent into mental illness years earlier. Each fact revealed from the back story has increased resonance when laid over the present-time story. In writing your own story, try to reveal the elements of the back story so that they add depth and meaning to your writing.

If you elect to use a narrative method to communicate your exposition to the audience, it's not necessary to present it like a bulletin tacked to a post. Such writing is uninteresting and usually feels like an unnecessary detour to the audience. Try approaching these expository sections as minor plot points in your story.

A piece of back story that can stand on its own makes a good diversion from the linear progression of the main plot. If the piece is a story in itself, with its own arc and its own resolution, it can work as a welcome change of pace in a story that is moving relentlessly forward. If you can divulge important information by placing it in the context of a subplot or other digression, you will have accomplished the task of exposition artfully and in a way that is relevant to the main plot. It's likely that your audience will hardly notice that they are being fed crucial information if they are enjoying an intriguing tangent.

SHOWING VS. TELLING

Exposition will work differently depending on what narrative form you are working with. Elements of exposition and back story function far differently if you are writing a screenplay than if you are writing a short story or novel. In a short story or novel, you can introduce these elements wherever and however you choose. A bit of history about a character can be inserted at the proper moment and go on for several paragraphs or even pages. When the digression is finished, you can move smoothly back into the story. The in-depth description of a character can be inserted almost anywhere in a printed work. However, with plays and screenplays, it's difficult (if not impossible) to have the on-screen action just veer into a narrative tangent. In these cases, it is even more important to work character and back story information into what is happening in the natural flow of the drama. A character's off-hand comment can resonate deeply if it describes something central to that character or another one in the story. And, as in all writing, actions always speak louder than words. Sometimes novelists rely too heavily on their ability to *tell* the audience what they wish them to know about a character, when *showing* them would be much more effective. In screenwriting, the only means of exposition is through the actions and dialogue of the characters and this fact can make screenplay exposition much more interesting than in a simple narrative. Even in writing for print mediums, I would recommend using these more indirect means for communicating exposition. It is quite simply far more elegant, creative and effective to show an audience information through action and the flow of the drama, since this is how we usually learn such information in real life.

But if you do elect to stray from the linear progression of the story, there are a number of pitfalls to avoid:

- Avoid making the subsection too long. It is very easy for a reader to get lost in the tangent. I've read many stories where I had to flip back through the book to where the main story left off just to reacquaint myself with what was happening.
- Be sure that your subplot story is well developed. It should have its own form, rhythm and arc. The drama of the subplot story should be sufficient to maintain the audience's interest on its own.
- It should nicely dovetail out of the main story and back into it.
- Beware of becoming too enamored of your subplot story. Some

authors, weary or bored with their main plot line, will develop elaborate, detailed subplots that can actually become more interesting than the main story. They may also be so stylistically different from the rest of the work that they become an ill-fitting piece of the overall work.

Remember, the elements of exposition are fully in your control; they are the tools of surprise and for drawing meaning from the events in your plot. Think of them as trump cards in your hand. You want to become skillful at playing them at the precise moment they will be most effective to your plot. Like a successful card player, you don't want to waste all your trump cards early in the bidding, so hold these elements until they can do your story the most good. Exposition can often be the breeze that blows away the smoke of mystery at the proper moment, revealing new information that will resonate with your audience.

Raising the Stakes

Several times in the preceding section you've heard the term **raising the stakes**. Writing is not life. Some writers may aspire to realism, but realism and reality are two very different things. An unedited manuscript detailing your life, or most people's lives for that matter, wouldn't be a very exciting book. Most of our lives are spent doing mundane things that aren't the stuff of great drama. The arc of life has a lower pitch, and, in reality, plot points and climaxes are rarely reached at times when a good writer would schedule them. On the other hand, life does spin out some of the best tales. "Truth is stranger than fiction" is certainly true, but what makes that truth interesting to read is the author's ability to fashion that truth into the most compelling drama.

We keep reality at arm's length in creating fiction. This means creating better drama by manipulating facts—and one way we create more compelling drama is by raising the stakes. Rarely do time and circumstance merge in the most dramatic way. It is one thing for a character who is a lawyer to take on a controversial case, but if we find out that the opposing counsel is his best friend—that's raising the stakes. Such coincidences (that we'd never believe if someone described them in real life) are much more easily forgiven in the realm of drama.

REALITY VS. REALISM

Reality is the universe as it actually exists in the experience of ordinary (sane!) people.

Realism is a stylistic approach to art or writing that strives for a faithful representation of reality.

The key distinction to draw from this is that realism is a *representation* of a thing—not the thing itself.

Raising the stakes is that event in a plot that takes the characters and the drama to the next level. It may be an unexpected occurrence, an inevitable event or a coincidence for the characters, but it occurs in such a way as to bring the events in the story to a higher level of tension. Increasing the characters' stakes in the situation will drive your plot and your audience toward the climax. Without these well-defined, well-placed events, your story will be flat, and the ascent to the climax will be dull. While the major plot points, plotted on our arc graph, draw a steady upward progression, within that progression there are quantum leaps that are critical to good dramatic plotting. Think of each instance of raising the stakes as a quantum leap.

 **DRAMATIC COMPARISON**
RAISING THE STAKES

Here are examples of raising the stakes from our classic stories:

STORY	RAISING THE STAKES
Casablanca	Rick's discovery that his old flame Ilsa is in town
	Ilsa declaring her love for Rick when she visits his apartment
". . . Usher"	The death of Usher's sister
	The arrival of the thunderstorm
Moby Dick	The sighting of the White Whale
Hamlet	The arrival of the players, and Hamlet's inspiration
	The killing of Polonius
	The death of Ophelia

STORY STARTER
RAISING THE STAKES

Here are some suggestions for ways to take a quantum leap in your writing.

A new wrinkle

While you want to lay out the conflict in a clear way early in your plot, try holding back some key fact that will make the character's plight even more difficult.

- Have your protagonist appear to overcome the conflict you introduced at the inciting incident, only to have him discover that the *real* problem lies elsewhere.
- Have one of your protagonist's supporters turn against him or die. The loss of an ally will make the protagonist's path different and more difficult and may inject a new theme of betrayal or loss into your plot.
- Have your protagonist discover that his actions have had some unanticipated effect (positive or negative).
- Have the protagonist realize that the conflict has impact beyond his own life.

Example: In *The Fountainhead*, Dominique realizes that the man she desires is the man whose work she has railed against in print.

Break a stalemate

The best drama comes when opposing forces appear to be almost equally matched. The most obvious example of this is any book or movie about a military battle. There is usually a point in the battle when the two sides are hunkered down in the trenches, face to face, with neither party appearing to have an upper hand. Introduce an element that allows the two warring factions to break the stalemate. When this happens, the story's drama will always escalate as the new circumstances play out. The break of the stalemate doesn't have to be in the protagonist's favor either. It can often give a story a boost, particularly if the protagonist's situation worsens before it improves.

- Have an unsung character (or the protagonist) suddenly take action where previously she expressed unwillingness.
- Have nature or fate (*deus ex machina*) intervene to change the situation.
- Have characters find an unexpected element of common ground or a common goal, turning adversaries into allies.
- Have a character discover an untapped well of strength.

Example: In *Dances With Wolves*, Dunbar and the Sioux are attempting to speak with each other. When Dunbar figures out that "tatonka" means "buffalo," the conversation and the relationship make a quantum leap.

Revelation

The quantum leap of raising the stakes is often accomplished through use of a surprise revelation. The revelation can be an actual plot point, where some action occurs that gives the characters new information, or it can come from exposition. This was referred to in the last section when we discussed the careful placement of exposition.

- Reveal a previously undisclosed fact about the characters or situation. This new fact somehow changes the characters' perspective on their situation and thus alters the action and the drama in the plot.
- Reveal a bit of the back story that the audience and/or the characters were previously unaware of.
- The revelation may come to the audience only when the protagonist unveils something about himself.
- Revelations in which the protagonist *and* the audience learn the new piece of information simultaneously are very effective. This sort of raising the stakes not only increases the dramatic impact of the story, it also engenders sympathy for the character since the revelation becomes a shared experience.

Example: In *Return of the Jedi*, Luke discovers that his enemy Darth Vader is his own father, Anakin Skywalker.

Surprise turnabout

Sometimes the stakes in a story are raised through an event that comes as a surprise to both the characters and the audience. This change of fortune can be like the breaking of a logjam, releasing not only the logs, but the water built up behind it, giving the story a rush of dramatic energy.

- Insert a surprise obstacle or setback for the protagonist.
- Give your protagonist a sudden, rapid advancement against the conflict, allowing him to leap ahead, seemingly overcoming all obstacles.
- Either of these turnabouts will nicely set up your character for another turnabout—like a double cross—either insuring victory when all seemed hopeless or dashing the protagonist's hopes to pieces.

Example: In the book *Primary Colors*, the protagonist's opponent in the election is struck ill, and Stanton seems to have the nomination tied up. Then another politician enters the race reluctantly, taking the lead. He then mysteriously drops out, clearing the way for Stanton's final victory.

The key is to keep the audience guessing, introducing elements that are both believable and dramatic. This is one area where over-reaching is a serious mistake. If a story is moving along well and the author suddenly raises the stakes too dramatically, he will lose the audience.

Every audience and author have an unspoken pact: The reader agrees to suspend disbelief, to give the author a little flexibility with reality in return for good drama. The author accepts the audience's forbearance and promises not to abuse that suspension of disbelief.

If you overreach when raising the stakes, you break the pact between author and audience, the artificial world of the story is shattered and the audience is likely to desert the author in midstory.

On the other hand, if you throw your readers a well-timed, well-crafted curveball, their gasp can be almost audible and they will dive deeper into your story and grow closer to your protagonist. A skillful raising of the stakes is one of the most exciting accomplishments for a writer and one of the most enjoyable aspects of experiencing a story for an audience.

Suspense

If we boil down this notion of raising the stakes, what we are really talking about is *suspense!* The gradual increase of tension is necessary in almost any story. However, creating suspense is a difficult and complicated task. It takes a clever mind and a subtle touch. Too often in modern writing, tension is created only by stringing together outrageous, sensational and explosive events. In movies, horror and carnage substitute for the real, satisfying experience of suspense.

Suspense can be created in any story, from a gripping action novel to a drawing room comedy. The elements of suspense are largely the same for either undertaking, but for the purposes of this section we will focus primarily on suspense or action stories, not because these

---

Every audience and author have an unspoken pact: The reader agrees to suspend disbelief, to give the author a little flexibility with reality in return for good drama. The author accepts the audience's forbearance and promises not to abuse that suspension of disbelief.

---

subtler forms of comic suspense aren't relevant or interesting, but simply because it's easier to illustrate the use of suspense where it is a central element in the plot.

An acknowledged master of suspense is film director Alfred Hitchcock. I'll use examples from many of his movies in this section to illustrate the use of suspense. An earlier master of suspense was American writer Edgar Allen Poe, and I'll discuss his techniques as well.

Creating suspense is the ultimate balancing act. Like for a circus acrobat, writing suspense involves the precise balancing of several factors, each of which depends entirely on the others.

Elements of Suspense

- Suspense is the audience's anticipation of what will happen next, the delicate balance between not knowing, yet wanting to know.
- Suspense is the precise control over what the audience knows and what it doesn't know. Creating suspense is all about revealing part of the picture, but not the whole picture. Knowing a little bit about a situation, an audience will almost always desire to know more, and it is the author's withholding of this knowledge that creates suspense.
- Suspense is also the clever balance of timing. It is giving the audience a piece of information and then knowing just how long you can keep them waiting for the other shoe to drop.

By balancing these three elements, you will create a fine, taut quality to your work that will enhance the story's forward momentum by keeping the audience turning the pages to discover what comes next. As you can see by comparing these three elements, each is intrinsically dependent on the others, and the art of creating suspense is managing all three elements successfully. Some of the basic methods for creating tension are easily defined and can give you a good starting place to determine how to manage suspense in your plot.

Time Bomb

One of the most effective means of creating suspense could be called the ticking time bomb. Hitchcock used this one marvelously, using an actual time bomb in the movie *Sabotage*. The idea is to set a figurative clock ticking, limiting the time frame in which the events of your plot (or some subset of those events) can occur. In *The Man Who Knew Too Much*, one of Hitchcock's perennial favorite heroes, Jimmy Stewart, plays a man who knows that an assassination is going to occur. He must race to find out who will be assassinated and where the assassination will take place. In the climactic scene we know that at some precise moment during the musical score that a symphony is playing the fatal shot will ring out. The music becomes the fuse of the time bomb, marvelously creating suspense as the audience is glued to the action, waiting for the music to reach its crescendo.

The time bomb can be started as early in your plot as the inciting incident. Or you can use a smaller time bomb to create tension in a single important sequence. The key to the time bomb method is to put the protagonist in a circumstance that must resolve itself in a given time frame. As the hero struggles to resolve the situation, the audience will be acutely aware of the passing of time, and their concern for the hero will grow incrementally as each moment passes.

Puzzle

Another way to create suspense is to give the audience just a piece of the puzzle, a fragment, denying them the other pieces until later. This is particularly effective in stories that have a mystery component to them. It is also effective because you can keep offering your audience more fragments, unconnected pieces of the puzzle, not allowing them to connect the pieces until the climax of the plot. In *Rebecca*, another Hitchcock film from a book by Daphne du Maurier, we are given the story of the first Mrs. DeWinter a single piece at a time. At the beginning of the plot we know very little about her, and what we do know is seemingly unrelated and irrelevant. As the plot progresses, the new Mrs. DeWinter (the character ironically is never given a first name!) slowly learns the tale of what happened to her husband's first wife. Still, the pieces don't make sense until the very end when the evil Mrs. Danvers recounts the entire tale, including the crucial puzzle piece.

This technique is wonderful for drawing in an audience because, unlike the ticking time bomb, the audience is challenged to figure out the missing pieces and to draw the connections between the pieces that they are given. This will keep them not only turning pages or glued to their seats, but it will also set their minds awhirl trying to out-guess the author!

Truncating

Another means of fragmenting the audience's understanding of events and to create tension is to truncate a scene. There are two ways to do this: One is to start a scene late, after some unseen crucial event has taken place, and the other is to cut out of a scene before its action has been completed.

Example one. Two characters are engaged in a heated argument. They are yelling and screaming at each other until one of them makes an angry threat and pulls out a gun. Then jump immediately to another scene—only in this one, the character who was threatened is conspicuously absent. Did the other character kill him? The audience will be left wondering and you will have created suspense.

Example two. You start a scene where a husband and wife are standing outside of their home. They aren't speaking to one another, but the husband gets into his car and drives off. The wife then goes on about another piece of business with another character. What has happened? your audience will wonder. Did the husband leave her? Did she kick him out? Or has he just left on a routine journey? Discovering the answers will keep your audience involved in the story.

There are two elements involved in building suspense throughout your story. First is creating suspense in an individual scene or sequence, like in the above examples. A greater challenge is maintaining the tension from the beginning of a story to the end, establishing tension in the opening scenes and keeping the audience guessing until the climax, and possibly beyond.

The pace at which you build suspense (stretch the rubber band—see p. 69) in your plot is key to reaching the proper point at the proper moment. The building of tension should be gradual, with periodic spikes in tension along the arc of the story, which will likely correspond to the major plot points. There is danger in both building the tension too gradually or too soon and in building it too fast.

Building Suspense Too Slowly

Building suspense too gradually will make it difficult for your audience to stay involved in the characters and in your plot. The plot that mean-

THE RUBBER BAND METAPHOR

One way of thinking about the suspense in your story is as a rubber band. You, the author, stretch the rubber band gradually over time, making the drama in your plot more and more taut with every event, every plot point.

This metaphor can come in handy if you keep it in the back of your mind as you write. After each scene or sequence you write, ask yourself, "How did this event stretch the rubber band?" Every rubber band has a breaking point, a point at which releasing one end will create the maximum amount of "snap." That snap is the blow you want to deliver to your audience with the climax of your plot. Therefore, try to gauge the stretching of your rubber band so that you reach that point of maximum elasticity right at the moment you want to unleash it—the climax.

ders aimlessly for pages and pages makes it impossible for the audience to commit the emotional investment necessary to carry them through. Today's most successful writers know how to set the hook of suspense early in their work, so that the audience is compelled to follow the story.

In today's difficult publishing world, most agents and editors will give an author only a mere thirty pages to hook them. If the agent or editor isn't hooked in that short time frame, he will return the manuscript with a "thanks, but no thanks" letter.

Plan your story so that the tension that must carry through to the climax is established early. I recommend you plant the first seed of tension in the few pages before the inciting incident occurs, then sprout that tension in that inciting incident. From there, build it steadily, planning so that new elements, fresh fuel, are added to the tension at regular intervals. One frequently made mistake is setting the tension early, during the inciting incident, but then forgetting about it until the story approaches the climax. This often happens when the author, after initiating the story, spends the next long section presenting endless

In today's difficult publishing world, most agents and editors will give an author only a mere thirty pages to hook them. If the agent or editor isn't hooked in that short time frame, he will return the manuscript with a "thanks, but no thanks" letter.

exposition—to stretch the rubber band a little bit, only to release it. Even if you hook the audience by the time you reach the magical page thirty mark, you will still lose them if the story goes slack after that.

Building Suspense Too Quickly

It is equally important not to stretch the rubber band all the way to the breaking point too early in your plot. This will make it impossible to maintain that suspense for the long haul to the climax. The result is that either the tension will gradually dissipate or the audience will become desensitized to it by the time the climax arrives. This latter scenario is what happens in many of today's explosive action movies. Audiences are bombarded over and over again with scenes that in a normal film would be climaxes themselves, until their capacity for thrill is completely overwhelmed. The result is a story that, in spite of the enormous pyrotechnics, seems flat.

Masters of suspense like Poe and Hitchcock knew how to take the slightest tension and grow it without need of explosive action. Poe created one of the most suspenseful stories of all time using nothing more terrifying than the beat of a heart. The secret is to increase the level of *relative tension* gradually. This means that while the story may never produce true fireworks, each plot point increases the tension incrementally so that relative to the plot point before it, the suspense has grown considerably.

The first skill in creating tension you must develop as an author is knowing how to stretch the rubber band, using the techniques we described earlier for keeping your audience guessing. As you master these techniques and develop your own knack for writing compelling drama, you will also master the skill of pacing the growth of your plot's tension. The final element involved in writing tense, compelling stories is knowing when the rubber band is about to break.

The best suspense writers know the exact moment when the rubber band of suspense will stretch no more, and they release the rubber band with a snap, unleashing the climax of the story. The key is gauging when an audience can take no more suspense and needs a final resolution to the story. Again, many modern authors have lost control of this delicate art. How many books or movies have we experienced where the author simply went too far? Creating suspense has an inherent quality of pushing one's luck with the audience, as you ask them to believe, and even be complicit, in thrilling events, but there is a fine line between creating suspense and going too far. We've all experienced stories that we were fully engaged in, rooting for the characters and completely absorbed, but then the author either asked us to believe one thing too many or asked us to wait just a little too long. Suddenly, the rubber band doesn't release with a satisfying "snap"; rather it breaks and the integrity of the story falls into chaos and disarray. To control this rubber band, to stretch it without breaking, requires that the author be able to disengage from the process of writing the story, to go back to the story as a reader and decide if the suspense has been stretched too far. If you have even the slightest inkling that it has—you are probably right. Revisit the structure of your story and rewrite it so that the story "snaps" at the right moment. Look at your story plotted against the plot arc. If it seems that you've gone beyond where you'd originally intended to place the climax, you need to reel in the story. Often, as writers, we get on a roll and add things to our plots that we hadn't intended in the planning stages. This riffing on the plot isn't a bad thing, and can lead to some of our most creative work, but we always need to be able to return with the objective eyes of the architect to determine if the improvisation works within the story as a whole. By going back to our original plan, we can almost always (assuming we did our planning well) divine the proper moment to release the tension in our story.

So, as you build the events that create suspense in your plot, keep the rubber band metaphor in mind. Be sure that you are stretching it steadily until the moment at which it is ready to snap.

Restricting Perception of Events

As we've seen so far, one of the primary keys to creating suspense is limiting what the audience knows. Give your audience the what you don't know *can* hurt you message. Keep the audience guessing and wondering what is going to happen next by fragmenting and truncating the information you pass them. This is what creates suspense. Another way to restrict your audience's perception of events is to limit the frame or the scope of your story. There are several ways to do this.

Limited narrator. In most fiction the writing is in the third person, omniscient view. This narrative voice affords the author the ability to jump from one person's mind to another's, showing various perceptions of events, basically being everywhere at once. This gives the audience a very broad perspective on events and allows the author to create some very interesting contrasts and comparisons. But it also may allow the author to give the audience too much information, undercutting the potential for suspense.

One way to address this issue is to use the third person, omniscient view, but restrict what information you give the audience about characters other than the protagonist. Don't reveal every nuance of what is happening; save some information to create suspense. Stick with the protagonist and allow him to be the means by which the audience discovers new information.

For a more direct approach to limiting the audience's frame of knowledge, try putting your story in first person. If the story is told from the perspective of just one character in the story, your audience will know only what that character knows and will make the various discoveries throughout the plot along with that character.

First-person narrative has been used to great effect in many novels, particularly in the classic detective novels of the 1940s. Readers were thrilled by the adventures of Sam Spade, who spun his detective yarns in the first person. The reader traveled on the journey along with the character (rather than having the journey recounted in third person) and was drawn deeper into the plot by a sense of complicity with the protagonist. In these stories, whatever tension the character felt was felt simultaneously by the audience.

The first-person narrator doesn't necessarily have to be the protagonist in your story, either. It is often very effective if the narrator is a third party to the action, a mere observer, and one whose perspective on events is limited. *Moby Dick* is a terrific example of such a story. Ishmael, a simple deck hand, narrates the story of Captain Ahab. His understanding of Ahab is limited, but we learn about the protagonist gradually as Ishmael signs on and makes the whaling voyage. Since Ishmael hadn't previously been to sea, we also get to discover all the wonders of a sea voyage through his virgin eyes. Captain Ahab is a mystery to him at first, and the audience learns about Ahab along with Ishmael. In short, Ishmael's discoveries become the audience's discoveries. The biggest advantage of this type of narration is that the narrator can't necessarily see into the psyche of the protagonist, allowing suspense and tension to grow.

Limited space. Restricting the space in which your story takes place is another excellent way of creating tension. This technique works in a couple of ways.

- First, there is the "no way out" factor. By keeping your characters, particularly protagonist and antagonist, in the same, preferably small, space, you greatly increase the power of their interaction. Since there is no escape, they have no option but to confront the conflict between them.

- Second, there is the "too many rats in the cage" factor. Characters confined to a small space are by nature going to become more agitated and irritable, increasing the chance for dramatic fireworks.

These two factors illustrate why some of the most tension-filled dramas ever written take place in confined spaces like spacecraft (*2001: A Space Odyssey*), ships (*The Caine Mutiny, Moby Dick*) and even submarines (*Das Boot*). By confining their characters, these authors guaranteed that their stories would pack a dramatic wallop. Hitchcock created life-and-death suspense in *Lifeboat* by confining all the action and all the characters to one small lifeboat afloat in the ocean. In such small spaces there is nowhere for the characters to retreat and very little room for safety valves where tension between characters can be vented.

When used effectively the tension created by the small space can even translate to feelings of claustrophobia in the audience. I remember seeing the German submarine drama *Das Boot* many years ago and being so anxious about the close quarters that I kept looking up to the theater ceiling just to remind myself that I wasn't on that boat with them. By the time the movie was over, I couldn't wait to go outside and take a deep breath! Similar experiences can be created without the power of the cinema. When I read Stephen King's short story "Rita Hayworth and the Shawshank Redemption," I had to keep looking around to remind myself that I, too, wasn't in prison. Needless to say, if you can create such confined spaces where your characters have little to hide behind, you will certainly create memorable drama.

Limited time. The time factor is the other dimension of your plot that you can restrict to create suspense. Again, there are a couple of ways to do this:

- You can, as mentioned before, start the ticking time bomb. If you write a short story in which a time bomb is literally set in the opening scene to go off in thirty minutes, the tension in your story can be increased with nothing more than a simple glimpse of the clock ticking toward zero.
- Restrict your story to a distinct interval of time, one day, for instance. If an entire story must occur in a day, or a week or a season, you've given your plot a finite time frame, again creating a "no way out" scenario. Only now instead of it having to occur in a defined space, the story must resolve itself within that given time frame. You can set this frame as simply as saying "it all happened that summer." By defining it clearly from the top, you will be able to use the simple passage of time as an element of suspense.

Again, Hitchcock was a master at restricting time. In his film *Rope* he attempted the difficult task of filming an entire story in real time. He used several clever devices to disguise the breaks in the action, which were necessary because the camera could only hold about twelve minutes of film at a time. But his murder mystery unfolded in real time and in real space. In this case there was truly no escape for characters or audience, as the action was confined to the space of a single apartment and the one hour and forty-five minutes between the murder at 7:30 and when the murderer is revealed at 9:15.

The Twist

Suspense for its own sake is of little value in a plot. Like books and movies that can only shock without ever thrilling, suspense doesn't really contribute to a plot's effectiveness unless it pays off somehow. The most obvious way it can pay off is with an exciting climax that ties up the loose ends and answers all the questions that created the suspenseful environment. There's another element that can help suspense pay off, and, when used most effectively, can greatly increase the suspense in a plot. This is the plot twist. For the purposes of this section, let's define the plot twist as the unexpected element in your story, a turn of events that takes the audience by surprise.

A plot twist often raises the level of drama in a story from the ordinary to the extraordinary. Think of the stories you've encountered where there was a twist so unexpected that it not only changed the whole tenor of the story but also opened up a totally new perspective on the story. One of the best plot twists ever was in the film *The Crying Game*. The twist in that story was so shocking that audiences and critics actually managed to keep it secret. Most audiences can't resist telling others good plot twists, but in this case, the twist was so extraordinary that nobody wanted to ruin the surprise for anyone else. If you remember (if you haven't seen the movie, skip to the next paragraph) your reaction when you found out that the protagonist's girlfriend *wasn't* a girl, you know how a cleverly designed plot twist can completely transform a story. The twist in *The Crying Game* adds a whole new dimension to the main character. How will the revelation affect his feelings for his lover? Will he lash out at him for the deception? It also completely reframes the friendship. It adds dimension that didn't exist before to both the individual characters and to the relationship between them.

The secret to good twists, like most elements in creating suspense, is maintaining a careful balance between the unexpected and the impossible. An outrageous plot twist that defies reason and plausibility can shatter a story's credibility, and a clichéd, hackneyed plot twist that's been seen a dozen times before adds nothing to a story, except to increase its predictability. Giving your plot a good twist isn't an undertaking that begins at the moment the twist occurs. The seeds for it must be planted well in advance. Creating the plot twist is like setting a good trap. You lay the snare, then carefully cover your tracks, concealing any evidence of what you are about to spring.

Some plot twists will occur as part of the climax, paying off the suspense you've built up in a completely surprising way. Climactic plot twists require delicate handling. Remember that you've taken your audience on a rather long journey, you've outlined the conflict for them and they've witnessed the character's drive toward his goal. To turn that conflict and that goal upside down with a plot twist is no easy task. It's entirely possible that you'll lose the audience at this critical moment when they are looking for the final piece of the conflict to be settled. To deny them this is to risk their sympathy and to risk the effectiveness of your resolution. Think hard before using a plot twist at *the* defining moment of your plot.

I believe a better place for a plot twist is right before the climax. A properly designed twist at this time can be just the catalyst that is needed to bring the story to its pinnacle. The use of plot twists takes us back to the very essence of what we've been discussing in this section: raising the stakes. The plot twist is the trump card when it comes to raising the stakes in a story.

STORY STARTER

PLOT TWISTS

A few of the things a plot twist can do include:

- Raise the stakes for the protagonist
- Throw the audience off the trail
- Act as a catalyst for getting a reluctant protagonist to act
- Deepen the resonance of a character or relationship

Another good example of a plot twist is in the movie *Psycho*. Throughout the plot we are led to believe that the murderer is Mrs. Bates. The glimpses we see of the killer clearly point to her. But, as most of us know, the killer turns out to be Norman. Hitchcock cleverly plants the seeds of doubt early. We hear Mrs. Bates's voice, but never when Norman is on screen. We see her clothes, but never her face. On the other hand, Norman, with his stuffed birds and laconic manner, is clearly a rather creepy fellow. All this adds up to a crucial combination of two elements. The first is evidence that one outcome is likely, but, at the same time, the author is planting doubt about that outcome, creating tension and setting the audience up for a thrill.

Plan the twists just as carefully as you would any other portion of your story. As you plan the action leading up to the twist, choose all the clues you will leave concerning your twist, no matter how small, and determine where you intend to place them. This is one area of plotting where you can't be too detailed.

Sometimes, you won't find the twist in your story until you've already written a large portion of it. Be sure you don't just drop it in and move on. If this happens, and the perfect plot twist doesn't come to you until late in the writing process, work your way backwards from the point of the twist, plant the clues and then cover the trail. Often you'll find that many of these clues were already planted in the writing of your story, and all you'll need to do is draw them together, highlighting their meaning within the newly discovered context of the plot twist.

These elements—suspense, limiting the frame and the plot twist—

are all ways of raising the stakes in your story. They will provide you the quantum leaps you need to propel your characters and your story toward the most important piece in the drama: the climax. Everything you do in your story should, directly or indirectly, point the audience toward the explosive moment when everything in the story is at risk. Use these elements to weave together the themes and ideas that give your story its richness. Then when your audience reaches the climax, you can be sure that they won't be disappointed.

CHAPTER FIVE

The Climax and Resolution

The climax of your story should occur at precisely the moment when the rubber band we discussed in the previous chapter is about to break—the moment at which tension is at its maximum. It is probably the most important moment in your plot and certainly the time when all the hard work you've put into building the rising action of the story will come to fruition. Since so much is at stake, it's a critical moment both for the characters in your story and for the success or failure of your tale.

Obviously, a successful climax is impossible if the rising action that's led to it has been a failure. However, a successful rising action can also be squandered by a poorly timed or executed climax. The importance of this moment really cannot be overstated. Therefore, we must look closely at how to properly execute the climax so that you deliver your audience the most devastating possible blow.

Two Phases to the Climax
The first phase is something we talked about earlier—the crisis. The crisis is the movement in the story that immediately precedes the climax. You can think of it as a slightly enlarged view of the climax that encompasses the final moment before the ultimate confrontation in the plot. The crisis can be thought of as the point of no return, the

moment in the story at which the protagonist is left but one course of action. The crisis also includes a short time after he crosses this point before acting, which is often a time for emotional processing of the situation, and the preparation for the final action. These two pieces together, the point of no return and the processing of the situation, are the crisis of the story.

The climax phase is the ultimate action of the story. This is the moment when the protagonist, faced with no other alternatives, confronts his conflict face to face. The outcome of this charged confrontation is what will be left to play out in the final piece of your plot, the resolution.

DRAMATIC COMPARISON
CRISIS

STORY	CRISIS
Casablanca	Crisis begins with Rick discovering that Ilsa has sneaked into his apartment.
". . . Usher"	Crisis begins when the sound being described in book Narrator is reading is heard in the house.
Moby Dick	Crisis begins with sighting of white whale and the initiation of the chase.
Hamlet	Crisis is set off with the return of Laertes to the palace.

Constructing the Climax: Choosing the Proper Moment

The placement of your crisis and resulting climax in your story's time line will help determine how effective it will be. To make this determination, you must have a good feel for the tension and rhythm in your story. Just as a musician knows beat four by knowing beats one through three, the writer knows the moment of the climax by knowing the rhythm created by the rising action.

If you take the time in advance to plot your story carefully and completely on the arc, you'll have no trouble knowing at what point the climax will happen. If you've placed these steps properly, you will see that all of your themes, plots and ideas have converged at this point. Essentially, all your plotting has led you to this moment when there's nothing left to do but unleash the climax of your story.

Hazard: The Late Climax

What gets many writers into trouble is trying to finesse this moment a bit too much. Frequently, writers come to this point without having hit all the points they originally intended in the planning of the story, so they extend the story to slip in these other elements or themes. Unfortunately, we've already stretched the rubber band to the breaking point, so instead of releasing its energy with a smart "snap," we prolong the moment, dissipating the tension. The anticlimactic, delayed "snap" is more like a thud. The author has lost the concise, forceful impact that the well-planned story potentially possessed.

If you arrive at the moment of truth—the climax—and you've neglected some points or themes that were crucial to the story, the solution isn't to delay the climax. The only recourse is to go back to your plot outline and figure out where you can work those points in earlier in the story. This will require some finesse and possibly some retooling of the whole rising action. But this is a much more effective solution than forcing a fit or prolonging the plot's journey to the climax.

Rhythm

Normally, the rhythm of a story is something that the reader experiences unconsciously, but the author must be aware of it and regulate it. If the major plot points are the story's organs, the rhythm is the heartbeat.

The act of writing is much akin to music. Once you've outlined your story and plotted it on the arc, as you begin the writing process, try to tune into the "rhythm" of your story. Remain aware of the pacing of your story but tune into the rhythm.

Varieties of Rhythm

- The rhythm of the plot points, which increase in frequency and impact as you approach the climax.
- The rhythm of the tension, the gradual stretching of the rubber band.
- The rhythm of the characters, as their relationships intertwine and as the audience becomes increasingly involved in their lives.

Just as the musician learns to hear the time signature of a piece of music without reading it on the page, with practice you'll learn to "hear" the rhythm of your story. This skill will help you in placing all the key events in your story, not just the climax. The best method for learning this is simply practice.

EXERCISE
FINDING THE RHYTHM

Part one

Start with short stories. Read several and try to get in touch with the rhythm of the plot. Mark with sticky notes the key moment in each major plot point. Notice the distance between them and their relative intensity.

Part two

After doing this with a couple of short stories, try a play or novel. Mark the key moments in each major plot point, but before you reach the climax, try to predict where it will occur.

Part three

Later, take the same novel or play and try to tune in to its rhythm. Chart the major plot points and try to understand how the author is regulating the rhythm in order to lead his audience to the climax.

It's important in striking the climax at the right moment that you get the feel for the rhythm you've developed in your own story. Often, however, in writing a longer work, the author will begin to lose touch with the rhythm of the plot since it happens over so many pages and probably over many months of work. This can make it difficult to both feel and write transition into the climactic portion of your plot.

If you have a good grip on the rhythm at the outline phase, you'll be less likely to lose it later. If you do lose the rhythm, one solution is, ironically, to stop writing.

When you arrive at the point in your outline where you've plotted the climax, stop writing. As you feel the story reaching the crisis, take a break. Go back and read what you've written. During this read you can reacquaint yourself with the rhythm of your story and make any necessary adjustments. Once this rhythm is working in the rising action, and once you've gotten familiar with it again, you will be able to launch into your climax with a fresh perspective and also with a

If you have a good grip on the rhythm at the outline phase, you'll be less likely to lose it later. If you do lose the rhythm, one solution is, ironically, to stop writing.

clear awareness of where your audience will be with the story. But if the rhythm leading into your crisis is off, even the most well-conceived climax will be compromised. This is the time to go back and rework your outline, and examine the basic building blocks of your plot.

Constructing the Climax: The Proper Setting

Equally important in executing a satisfying, devastating climax is choosing a compelling setting. Many otherwise excellent stories are compromised by the author's poor choice of a setting for the climax. The setting should help in the climax's overall goal of tying all the ideas, themes and subplots together. Here are some things to consider in choosing the setting for your climax.

Theme

Relate the setting of the climax to the themes you've been developing in your story. By setting the climax in a location that has resonance with the themes of your story, you will increase its impact.

The climax of the movie *Field of Dreams* takes place on the baseball diamond. While much of the film has taken place on a road trip, the subject of baseball is obviously central to the film. So rather than have the climax occur during the road trip or in another location, it happens right there on the field. Roy's problem with the past and his relationship to his father, as well as his financial problems, are played out *together* in that most potent location. The confrontation about his finances could've taken place in a bank, but it was more effective to bring the bank to him. It gave the filmmakers the chance to tie these events together so that they could rebound off one another. The baseball diamond in Roy's field becomes ground zero, where all his problems are finally confronted. It also allows subtle, inexplicit metaphors that most people can relate to, like "the ninth inning" and "two strikes," to quietly add to the drama. By setting the scene at the diamond, the themes of the relationship between father and son and the redemptive, incorruptible power of baseball are brought together.

Consider the themes of your story, and try to find a setting for the climax that will bring them into the sharpest possible relief. Allow the setting to emphasize your themes, as well as support your drama. A character who is "on the edge" in the plot should possibly find himself on some literal edge in the climax. A character struggling to find his identity may reach his climax in a place of absolute solitude.

Emotion

The setting should also have an emotional charge for the protagonist. A climax in a restaurant is much better if that restaurant holds difficult memories for the character. Whatever the location, the climax will be more effective if it holds some special meaning for the character, perhaps some meaning that's been brewing for a long time.

Many journey-based plots will spend much time describing or contemplating some special location for the protagonist, building up its mythology over many pages, without ever revealing it until that climax is reached. The location may also be the physical manifestation of the character's goal. In *The Wizard of Oz*, Dorothy spends the entire rising action trying to get to the Emerald City. It is a place that has loomed in the distance for a long time and has held the promise of fulfilling her wish. When she arrives, the anticipation has been so great that the city takes on a larger-than-life quality for Dorothy.

The protagonist may also be returning to a place that we've seen earlier in the story, perhaps of an earlier defeat. The "I shall return" template can be very powerful, returning the character to the site where he experienced his lowest moment or where his greatest fears live. In *Vertigo*, Jimmy Stewart's character finally exposes the ruse being perpetrated against him by dragging Kim Novak's character to the top of the bell tower. Stewart's strengths as a detective are displayed when he describes how he was fooled, and his weakness, his fear of heights, is challenged as well. The result is a climax that is both powerful and memorable, tying together the themes of fear and illusion that Hitchcock explored throughout the film.

Whatever the location, it should be a place that exposes the character's deepest vulnerability and provides a place for his weaknesses as well as his strengths to shine.

Constructing the Climax: Less Is More

When it comes to the crisis and climax of a plot, the worst course of action is to drag it out.

- Distillation is the key to climactic success.
- The most effective climaxes occur in the space of a single scene.

As soon as your protagonist reaches the moment of crisis, the next scene you write should be the climax.

- The climactic scene should be as concise and to the point as possible.

Economy is important in all writing, but at this point in a story it is particularly crucial, because you've raised the drama of your story to its highest point. Keeping it there for any extended period of time will be extremely difficult, if not utterly impossible. You are burning dramatic energy at a very high rate, a rate that is unsustainable for very long. The state of crisis that your characters are in is also unnatural. Therefore, you must strike quickly and fiercely at this moment, releasing all of the pent-up tension in one lightning stroke. Think of the climax of your story as almost a physical blow to the audience and the characters. You want this *coup de grace* to be sharp and concentrated, focused on this small moment in time. A broader, more diffused climax will dissipate and absorb the energy you've worked so hard to create.

Constructing the Climax: Pulling All the Strings Together

The more effectively and efficiently you can pull all the story's strings together for this single scene, the more impact your climax will have on the characters, and thus, the audience. Remember that we are trying to tie up all the story's subplots, subtexts, themes and ideas. This will give the plot the release that the audience needs to be satisfied. This moment is when you will begin to answer the questions you've been asking throughout your story.

Hazard: The Kitchen Sink

In drawing all these various strings together, be careful not to throw in new strings for the audience. This is what I call "the kitchen sink" factor. There is a desire sometimes to throw every conceivable idea into the climax of a plot. Frequently authors will figure that the climax is the moment when they can pull in every wild, disparate idea they have. The impulse is often to really "pour it on" dramatically. What this accomplishes, however, isn't heightened drama or a more devastating climax; it usually just muddles things. In most cases this urge to throw in everything but the kitchen sink results from a plot that hasn't raised the stakes sufficiently or hasn't focused effectively on delivering the reader to the climactic dramatic moment. This is akin to the poor filmmaker who tries to compensate for his plot's weakness by filming bigger, noisier explosions.

Often, authors will, in this climactic moment, discover new ideas and new meanings in their work. While this is a valuable experience, and the craft of writing is at its best when new discoveries are being made in the midst of the process, you have to be careful about throwing your audience a curveball.

 QUICK QUIZ

CLIMACTIC DISCOVERIES

If you make this sort of discovery while writing the climax to your plot, evaluate this new information and decide how it fits into the story.

Is it an interesting diversion, but one that defocuses the climax you've worked so diligently to deliver?

Are the issues your plot has been dealing with somehow different or have they changed from what you originally thought?

Using the answers to the above questions, you need to decide how to deal with this new information. If it is important enough to come out in the climax, you will need to go back into your story and work this new theme, character trait or other information into the whole story. If the new discovery is just an intriguing side note, then you may want to work it into another scene or do away with it.

I know this sounds cruel and painful—to reject an interesting idea—but remember the old writer's saw: "Writing means killing your children." Not every idea, not even every good one, has a place in a given story. Try to remain focused and disciplined in your writing, and the end result will almost always be superior.

Don't hit your audience with something from left field. This will result in a confusing, dissatisfying ending to your plot and leave your

I know this sounds cruel and painful—to reject an interesting idea—but remember the old writer's saw: "Writing means killing your children." Not every idea, not even every good one, has a place in a given story. Try to remain focused and disciplined in your writing, and the end result will almost always be superior.

audience feeling ripped off or betrayed. The climax of your story is the time for all your efforts to pay off, not the time to start the audience on another set of issues and ideas. Be careful that the climax doesn't feel like the inciting incident of another story—a hard-hitting scene, but one that opens up a new line of action, instead of paying off the action that the audience was already so heavily invested in. Since you want this scene to be quick and impactful, there isn't time to introduce much new information. It's usually best to deliver on the promises you've made your audience leading up to the climax, but there are exceptions to this rule.

The Surprise Ending

The unexpected climax is one of the most time-honored conventions in writing. Particularly in mysteries and thrillers, this sort of ending is almost a genre convention. These types of endings, however, are extremely difficult to do and require even greater planning than ordinary plotting. The key to the surprise ending is for it to be believable, and believability means having planted the seeds of the surprise early. These seeds must be well disguised and mustn't put an undue strain on the plot's overall plausibility. If your surprise ending is too surprising, your audience is likely to react with a disgusted, "Yeah, right," and never finish your story, let alone read another. While the surprise climax should catch the audience off guard, it must also immediately bring those carefully placed clues into sharp relief so that the audience is left gasping, "So *that's* what that meant!"

In the case of the surprise climax, speed is even more of the essence. The surprise should reveal itself quickly, instantly causing the rest of the story to make sense, before hastily proceeding to the resolution. If you take too long to reveal the surprise, the effect will be greatly reduced, like turning on the lights five seconds before shouting "Surprise!" at a birthday party. Don't give your audience the chance to figure out the surprise before you've sprung it. In George Cukor and Joseph Mankiewicz's *The Philadelphia Story*, there are three candidates to be the groom in Traci Lords's wedding: George, her fiancé; C.K., her ex-husband; and Mac, the reporter. Until the final moments of the film, the outcome is anyone's guess, and Traci's eventual choice makes for quite a surprise ending.

Different theories put the climax at different points in proximity to the story's end. I believe that the most effective climaxes occur close to the story's end: Once you've unleashed the climax of your story, there usually isn't an awful lot to keep the audience's interest. We'll talk about resolutions in the next section, but in my opinion, plots work best when the climax is the penultimate major plot point in the story. The final beat is the resolution.

It's been said that "the first rule of comedy is to leave the audience wanting more," and this applies to storytelling too.

Once you've left your audience breathless with the unfolding of your plot's climax, the best next move is to head quietly and meaningfully into the resolution. Your audience's stamina will probably be waning, and if your climax has been successful, they will be satisfied and ready for the story to resolve itself.

DRAMATIC COMPARISON
CLIMAX

STORY	CLIMAX
Casablanca	Scene at airport when Rick makes Ilsa go with Laszlo (probably one of the most famous scenes in cinema)
". . . Usher"	Approach and appearance of Usher's sister at the bedroom door after being buried alive
Moby Dick	Battle with the white whale, Moby Dick
Hamlet	The death of Hamlet

The Resolution

This is the final movement of your plot, and, with the climax successfully past, it is a chance for writer and audience to relax a little, to bask in the afterglow of a good dramatic ride. But this lower level of dramatic tension doesn't mean that the writer should go to sleep. On the contrary, now is the time to reinforce your message, the time to enjoy the characters you've been traveling with and the time to encourage reflection in your characters and in your audience. I like to think of it as akin to the follow-through of a good tennis stroke.

It's been said that "the first rule of comedy is to leave the audience wanting more," and this applies to storytelling too.

The impact has been made, but somehow the continued action is important to the trajectory of the ball.

The resolution of your plot must be as well thought out as everything else you've done thus far, but it also has a little more leeway. That is, if you follow a few simple guidelines you can alter the resolution of your story as you write it without disrupting too much of what has gone before.

No Wild Conclusions or Extrapolations

Having just come through the turbulent experience of writing a story, you will probably have made many interesting discoveries about your characters during the events that have just transpired. Remember, as the storyteller you've been on a journey just as much as your audience has. You will probably reach the end of the climax with a head full of ideas, and you'll want to express them all in the short space of the resolution. While these spontaneous discoveries are a part of the magic of writing, be sure to edit these conclusions carefully. Avoid jumping to conclusions that aren't necessarily there or reaching for meaning that may not have been written into the text. This will confuse readers and make them feel as if they missed something. You also risk obliterating the points that your work actually *has* made.

Avoid Restarting the Dramatic Curve Too Quickly

Some writers arrive at the resolutions to their stories eager to send the characters on their way into the next movement of their lives. This is a good way to leave a story, the "riding off into the sunset" approach, but be careful that you don't leave the audience hanging. If you begin another compelling adventure in the characters' lives, the audience will be left wondering how *that* story turns out.

Leave Your Audience Wanting More

But don't frustrate them by starting and then aborting another story. The exception to this, of course, is the serial—in which case, you will be writing another story and will want to use this time to catch your audience's interest in the next installment. My suggestion in most cases is to keep the dramatic action in your resolution subtle. Don't launch into great adventures only to write "the end." Instead, drop hints as to where the characters are headed and how they will live

---

TAKE A BREAK

One way to avoid resolution pitfalls is to take a break from your work after you've written the climactic scene. Give yourself a day or more to achieve some distance from your story. Writing can be an engrossing, immersive process and it is easy to lose perspective as you are carried away by the power of your own words. Step back, read a book for a change or go to a movie. Let the ideas you've stirred up during your writing settle back down. Once you've done this, go back to your work and write the conclusion. What will have stuck with you is probably what is most relevant to the story and the kind of action or information that truly belongs in the resolution. If necessary, reread what you've written and give yourself some time to think about it. This will help you to approximate what the audience will have experienced, and you should end up with some good insights as to what they need to know or what points they might be thinking about that you want to reinforce.

---

now that the drama of your story is behind them. This will leave the audience interested in how their lives will proceed, but is subtle enough that they will be able to "write their own ending" to the characters' stories.

Keep It Brief

The "kitchen sink" tendency can sometimes rear its ugly head in the resolution of your plot, too. The urge to reinforce every point and theme in your story will be strong as you deal with the rush of emotions let loose by the climax. But after the climax, the plot will quickly lose momentum, and the farther you get from the high point of the central drama, the harder it will be to maintain audience interest. A resolution that is too long will dilute the warm afterglow the audience feels as your plot plays out its final notes. Approach your resolution with the same discipline you exercised in the rest of your plotting.

Stay Focused

You will be tempted to get sloppy at this point as your project nears completion. Chances are you will be anxious to finish the draft, and you might even be a little bit weary of your story and its characters. This is why it's a good idea, as mentioned above, to take a break from your work before approaching this final effort.

Throw the Audience a Bone

It's fashionable to write plots that are very dark and leave audiences with ironic or ambiguous endings, I won't make a judgment about those sorts of endings, which can be as thought provoking and compelling as happy endings. And, I'm certainly not recommending that you soften up your ending in order to give the audience the warm glow of "happily ever after." However, it's important to remember that you've asked your audience to go on a long and potentially difficult journey with you. They deserve some sort of reward from you for their attention, and (though the story itself should have been its own reward) I believe that even the most dark, ambiguous ending becomes more satisfying, even bittersweet, if there is some note of hope or other reward awaiting the characters and the audience in these final moments. Many writers, perhaps afraid of seeming soft, will make their stories unrelentingly dark, dour and tense. While this can make for great writing, it can be very hard on the audience.

The Fillip

Another element of the resolution that can help to deepen your story's resonance while also adding a small, interesting dramatic element to the end of the plot is a fillip. A fillip is a minor dramatic element that occurs after the climax and puts a slightly new or different spin on what we know about the characters. It can be a bit of irony revealed in the final moments, or it can be a remarkable coincidence.

What this element can do for your story is propel the audience through the resolution, give them a treat for their trouble and, hopefully, some additional elements to think about and to take away from your story. The fillip can add a new dimension to the resolution of your plot and will break up the predictable, often linear, summation with a compelling tidbit of information. Some different kinds of fillips:

Coincidence

As you wrap up the plot, it is sometimes interesting to throw in some element of coincidence. This will express the notion that events in the story were somehow not just the outcome of mere chance, but that there was some sort of larger force at work. As your audience considers the characters' good or bad fortune at the climax, they will be forced to ask themselves, "Was it just luck?" The larger force doesn't have to be an obvious *deus ex machina* (though maybe it is); it could be the possible intervention of a minor character. Either way, it is a great means of emphasizing the odd way the world often works and will relate to the real world your audience inhabits where strange coincidences happen almost daily. The real goal is for the fillip to spur much thought about how and why things work out the way they do. The coincidence can also be used to draw together plot elements that may not have been associated during the rest of the story. On the larger canvas of a novel or an epic movie, you may use the fillip to make the connection between events that were distant in either time or location, showing how they somehow came together in a meaningful way for the characters.

Irony

A particularly popular element in literature is the use of irony. While many writers employ irony relentlessly in their work, it often makes a great fillip in the resolution of the story. If the outcome of the climax is in any way dark or ambiguous, you will most certainly have the elements of an ironic fillip in place. Again, the goal is to cause your audience to marvel at the strange way the world works and to point to the possibility of larger forces at work. Irony can also cause the audience to question their assessment of the outcome of the plot's conflict. In the movie *Titanic*, the present-day sequence that ends the film reveals that the search for the "Heart of the Ocean" diamond was fruitless all along, since Old Rose had it from the beginning. The irony of her throwing it back into the ocean gives the film a bittersweet ending.

Twist

It's also possible to create a dramatic fillip in the resolution by putting an unusual spin on the outcome of the conflict. This could mean that a positive outcome may turn out to cause more problems for the protagonist or that a negative outcome may work out for the better. This type of turnabout is a sort of post-climactic plot twist. Be careful not to start another whole story, but a subtle change of direction will add depth and ambiguity to the outcome of your plot, giving your audience lots to think about. At the end of *Wag the Dog*, the ruse that the producer perpetrated has successfully deflected attention from the president's philandering. However, the producer refuses to keep quiet and ends up being killed. This puts a very different spin on the film, making the comical politicians considerably more sinister.

Projection

One of the strongest uses of the fillip is to give the audience a bit of data that they can use to project the course of the characters' futures. Very often a sort of postpartum depression sets in with audiences when an engrossing story with wonderful characters comes to an end. The best stories always leave us a little saddened that they're over, and often we have invested so deeply in the characters that they've become like real people. We wonder what will happen to them next. The fillip can give your audience some evidence that they can use to project the next (unwritten) chapter in the story. Whether you forecast a rosy future or a darker one, the audience will be left with something to entertain their minds after the lights have come up or they've closed the book. In Elmore Leonard's *Rum Punch*, the final scene shows the beleaguered flight attendant leaving town with the money that she's scammed. She announces to her friend that she's going to Spain. This bit of information gives the audience a clue as to how the character's life will continue.

Final Impressions

The most important thing about resolutions is that the audience will probably remember this part of your plot quite vividly. Coming at the end, it may likely be the impression that will stick with them over time.

WORD OF MOUTH

Since any dramatic art relies heavily on word of mouth to draw in more audiences, you want your audience to remember your resolution fondly. We've all had the experience of reading a book or watching a movie that had a less than satisfying ending. Ask yourself if you ever recommended such an experience to someone else. Probably not.

This isn't to say that your plot must conclude with a happy ending. On the contrary, some of the most satisfying and memorable endings in literary history weren't happy. No one would argue that Shake-

DRAMATIC COMPARISON
RESOLUTION

STORY	RESOLUTION
Casablanca	Rick shoots the German officer and Renault turns patriot
". . . Usher"	The house crumbles as the Narrator flees
Moby Dick	Ishmael's rescue
Hamlet	Fortinbras arrives at the palace

speare's tragedies suffered as a result of unhappy endings, and often the most thought-provoking endings are the darkest. The key is to be sure that your resolution reinforces the messages you wanted to send when you started writing. Whatever it was that compelled you to tell the story you have told should be emphasized as you write the final pages, so take the time to refocus yourself before plunging into your resolution and be as clear about what you want to convey as you possibly can be.

Building the Plot

CHAPTER SIX

Using Plot Archetypes

With a thorough understanding of the pieces that make up a plot, we can begin to examine the mechanics of how plots function in actual stories and how those pieces can be manipulated to create the greatest effect. Before we go into the actual process of building your own plot, it's useful to take a look at some common plot structures.

Over time many different plot archetypes have formed. As storytellers began creating sophisticated plots, certain recurring themes eventually formed themselves into story patterns as more and more stories were written which used similar patterns to explore variant themes. Eventually, these story patterns became informally codified, with established conventions and plot components. These story patterns matured and split into subgroups or lost favor and disappeared. The strongest of these story patterns have survived to this day as plot archetypes.

These plot archetypes have become pillars around which many of our greatest stories have been built. How many different archetypes exist depends mostly on whom you ask: Some theorists have said that there are as few as four different story patterns, while others have claimed twelve, twenty or thirty-six. The actual number really depends on how detailed your definition of a story pattern is. I'd prefer not to settle on any set number of story patterns, but I've chosen nine differ-ent story patterns I think are worthy of discussion and make for good examples of how these story patterns function.

One of the interesting things about these plot archetypes is that in spite of their inherent similarities they have spawned a tremendous variety of stories. The strength of a plot archetype seems to be its ability to give authors a strong bedrock on which to build. As you'll see in the discussions of the specific archetypes, many great stories have been told using the same story pattern.

Plot archetypes accomplish two things:

1. They provide a foundation and sub-frame on which an author may build her story. By relying on the conventions of the archetype, the writer is able to focus her efforts on other elements of the writing. The archetype also provides a rich source for making comparisons and contrasts between the author's ideas and the conventions of the archetype.

2. The author can assume a certain body of knowledge on the part of the audience. It's likely that the audience will have read other sto-ries of this archetype and will be familiar with the conventions. Upon that basis, the author is free to explore the archetype and use it as a prism through which the audience can experience the story. The audience, too, benefits from these archetypal story pat-terns since it can more easily follow the story and understand the underpinnings of it.

Both audience and author also get to reap the benefits of the force of every great story of that type that was ever told. Comparisons to the same archetypal stories that came before become automatic and the author is able to communicate in a kind of shorthand. The author can evoke images, emotions and events of other stories, creating richer textures and deeper meanings. The force of history behind a story written in an established plot archetype can also lend a great deal of scope to a story, allowing a small and intimate story to express global themes, while still focusing on the personal. The author is thus able to evoke those other great tales to draw connections to her own story.

Rules Are Made to Be Broken

One of the other characteristics of plot archetypes is that they eventu-ally inspire writers to begin playing with their conventions, challenging them and even satirizing them. Such experiments often rejuvenate a stale story pattern. Writers like Graham Greene have created memorable satire by making fun of genre and story conventions. In his book *Our Man in Havana*, Greene did a wonderful send-up of a pursuit story and the whole genre of the spy novel. The film *Airplane* hilariously mocked the catastrophe-story pattern. Mel Brooks has made a career of sending up various archetypes and genres. *Blazing Saddles* made fun of both the vengeance archetype and the western, while *Young Frankenstein* satirized the monster movie and the betrayal-story pattern.

Other writers have chosen to experiment by mixing different story patterns or subverting story patterns, throwing out key conventions while preserving others. In the film *Weekend*, French filmmaker Jean-Luc Godard challenged the journey archetype and the road movie by preserving most of the archetype's conventions, while refusing to allow his protagonists to ever arrive at their destination.

Nine Archetypal Plots

Archetype: Vengeance

CONVENTIONS OF THE REVENGE PLOT

- Protagonist loses something dear.
- Rising action involves pursuing revenge. Sometimes the audience also discovers source of protagonist's vengefulness.
- Protagonist is passionate about goal.
- Protagonist faces defiant obstacle.
- Climax is always the moment of vengeance.
- Protagonist faces moment of questioning of his vengeful motive.
- The conflict has little ambiguity.

Examples:

- *The Tempest* by William Shakespeare
- *Moby Dick* by Herman Melville
- *Rob Roy* by Sir Walter Scott
- *The Outlaw Josey Wales* directed by Clint Eastwood

The revenge story goes back to biblical times. It is a natural story pattern because the act of vengeance is a natural magnet for involving drama. Revenge is one of those emotions that lives very close to the surface in man and is one that lends itself to colorful expression. The dramatic theme of vengeance also creates ideal conflict. Conflict is obvious and compelling to the audience in a revenge story. The protagonist's motivation is obvious and drives the plot. It is also very easy to gain momentum with such a story. The protagonist's work is cut out for him; he is motivated and usually passionate about his quest.

The revenge plot also uses the antagonist in a straightforward, pow-

DRAMATIC COMPARISON
VENGEANCE

Let's look more closely at two different tales of revenge.

Vengeance fails

Herman Melville's *Moby Dick* is the story of Captain Ahab and the crew of the *Pequod*. It follows the template of the revenge plot perfectly. The story begins with Ahab hiring the crew that will accompany him on his hunt for the white whale. Early on, the audience learns that it was during an encounter with the whale that Ahab lost his leg. Melville describes in detail Ahab's wooden leg and the pain, both physical and emotional, that Ahab feels from his loss. As the story goes on, the audience learns more about the encounter with the whale and delves deeper into Ahab's obsession with avenging his lost limb. As is the convention in revenge stories, the climax of the novel occurs when the *Pequod* finds its quarry and the battle with the giant whale occurs. Ahab's quest for vengeance fails and costs him his life, his ship and most of the crew, but his quest for revenge propels the story unrelentingly.

Vengeance succeeds

Shakespeare's *The Tempest* takes a gentler, less obsessive approach to revenge. Prospero is exiled by his evil brother Antonio. On the way to his exile he is shipwrecked on an exotic island. Suddenly endowed with magical powers, Prospero begins exacting his revenge. Along the way he must make peace with a beast who rules the island. Eventually, Prospero's new powers are put to work and he conjures another storm like the one that shipwrecked him. This time the storm brings his brother Antonio to the island and Prospero confronts him. Suddenly, Prospero, who was unceremoniously put in a boat and sent away, has power over his marooned brother. Prospero's vengeance succeeds.

erful way. Some of drama's best villains have come from this plot archetype. Antonio in *The Tempest* or the white whale of *Moby Dick* are evil or, at least, destructive beings. The revenge plot involves events that are deeply personal to the characters involved, and thus the conflict is usually a pure one with less ambiguity than in other stories. The protagonist feels wronged, while the antagonist somehow feels justified in his action.

One way that vengeance plots play with the idea of ambiguity is in questioning or forcing the audience to question the righteousness of the protagonist's quest for revenge. In *Moby Dick*, the sailors on the *Pequod* are dragged along as unwitting victims in Ahab's quest for vengeance against the white whale. Even when the book was first written, readers had to question the human price of Ahab's obsession, and the modern reader can't help but wonder about the environmental impact of it. In Euripides' *Medea*, the scorned woman kills her children to exact vengeance on Jason, who has deserted her.

In either story the reader cannot help being moved by the protagonist's strong emotions and the force of passion. Revenge plots capitalize on hatred, one of man's strongest emotions. The force of this emotion gives audiences a wild, thrilling ride, while asking them to question and judge this emotion. These stories connect so strongly with audiences because desire for vengeance is one that most people have experienced, but few people have indulged. Who wouldn't enjoy exacting a price on someone who has done them wrong and vanquishing a hated enemy.

Archetype: Betrayal

The archetype of betrayal has long been the source of wonderful melodrama, for it provokes strong emotions in both the betrayer and the betrayed. Passion, jealousy and scorn are all an integral part of this juicy story pattern. At the root of any betrayal plot is the element of trust, and every story of this type must begin by establishing a close, trusting relationship between two parties either through action or back story. Without this trust, without a tight bond between the characters, the act of betrayal will be weak and may even seem casual. It is critical that the audience be allowed to experience the closeness, even interdependence, of the two individuals. Once that is established, all that needs to be done is to give one party a compelling reason to

CONVENTIONS OF THE BETRAYAL PLOT

- Trusting relationship is established and then smashed.
- Betrayal plots often have elements of the revenge plot in them.
- Difficult decision to betray makes for a better story.
- The more personal the betrayal the better the effect created.
- Feelings of guilt and humiliation exist in victim who asks, "How did I provoke this?" "How was I deluded?"
- The love triangle is a primary source for stories of betrayal.
- Political intrigue involves betrayal of the state or of the comrade, as well as treachery, treason and traitorousness.

Examples:

- *Othello* by William Shakespeare
- *Madame Bovary* by Gustav Flaubert
- *Heartburn* by Nora Ephron

betray the other. The more compelling this reason, the more difficult the choice will be and the more sympathetic the betrayer can potentially be. If the reason for the betrayal is more base, more sordid, the more it is likely that the betrayer will be viewed as villainous. Callous, self-interested betrayers make for terrific villains. The audience will surely be outraged that someone would commit such an act so nonchalantly, and usually with such relish.

The betrayal plot often works closely with a revenge plot as well. The two are a natural fit. The betrayed party will surely wish to avenge the injury done, so it is easy for the betrayal to turn back upon itself, into a quest for revenge. In this case the plot takes on a twist with the betrayed party refusing to be a mere victim, but insisting that reparations be made or some price exacted from the treacherous party. In these stories, the first part of the plot follows the conventions of the betrayal plot and the later portion is more of a revenge story.

Betrayal plots work best when the betrayal is a difficult decision. When the temptation is great or when it seems justified, the moral dilemma faced by the character will be far more textured and complex. The audience will be torn as to where to put its sympathy, and these sorts of choices—ones so agonizing—are ones that most audiences are familiar with, even if not at such a dramatic level. The harder the choice, the more complicated the ramifications will be, and the greater

DRAMATIC COMPARISON
BETRAYAL

Antagonist betrays

Iago from Shakespeare's *Othello* is a great example of such a traitor. A personal slight—being passed over for a promotion—is the act that sets Iago on his traitorous and ultimately deadly course. Though he is clearly a trusted officer among Othello's ranks, he brazenly fabricates suspicions in Othello, first about Cassio and later about Othello's adored wife, Desdemona. Iago's motive is blatant self-interest, and it makes him one of Shakespeare's most hated villains.

Protagonist betrays

In *Madame Bovary*, Emma betrays her loyal, though boring, husband in order to pursue her adulterous affair. In this tragic story the protagonist is the betrayer who later pays the price of her actions. It is possible, however, to view Emma as betrayed by her own feelings and by her society, which leaves her no dignified way out of a bad marriage.

---

emotional pain it will cause in both parties.

The party that has been betrayed in these types of stories generally feels several different emotions, and these emotions lead to different actions. If the betrayed character just feels angry and hurt, it is likely that he will simply set out to exact revenge from the offending party. However, you can make your plot more interesting if the betrayed character also feels some guilt and some humiliation. It's possible that the character's reaction isn't merely one of anger. Maybe it's also one of questioning: "What did I do to cause such a betrayal?" Or, it may be one of humiliation: "How could I have been so duped?" This will lend a different and decidedly more complex layer to your character's actions. A betrayal may set off a deep questioning of the character's own loyalties or skill at judging character. It may even call the character's self-esteem into question.

Betrayal plots tend to come in two main varieties. The most popular, a classic plot archetype, revolves around the love triangle in which lovers or spouses betray one another for other lovers. These stories are wrought with passion and a simple, direct route right to the very core of the characters' personalities, something that many people can relate to. The other main variety involves the political traitor. The spy novel has depended upon this archetype for years. The issues in these stories aren't quite as personal as in a love triangle, but the consequences tend to have a much larger scope with whole nations hanging in the balance.

Archetype: Catastrophe

This story pattern falls on the opposite end of the spectrum from the revenge plot. While revenge stories are almost completely driven by the protagonist, these stories are about overwhelming forces that scoop up the protagonist and carry him away. The drama of the story comes in the ways the protagonist finds to cope with what is an almost impossible situation. With the exception of some extreme comedies of errors, most catastrophe stories are dramas.

The catastrophe plot usually starts in a situation where things are, if not pleasant, at least under control. The inciting incident is the first disaster. Sometimes this disaster is of the protagonist's own making, often resulting from some sort of discontent that has caused the protagonist to upset the status quo. Other times the disaster is initiated by external forces, an antagonist or nature itself.

Ironically, the rising action of the story is more akin to a falling action. Things go from bad to worse as the protagonist struggles to

---

CONVENTIONS OF THE CATASTROPHE PLOT

- Story starts while circumstances are good.
- Events are out of the protagonist's control.
- Rising action proceeds with a slow mounting of problems.
- The climax comes at the time when the protagonist experiences the ultimate loss.
- Resolution concerns what is salvaged and/or the moving onward.
- Themes tend to be about people coping with impossible situations, man's inhumanity to man and the power of nature.

Examples:

- *The River*, a film starring Mel Gibson and Sissy Spacek
- *The Grapes of Wrath* by John Steinbeck
- *A Farewell to Arms* by Ernest Hemingway
- *Airplane* directed by Jim Abrahams

DRAMATIC COMPARISON
CATASTROPHE

Natural catastrophe

In Steinbeck's *The Grapes of Wrath*, the Joad family, once a subsistent, if not successful, group, is forced to leave its Oklahoma farm because of a blight and the Depression. They travel west to California, in hopes of realizing that state's promise of abundance. They arrive to find thousands of families just like themselves and economic conditions that are no better than what they left in Oklahoma. Stripped of property and dignity, they sink into poverty and move from place to place hoping simply to survive. Steinbeck uses the endless string of catastrophes to comment on man's inhumanity to man during times when sticking together is the only means of survival. The author provides precious little comfort in *The Grapes of Wrath*, so little in fact that the smallest act of kindness that occurs near the end of the book has enormous impact.

Man-made catastrophe

Hemingway's *A Farewell to Arms*, the story of an ambulance driver in Italy during World War I, is a classic catastrophe plot that uses war as a source of misery. While Hemingway is known as a writer of enormous romantic power, this story's romance seems doomed from the start and the audience is given an unsparing view of war. As the convention dictates, the story begins on its highest note as the ambulance driver falls in love with a beautiful English nurse. Unable to bear the horrors of war, the driver deserts his unit and escapes with the now-pregnant nurse to Switzerland. Just as it appears they may live happily ever after, the woman dies in childbirth, leaving the man alone and on the run. Again, little comfort is given to the protagonist, and the audience must be content with his mere survival.

In both of these stories the traditional plot arc is turned upside down as circumstances become steadily worse for the protagonists. The appeal of these stories can only be explained by the concept of catharsis. The audience derives some sort of relief from experiencing these horrors vicariously. This story pattern demands stories that are often powerful, but mostly joyless.

survive. Often during this section the protagonist undergoes some sort of change, realigning priorities or regaining lost focus. Events are almost always out of the protagonist's control. As the things get worse, the protagonist tends to suffer or fight nobly, but unsuccessfully, the forces working against him.

The low point for the protagonist, interestingly enough, comes at the climax. It is in this moment that the protagonist suffers the ultimate loss or the ultimate indignity, and the injustice of the situation is made plain for the audience. In this moment the protagonist is most powerless. In spite of all his efforts, the battle seems lost and the future is bleak.

What is so unusual about this plot archetype is that the arc we are accustomed to following has almost been inverted. The rising action is the time where things get worse. The level of the drama rises, but the protagonist's fortunes sink. The high point—the climax—actually becomes the low point. The resolution is where some hope or relief is granted to the protagonist and the audience.

Archetype: Pursuit

This type of story is so compelling that the chase, as a set piece (the centerpiece of one section of a story) if not an overall plot archetype, has become a staple in modern literature and film. In action films the chase scene is now a cliché and a de rigueur piece of any story. What makes pursuits so compelling is that it is easy for both author and audience to identify the parties and issues involved. While it's entirely possible to complicate the issues of the chase, few story structures present this kind of opportunity for straightforward storytelling.

Like the vengeance plot, the chase has a built-in dramatic engine, with a clearly defined goal (catching the pursued) and obstacle. The act of pursuit defines the forward momentum of the story and can even be used to control it. The level of tension can be dictated by how close predator and prey are to one another. The chase also gives the author a natural means of moving the story from one physical environment to another. Like the vengeance plot, the pursuit story is naturally predisposed to having characters with passionate feelings.

Pursuits tend to come in two basic types.

Physical pursuits. These are the stuff of great action thrillers, whether on the page or screen. Physical chases lend themselves to

---

CONVENTIONS OF THE PURSUIT PLOT

- Inciting incident is the moment when the conflict that will result in the chase is established. One party flees, another sets off in pursuit.
- Rising action sees the pursuit develop with complications for both pursuer and pursued. Often there is a close call in which the quarry is nearly caught.
- The climax always brings about the moment when the pursuer and pursued ultimately meet.
- Frequently the chase acts as a metaphor for larger themes and asks questions about the nature of things—like freedom.

Examples:

- *Les Miserables* by Victor Hugo
- *The Fugitive* directed by Andrew Davis
- *Moby Dick* by Herman Melville

---

sweeping, freewheeling stories packed with action and excitement. Frequently, crime stories and westerns contain this story pattern since it lends itself to the overall idea of crime and criminals. Physical pursuit stories often require both protagonist and antagonist to overcome considerable physical obstacles, like long distances, harsh environmental conditions and other challenges to personal endurance.

Psychological pursuits. These contain chases that are less literal and contain less spectacle, but can be no less thrilling. An excellent example of this is the Thomas Harris novel *The Silence of the Lambs*, which was later made into an Academy Award–winning film by director Jonathan Demme. In the story, a young FBI agent (Clarice Starling) is on the trail of a serial killer. In order to find and capture the murderer, she is forced to align herself with another convicted serial killer, who also happens to be a brilliant, twisted psychologist (Dr. Hannibal "The Cannibal" Lecter). There are several, overlapping pursuits in this story. On the surface Clarice is chasing the murderer, Buffalo Bill, but the story is memorable because there are other pursuits happening: For instance, Lecter pursues Clarice, trying to get into her mind and find her vulnerabilities. He seems to be a natural-born hunter. Also, his work as a psychologist has required him to chase his client's neuroses. He obviously finds great amusement in the act of pursuing others with his mind. The memories that Lecter unlocks in Clarice cause her to flee not only from Lecter's probing questions, but from her own past and its demons.

We've already discussed *Moby Dick* several times in the course of this book, and while earlier we defined it as a story of vengeance, just as strong a case can be made for it as a story of the chase. Clearly, Ahab's obsession with the white whale forces him into his desperate pursuit of the creature. It is equally true that he is being pursued by his obsession with vengeance.

 ## DRAMATIC COMPARISON
PURSUIT

A good example of a pursuit that combines a psychological chase with a physical chase is the movie *The Fugitive*. Dr. Kimball is fleeing from the authorities, while simultaneously chasing the One-Armed Man. The story becomes the ultimate game of cat and mouse as Kimball uses his wits to escape the pursuing marshall, Gerard. Though the eye-popping lengths that Kimball goes to in order to escape (remember the ultimate high dive?!) attract a lot of attention, the duel of wits between Kimball, Gerard and the One-Armed Man create just as many thrills.

In Hugo's *Les Miserables*, the idea of pursuer and pursued is twisted about repeatedly, causing the reader to question the idea of what it means to chase and be chased. Physically, Inspector Javert is chasing Jean Valjean, but when one considers Javert's obsession with catching Valjean, one is forced to question who is really being pursued. It can be argued that Javert is chased by his desperation and his rage. Meanwhile, Valjean's pursuit of peace and contentment is equally compelling for him.

Archetype: Rebellion

The emotions that these types of stories conjure up are ones that are familiar to most people and ones that aren't often expressed in real life. Other than during our teenage years, most of us don't do much rebelling and any we do certainly isn't the dramatic, romantic kind found in literature and film. So, like vengeance, rebellion is an emotion that we rarely indulge, but often fantasize about. Who wouldn't like to walk out of a job when working conditions are poor like in the film *Norma Rae*? The reality is that most of us simply cringe and bear our condition. Therefore, the rebellion story is a popular archetype since

CONVENTIONS OF THE REBELLION PLOT

- Protagonist is usually the rebel, not the person or thing rebelled against.
- Rebellion can be personal or political.
- Inciting incident is an act of injustice against some oppressed group.
- Rising action usually begins with a downward trend as the oppression grows.
- Moment of decision comes about one-third of the way between the inciting incident and the climax. This is the time when the character(s) decides to fight back.
- Climax is the moment of triumph or failure in the fight against the oppressor.

Examples

- *One Flew Over the Cuckoo's Nest* by Ken Kesey
- *The Caine Mutiny* by Herman Wouk
- *King Lear* by William Shakespeare
- *Macbeth* by William Shakespeare

it gives the audience the chance to live vicariously through another person, possibly one who is more courageous and possesses greater character than ourselves.

The rebellion plot also affords the opportunity to write about underdogs. Some of the greatest characters of all time, from Beowulf to Rocky Balboa, were underdogs. Everyone loves an underdog and it is easy for an audience to see themselves in the person of the underdog. Most of us feel overwhelmed by our circumstances from time to time, but we feel powerless to change our lot in life. Underdogs in rebellion stories show courage when regular people tend to walk away, and that makes them incredibly sympathetic to the audience. A strong, righteous underdog can rely on the sympathy of the audience. This type of story pattern also allows you to write about overcoming the odds in a very personal, very tangible way. The rebel who defeats his nemesis at the eleventh hour, who overcomes adversity and tremendous odds, is going to evoke strong emotions in the audience and cut a memorable figure.

As you may have noticed, one of the characteristics of many archetypal plots is that they deal with strong, relatively simple emotions. Rebellion is no different. In order for this story pattern to work, the conflict between protagonist and antagonist has to be clear and uncomplicated. Archetypes have survived because they provide neat, straightforward patterns that can be relied upon to evoke certain emotions. These patterns themselves are not subtle; it is up to the author to bring subtlety and nuance to his story.

The conventions of the rebellion story pattern dictate that in most cases the protagonist will be the rebel, not the one rebelled against. Since the definition of rebel is one who fights against an established power, the crushing of a rebellion will not make for a very heroic conquest. The oppressed group should be sympathetic and sufficiently overmatched so that its eventual success (if achieved) will be remarkable. The rebel's cause should be fairly clear, and the injustice he suffers should be adequately demonstrated, preferably within the scope of the story; showing the injustice as back story will take some of the sting out of it.

Rebellion plots usually begin with some act of injustice as the inciting incident, which isn't enough to spark the rebellion, but rather starts a period of decline in which the protagonist's situation deterio-

---

 ## DRAMATIC COMPARISON
REBELLION

Familial authority

A number of Shakespeare's plays concern rebellion. *King Lear* and *Macbeth* were about two very different kinds of insurgencies. In *King Lear*, Lear's daughter rebels against him, refusing to concede to her father's seeming tyranny. Her rebellion comes at a high cost as she is banished, but ultimately Lear sees the error of his ways. In *Macbeth*, the title character kills the king and takes his place, but ultimately his rebellion fails. The one constant in all of Shakespeare's plays about rebellion is that the cost of rebellion to both the oppressor and the oppressed is terribly high.

Political authority

In Ken Kesey's *One Flew Over the Cuckoo's Nest*, the rebellion is carried out by a bunch of mental patients. This group is the ultimate bunch of underdogs. Merely functioning is a challenge for them, but Kesey makes a persuasive case for the primacy of human dignity when they mount their own insurrection against their faceless, oppressive caretakers.

---

rates rapidly. One of the key elements in rebellion plots that is rare in many other plots is a fulcrum moment that occurs early in the rising action and is the *moment of decision*: The protagonist decides he can no longer endure the oppression and takes his first action toward changing his state. The climax is the moment when the rebel either succeeds or fails in his coup.

Another constant of rebellion plots is the notion of authority being challenged. Frequently that authority is political, but there are many influential rebellion stories where the authority is familial.

Archetype: The Quest

This story pattern has a certain mythic quality to it. Unlike the patterns we've discussed so far, this one really requires a bit of magic to make it work. While these stories are often written about actual journeys, the essence of these stories usually lies within some deep, inner journey. The myth of the quest probably has its foundations in man's earliest wanderings. These wanderings first took literary shape in the work of the Greek poet Homer's epic *The Odyssey*. This story of the wandering hero Odysseus has become the archetype for all journey stories and his name is synonymous with the very essence of the mythical journey, the odyssey.

These stories are special because the protagonist's outer journey

---

CONVENTIONS OF THE QUEST
- Stories often involve a journey back home either literally or figuratively.
- There is almost always an inner journey that the character is making that is paralleled by the outer journey.
- Characters in these stories have a strong sense of destiny; they aren't just on a trip, they're on a mission.
- These stories often have a strong sense of the supernatural or metaphysical at work.
- Protagonist's journey is frequently a search for truth or enlightenment.

Examples
- *The Odyssey* by Homer
- *Raiders of the Lost Ark* created by Steven Spielberg and George Lucas
- *Don Quixote de la Mancha* by Miguel Cervantes
- *Treasure of the Sierra Madre* by Bruno Traven

DRAMATIC COMPARISON
THE QUEST

Probably the ultimate quest is for the Holy Grail. This mythical hunt for the chalice of Jesus Christ has been the source for many wonderful stories. From the legends of Arthur and the knights of the Round Table and their desperate quest for the grail to the Hollywood version of this quest in *Indiana Jones and the Last Crusade*, mankind has been on a long literary quest for this ultimate religious symbol, which has created an almost endless string of stories, all based on the story pattern of the journey.

The quest for the Holy Grail points out an important characteristic of the journey plot. The protagonist needs to have a strong sense of destiny. It is this sense of mission that motivates the character to overcome a tremendous series of hurdles. Many of these protagonists feel a metaphysical, supernatural or even divine purpose guides their actions. This divine guidance generates characters who undertake their actions with great passion and conviction.

The quixotic hero also arises from this sense of destiny. Modeled on Cervantes' mad knight Quixote, these are characters who undertake seemingly impossible or ridiculous actions with the belief that they are divinely inspired. This hero has endured to modern times. The film *Field of Dreams* is about a farmer who goes on a rather quixotic journey, traveling across the country and finally turning a cornfield into a baseball diamond.

---

can be a source of tremendous adventure. Certainly Odysseus's travels had all the adventure any modern-day action movie director could ask for: sea voyages, battles, monsters, exotic locations and most importantly—beautiful women. The quest journey makes for terrific, gripping drama with lots of thrills for the audience as well.

But the essence of these stories and the source of their enduring quality is that the physical adventure is usually a metaphor for some other journey the protagonist is taking, a journey of self-discovery or of discovery of the past. The inner journey could be for some deeper meaning to the character's life or to life in general, but there is almost always some other nonphysical quest for the protagonist. This search for greater truth gives the protagonist the promise of finding something that will bring a missing peace and serenity to his life. Heroes in these stories are often restless, discontented people for whom something is missing, and the only solution is to undertake this quest.

The inner journey and the survival of the outer journey are often metaphors for life. Authors have frequently used the journey archetype to consolidate the vast sweep of life into a smaller, more focused length of time and arena. The journey becomes a microcosm for life, which the character is able to explore thoroughly during the span of the journey.

This archetype demands a protagonist who is passionate and possibly a bit crazy. Zealots are great protagonists for quest stories. These stories may also exhibit a kind of purity that is often missing in drama. The heroes are heroic by nature of their dedication to the goal. While they may create tremendous mayhem on the way, one cannot help but marvel at their singularity of purpose.

Archetype: Ambition

The ambition archetype is a very popular one, particularly in American film and literature where the roots of capitalism run deep. It seems that Americans' relationship with ambition is an uneasy one. We applaud the ambitious person who applies himself and overcomes obstacles and odds, but we are also cautious about how far that ambition goes and we demand the person be kept in check if he becomes too powerful or abuses power. These mixed feelings about ambition and

---

CONVENTIONS OF THE AMBITION PLOT

- Ambition is frequently driven by a desire for power.
- Pursuit of ambition requires a bargain of some kind or some sort of renunciation or sacrifice.
- Protagonist often has little power to begin with.
- Ambition is a double-edged sword; it may bring glory, but that glory is almost always mixed with pain or loss.
- Protagonist often experiences a fall caused by his ambitions.

Examples

- *Julius Caesar* by William Shakespeare
- *Macbeth* by William Shakespeare
- *Primary Colors* by Anonymous
- *David Copperfield* by Charles Dickens

DRAMATIC COMPARISON
AMBITION

In the book *Primary Colors*, the governor, who is running for president, comes from humble beginnings, circumstances well delineated early in the plot. Even as governor of a small state, Stanton exhibits an inferiority complex. He is a man with a common trait in ambitious protagonists—having something to prove to himself, to his family, to the world. The determination not to "take it anymore" is a common motivator for these types of plots.

Plays like *Julius Caesar* and *Macbeth* are cautionary tales about what happens when ambition goes too far. Caesar is allowed to lead the Romans to many great victories, indeed to the pinnacle of their power, but when he begins to behave like a tyrant, Brutus, Cassius and Casca conspire to kill him. His ambition crossed that line and must be stopped. The case of Macbeth is similar. The audience watches with relish and some dread as Macbeth plots his evil deeds. Some in the audience may be glad to see Macbeth made king, but when he kills his friend and ally Banquo and the wife and children of his rival Macduff, all sympathy for his character evaporates. He has gone too far, has allowed his ambition to rule his mercy and good sense. He must be stopped.

---

the ambitious person make for a wonderful plot archetype. The conflicting emotions—the desire for success and the wariness of its results—make for a rich canvas for an author. It also makes for protagonists who are ambiguous and who frequently have fatal flaws.

The first important convention of the ambition plot is that the protagonist is usually required to make some sort of deal, a compromise of something dear, in order to pursue his burning desire. Often this bargain involves sacrificing principles that the hero values, principles that were probably responsible for garnering the audience's sympathy. Sometimes the hero makes the deal hoping that he can maintain his integrity, but usually one compromised principle leads to another. The bargain often involves someone close to the protagonist whom the hero, tempted by ambition, is asked to forsake or betray. The ultimate act is the decision to pursue ambition at whatever price is necessary. At this moment the hero's destiny passes out of his control and into the control of the ambitious instinct and the hands of fate.

Once the bargain has been struck, it often involves another sacrifice by the protagonist—either materially or personally. In many common plots, the protagonist gives up home or family, creature comforts, material possessions and peace in order to pursue the desire burning within. These sacrifices usually provide some scenes of initial reservation, but since ambitious protagonists are notoriously discontented, it is usually not a difficult decision. This sacrifice serves to distinguish the protagonist from the average audience member. These acts of sacrifice cause the audience to understand the choice that the protagonist is making and to question whether or not they would be able to make that same choice. It's a bit of a reality check for the audience and helps to set the hero apart from ordinary people.

In order for the protagonist's ambition to resonate with the audience, he frequently comes from a circumstance in which he has little power. That powerlessness, whether recent or from childhood, is often the motivation for him to make the sacrifices necessary to achieve his ambition.

Ambition is almost always seen in drama as a mixed blessing. There is a reverence for the person who strives, who makes things happen and moves humanity forward. This primal urge is celebrated in most cultures, and honors are heaped upon those who display this quality. However, there is also a reluctance to give such people free reign. Part of the bargain involved in plots that use this ambition archetype is that the protagonist is allowed to pursue his desire, so long as certain lines are not crossed. Unfortunately, once ambition gains some momentum, it is extremely difficult to slow down. Shakespeare, in particular, examined this problem frequently in his works.

The final convention of the ambition archetype is the fall. It is common for the protagonist to undergo a fall, a central element in dramatic tragedy. Indeed, many of the greatest tragedies ever written were based on this archetype. Ambition stories tend to be cautionary tales that serve their glory with a helping of humility, reminding readers that ambition must never go unchecked and that the ambitious must be respectful of and grateful for the gifts they are given.

Archetype: Self-Sacrifice
The plot of self-sacrifice is a difficult one to pull off in these modern times. Morals and religious anchors are less powerful than they once

---

CONVENTIONS OF THE SELF-SACRIFICE PLOT

- Service is to a higher authority, a cause, an ideal.
- Religious undertones and often overtones are common.
- Story is usually built upon some moral imperative or a righteous cause.
- Moral issues in these stories are black and white. The difference between what is right and what is wrong is crystal clear.
- Protagonist usually believes he will receive some kind of greater (though usually less tangible) reward in exchange for his sacrifice.
- These stories help to connect us to our own humanity and the greater self that we believe lives inside of us.

Examples

- *Of Human Bondage* by Somerset Maugham
- *Schindler's List* by Thomas Kennealy
- *Antigone* by Sophocles

---

were, and the whole idea of sacrificing for a cause seems to have disappeared with love beads and tie-dye. Nevertheless, this has been one of the most enduring archetypes since the beginnings of drama. The conventions of this archetype are simple. A character gives up something (or, frequently, everything) in service to another person or some belief or cause.

This story pattern requires several elements for it to work properly. First there must be a well-argued or generally held belief in some set of ethics or moral code. Unlike any other story archetype, this one requires a set of agreed-upon "rules." It is critical for the audience to have a good understanding of where the moral high ground lies so that they can understand and sympathize with the protagonist's sacrifice. Without this, the story becomes rudderless and unworkable.

One reason this type of story is more difficult to do these days is that there are rarely any agreed-upon moral structures in our society. We've become a world bereft of black and white issues; everything seems to exist in shades of gray. This doesn't work very well in the self-sacrifice plot. The moral structure needs to be clear, and it's necessary for the character and the audience to consent to it. Without this consent, the audience cannot develop a sufficient stake in the character's actions.

The protagonist who is doing the sacrificing is usually obeying a higher authority than that of man, and for doing this there is the expectation that a greater reward, usually one that is spiritual or emotional, will be forthcoming. In many popular self-sacrifice stories, the protagonist gives up all his worldly goods for the sake of doing what is morally right. The reward for this action is a clear conscious and a true sense of righteousness.

While these stories seem to be somewhat out of favor, as our culture's moral compass begins to right itself, it is likely that we will see them rise again in popularity. These stories give us a glimpse of our own humanity. They support the notion that we can make change happen and that there are some things that are unquestionably right. These stories are so reaffirming because they ignite in the audience a feeling that maybe they are better people than they think, that they too are capable of such courage.

 ## DRAMATIC COMPARISON
SELF-SACRIFICE

The Greek play *Antigone* has religious beliefs as its root. In the play, Antigone is forbidden to give her brother a proper burial because his father, the king, felt his son had betrayed him. Antigone decides that the law of god supercedes the law of man. She buries her brother, sacrificing her own freedom when she is imprisoned by her father.

Probably the most well-known story of self-sacrifice is the biblical story of Jesus Christ, who suffered enormously, worked tirelessly and ultimately died for the sins of his fellow man. This is the ultimate story of self-sacrifice. Christ was left with nothing except for his faith in God and his belief that what he was doing was the right thing. Christ was sure of a higher reward. He knew that his suffering would bring him into heaven and would give the gift of faith and salvation to his followers. This is a common belief in self-sacrifice stories.

Archetype: Rivalry

Like many archetypal story patterns, this story's power is rooted in the fact that most people have experienced some form of rivalry in their lives. Everyone has wanted something that another person wanted equally and has had to contend for the prize. What this archetype does is juice up the melodrama and raise the stakes a bit.

CONVENTIONS OF THE RIVALRY PLOT

- Two characters of equal strength are contenders.
- Both characters share an object of desire.
- A forum exists for the competition.
- Object of desire is often another character, creating a love triangle.
- Sometimes the object of desire is a position of power or material wealth.

Examples

- *Ivanhoe* by Sir Walter Scott
- *Cyrano de Bergerac* by Edmond Rostand
- *Two Gentlemen of Verona* by William Shakespeare

The crucial element in making this plot work is creating the actual rivals. They need to be characters of nearly equal, but different strengths. This plot pattern affords lots of opportunities to compare the rival characters' strengths and weaknesses as well as their similarities and differences. The rivals should have an equally good chance at attaining the prize so that the contest will be even and the outcome won't be a foregone conclusion. One of the rivals should be your protagonist, but it's possible that both will have sympathetic qualities. Unless you're a very accomplished writer, however, it's not a good idea to try to make them equally sympathetic. Stories with two protagonists can be very hard on the audience since they are trusting you to give them clues as to whom to favor. Try to construct characters whose qualities contrast with one another so that each will be vivid and so that their qualities will create plenty of natural conflicts.

The object of desire also has to be worthy of these rivals' actions. Since these rivals will make enormous sacrifices and lock with each other in mortal combat, the prize for which they compete must be sufficiently alluring so that the audience will understand their desire. Often the object is a person, usually a lover, and the two rivals should love this person in equal, but very different ways. So, too, the object of their desire should be indecisive about the two suitors. They should each be appealing in some way, otherwise the object of desire is diminished.

If the object of desire isn't a person, it is usually a position of power or material wealth. Again, the object needs to be sufficiently desirable to cause the rivals to do what they will do to attain it. Often it is a good idea to have the attainment of the goal by one rival result in the subservience, or even enslavement, of the other rival. This will raise the stakes and make the contenders that much more desperate.

The final important element in the rivalry plot archetype is an interesting forum in which the contenders undertake their competition. Rivalry plots require lots of twists and turns, so you'll want to set your story in an environment that is rich with these possibilities. More than most plots, rivalries are highly dependent on the supporting characters within them. There are always lots of allies and enemies, people to betray the characters and people whose favor they curry to achieve their goals. Many historic rivalry stories have been set in royal courts, which offer two very important elements: lots of power, wealth and desirable mates *and* lots of people with not enough to do and eager to get involved in political intrigue.

Stories like *Ivanhoe*, with its labyrinthine plot full of alliances and adversaries, and *Cyrano de Bergerac*, with its conflicting courtiers, make for excellent rivalry stories. The environment of the plots provided their authors lots of possibilities for twists and turns. A royal setting also forces characters to maintain an air of dignity and civility, which provides for wonderful contrast to the underhanded dealings going on in the rivals' battle.

These plot archetypes can provide a great starting place for the creation of your plot. While you may wish to create your own story, independent of these conventions, you may still find that bits and pieces of them find their way into your plotting. These archetypes describe some of our most basic human interactions. It's entirely likely that your story will contain some of them, if not in whole, then in part. When you discover one of these archetypes working its way into some section of your story, refer to its conventions listed here and keep them in mind. Also keep in mind some of the classic works of literature that have put these archetypes to good use. They may inspire ideas for interesting ways to handle these archetypal situations.

These archetypes have acted as the foundation for some of civilization's greatest stories. If they were good enough for the Greeks, Shakespeare and other literary luminaries, they are certainly worth considering when we begin to design our own stories. Keep in mind that these story patterns have become archetypes because they've

DRAMATIC COMPARISON
RIVALRY

In the story of *Cyrano de Bergerac* by Rostand, Cyrano and his young pro-
tégé vie for the affections of a beautiful woman, Roxanne. Though he is
his rival's superior in every way, Cyrano feels insecure about his physical
appearance and cannot imagine that the lovely maiden would be interested
in him. He helps his rival, even though it is painful for him, ultimately
resenting him.

The Fountainhead concerns the rivalry of two young architects. One is
an unprincipled, but highly skilled young man who is an expert politician
and knows how to make people like him. He rises quickly, humiliating his
rival and stealing his ideas. The other man is a highly principled, but difficult
man whose career takes many detours before he finds success. He does
not resent his rival, but merely has contempt for him. In the end, the
principled man is successful, while the other man is left broken and alone,
his lack of principles having left his life adrift.

withstood the test of time, and they work. They address issues that
are central to man's life and ask questions for which we are still searching for answers. The archetypes themselves and the stories they've
inspired create a great source of ideas and a perfect starting place as
you begin to consider writing or rewriting your own story.

CHAPTER SEVEN

Creating Characters and Back Story

The "what if" Question

The best plots begin with this simple interrogative. Take a character or a situation and ask yourself, "What if?" It may have been just such a question that first inspired you to begin writing your story.

- The "what if" question takes life out of the realm of ordinary, every-day occurrences into the stuff of compelling drama. It's useful in giving birth to your central story line. It is also a crucial question to continue asking yourself throughout the creation of your story. As you develop each plot point in your story, ask yourself "What if?" and try to raise the level of the drama in your story.

- The "what if" question will help you to find undiscovered threads to be woven into the rich texture of your story. "What if" can help you find the ironic and the unexpected connections hidden within your work. At anytime during the construction or the actual writing of your story you sense there is an opportunity to raise the level of your story, to start a new thread or to make a meaningful connection, stop and ask yourself, "What if?" Each time you are about to write a scene which feels ordinary or dull, one way to transform it into a fascinating, meaningful event is to ask yourself, "What if?"

The "what if" question is really just a handy reminder, a technique for questioning your assumptions about what you are writing. One of the biggest hazards in writing, particularly if you are writing novels or other longer works, is lapsing into a kind of mundane laziness. As writers, it is easy to let the ordinariness of everyday life find its way into our work, to become comfortable or blase. We must challenge every assumption and question every decision we make about the paths our stories take. Asking "What if?" is an easy way to push our work out of the mundane and into the extraordinary.

WHEN TO ASK "WHAT IF?"

- When trying to decide what to write about
- When creating each plot point
- When choosing the elements of the conflict
- When your writing feels dull or uninspired
- When a scene feels slack

The "what if" question figures in every major plot point during the construction of the outline. It is also a good catalyst for creating subplots and developing your characters. It can even help you to add richness to the back story.

 **EXERCISE**

Take the topic of your story, the central idea, and try to improve it or put a special twist to it by asking, "What if?" Simply think of your story, ask "What if?" and then fill in the blank with the most outrageous, unusual thing you can think of. See if this starts you toward a new perspective on your story.

Ordinary People, Extraordinary Situations

One way to guide your use of the "what if" question and to create compelling drama is to take everyday people and put them into unusual circumstances. Some of the greatest drama of all time was created with this time-tested formula. Whether we're talking about a real-life character like Jim Lovell in *Lost Moon*, which later became the film *Apollo 13*, or the young lawyer in John Grisham's *The Firm* or even Mark Twain's *The Prince and the Pauper*, all these stories are made more compelling by throwing ordinary people into situations that are highly unusual.

The reason these stories work so well is that the protagonist's ordinariness makes her relatable and thus interesting for the audience which is itself made up of lots and lots of ordinary people. The extraordinary circumstances in which the character finds herself makes for gripping drama. The audience is left to wonder what they would do in similar circumstances, and the protagonist's eventual triumph over these circumstances is reinforcing and reaffirming to the audience who will like thinking that they too could have been as clever and crafty as the hero of your story.

Protagonists who are forced to use common, though maybe more highly developed, skills and faculties to overcome unusual situations also forge another bond with the audience in that there is no extra, supernatural force on their side. They are simply human beings forced to stretch their capacities beyond where most of us ever have to in our daily lives.

So as you begin to approach the construction of your story, think about your characters in terms of how you can make them easy for your audience to relate to. Figure out what common elements they can have with the people in your audience. Even superheroes in comic books usually have an alter ego who is a somewhat regular guy. Batman has Bruce Wayne—a millionaire, yes, but also an orphan who has a hard time relating to other people. Superman has Clark Kent—the mild-mannered newspaper reporter. These alter egos create a bridge between the character who is nothing like an ordinary person and the regular human beings who make up the audience.

The Protagonist—Just Like Me, Only Better!

The superhero also illustrates another crucial element that your Everyman character should have—and that's a little extra something. While audiences want a character who is much like themselves, they also want a character who is a little bit better, a bit more courageous or moral or stronger than they are. That is to say, they want a character to whom they can aspire. This will give the audience something extra to root for since the character they are learning about is someone they can relate to, but also someone they can admire. While the character has flaws that any regular person can relate to, she also has some strength, maybe hidden at first, that will enable her to overcome the conflict you've set out for her.

Once you've created a protagonist who has the proper characteristics of Everyman, you want to challenge that character in the most profound way possible. As we discussed earlier, think about what conflict will challenge that character most severely, what circumstances will draw the most out of that character and render the character in the most vivid relief.

ORDINARY PERSON	EXTRAORDINARY SITUATION
William Wallace (*Braveheart*)	Ordinary warrior leads oppressed Scots against tyrannical British government
Norma Rae (*Norma Rae*)	Ordinary factory worker organizes exploited workers in drive to unionization
Tom Joad (*The Grapes of Wrath*)	Ordinary farmer leads family westward in search of work and happiness, but finds only tremendous misery

While your audience seeks a character who is much like themselves, yet with that something extra, they also want to see that character live a life that they can only imagine. No one will be interested in a story of some ordinary guy's life—that's the life they're leading, so why would they want to read about it? So the secret to creating good drama is to take your ordinary character and put her into a situation that is exciting, dramatic and in some way unusual. While creating these extraordinary events, however, always keep in mind the character's Everyman nature.

CHARACTER	CONNECTION TO REGULAR FOLKS	SOMETHING EXTRA
Superman	Mild-mannered reporter Clark Kent	Faster than a speeding bullet
Mr. Smith (*Mr. Smith Goes to Washington*)	Ordinary citizen with a job and a family	A passion for the American process of government
Hucklebery Finn	Normal Midwestern boy of his day	Extraordinary determination and cleverness

Try to create the circumstances of your story in such a way that there is some connection to the sorts of events that the audience can relate to. This isn't usually a problem if the writing you do is ordinary drama or comedy. However, if you like to write science fiction or adventure stories, it may be a little harder to find the story's connection to the audience's everyday life. It's not essential that the audience make this connection; many excellent stories have been told in which the characters were in a world that was utterly foreign to the audience, such as William Gibson's novels about cyberspace. The world of *Johnny Mnemonic* is utterly different from reality. However, it is much easier for the audience to draw a connection to the characters and their situations if they have some small, recognizable handle to grasp. In Robert Heinlein's novel *Stranger in a Strange Land*, the Martian character lives in a human world. We come to understand him through the contrasts drawn between him and the human characters. Ironically, the more we learn about him, the more points Heinlein is able to make about us as humans.

 ## STORY STARTER

"WHAT IF?"

What if the protagonist has an unexpected personal connection to the antagonist?

What if the protagonist's dilemma has consequences for his family, his community or the whole world?

What if the protagonist is forced into an unfamiliar environment?

What if a reticent protagonist is suddenly forced into an active leadership position?

What if the protagonist is faced with a physical challenge (adventure or illness)?

For adventure stories like "Mountains of the Moon" or Jack London's "The Cruise of the *Dazzler*," it is unlikely that many in the audience will have been in these sorts of perilous situations (war, wilderness), but people have enough experience with these elements, through various media, to understand them. Being able to draw a connection to everyday reality, your audience will be able to develop deeper emotional ties to the characters and their investment in your story will be stronger, making for a more satisfying experience.

To create extraordinary situations in the realm of the real world, the best way to begin is with the "what if" question we discussed earlier. If you have a character you wish to write about with some sort of emotional, ethical or moral dilemma, but you still don't have a basic conflict for your plot, try looking at the character's everyday life and asking yourself the "what if" question.

For instance, you have a character who is a lawyer and is trying an important case. This is certainly a common situation in everyday life, but probably not the stuff of great drama. But "what if" the character who is trying this emotionally charged case finds himself opposing his best friend? Suddenly, you have the makings of a story. Or, maybe you have a man who was a soldier in World War II. Feeling a bit lost in his comfortable life, he decides to visit Europe where he fought. That's a common enough situation, but what if he returns looking for a woman he knew fifty years ago and instead finds a man who turns out to be a son he never knew he had. That is a formula for drama.

Distilling Life Down to the Good Stuff

The trick in creating drama and the essence of the "what if" question is distilling life down to its most interesting parts. If you were to read the story of your own life, day by day, it would probably make for pretty dull reading. "I sat at my desk and typed on the computer, writing a book." That's what I'm doing right now in my everyday life and it wouldn't make for very interesting drama. However, if you took your life and cut out all the dull stuff, you could make a pretty interesting story. Creating good plots is distilling a character's life down to just the good stuff.

That is what the biographer does all the time. No person's life is infinitely or continually fascinating. Even the most romantic figure has days when he didn't do much of note. So the biographer's job is to take the interesting or thrilling things a person did and make them into drama by stringing them together one incident after another. A simple "five years later he . . ." will do the job of excising the dull parts. That is what you are doing for your protagonist—cutting out the dull stuff. In most stories, you will focus your energy on one small portion of a character's life, a portion in which something of note happens.

Two Types of Distillation

1. The first type of distillation is to get a full understanding of the portion of the protagonist's life that the story will consider. Although you may have a particular story or set of events in mind, try to look at the character's total life. This way you will be sure to understand how the plot relates to the total world of the character. The next step is to draw out the slack. That is, pull the noteworthy events together to become the major plot points of the story. The events in between can easily be deleted altogether or distilled into simple, concise bits of exposition.

2. A second way to distill the world of reality into good storytelling is by limiting the focus of your story. In the early stages of your writing process, identify the most important part of the story. Be disciplined about narrowing as much as possible. Some writers put many pages or minutes between the audience and the inciting incident. This is unwise. Audiences (not to mention agents, editors and producers) won't make it through that long run-up. Stay focused on the part of the story that matters most. This process will take continual refining, and as you begin to prepare your outline, you may notice that you've got extra scenes or sequences that aren't central to the story. Think hard about cutting as much of these as possible.

Sometimes you'll create so fascinating and interesting a character that you'll want to tell large portions of her story. You may be so convinced of your protagonist's potential that you'll begin conceiving a story of epic scope. While epics are a staple of both film and literature, consider carefully whether you can pull off a story of Homerian or Michenerian scope. More than likely, you'll want to narrow the scope of your story. This isn't a bad thing. In fact, having a potentially powerful character will give you a huge advantage in writing your story. The distillation process will be easy and you'll end up with lots of possibilities for great writing.

When distilling the elements of your story, you may find it difficult to limit the story in terms of time, finding no logical way to pull out chunks of time. However, you may discover that you can distill and focus your story by concentrating on a single theme or thematic element. Then, you can use that thematic element to decide which pieces of your story need to be told.

For instance, in the film *Two for the Road*, directed by Stanley Donen and starring Albert Finney and Audrey Hepburn, the story focuses on the disintegrating marriage of a London couple. The film, however, focuses only on one small portion of the couple's life—their annual pilgrimage from London to the south of France. The trip is seen several times during the course of their marriage, from when they were newlyweds to when they are just weeks from divorcing. By focusing on the drama of this annual trip, the evolution of the couple's marriage is examined. The theme of the road plays well with the other themes of the film, marriage as a journey, bumps in life's road, etc. The setting of being on the road allows the audience to focus closely on the couple themselves, independent of family and social circle. It also gives the audience a chance to compare the couple at different points in time periods that are years apart.

The idea is to choose a thematic element, possibly a season or other time period, a place or a ritual that is central to your story, and then build your story around that element. The thematic element will make the process of distillation easy: Simply use only the events that are directly related to that element. You will have a wonderful theme to tie the events of your story together and also to keep your audience focused on just the ideas that you want them to explore.

Once the process of distillation has begun, you should find dramatic episodes that will probably make up some or most of the major plot points in your story. The next step in the process is to look through what's been distilled for details that are important to the story. Look for details that will relate more than just simple exposition and facts. Find the details that make connections between the major plot points, the ones that can bridge those plot points, or that can point out elements that tie them together.

If you can find a thematic thread running through these details, you will add an important bit of texture to the story. That thread could be a minor character whose words or actions comment on the central plot, or it could be a motif or metaphor that deepens the resonance of the story's themes. Look for these details within the major plot points and in the spaces between. While you want the process of distilling the story to its essence to be rigorous, you don't want to cut out elements that are important. These elements may find their way into subplots, back story or exposition and they need to be handled carefully. Equally important, however, is that they don't distract the audience from the important matters of the central plot.

STORY	THEMATIC THREAD
Being There	Gardens, gardening and growing
Dances With Wolves	Man's harmony and disharmony with nature
Cat on a Hot Tin Roof	Concealment—everything is hidden

The point of all this distilling is economy, one of storytelling's most prized virtues. There is no experience more enjoyable for an audience than a story that moves elegantly from point to point, without a wasted word. Economy must be exercised at every point in the storytelling process. It certainly must be observed in the constructing of the plot, but it must also be observed in the weaving of other elements into the plot. Subplots, exposition and back story are important to the story, but they are also often places where a work can get flabby.

The process of distillation should be a part of each step in your work, from the early plotting to the weaving of the various elements and to the actual writing of the story. Each time you go through one of these phases of development, go back through your work piece by piece and pull out any unnecessary information, and, ultimately, any unnecessary words.

Prewriting the Characters and the Back Story

While the primary thrust of this book is building your story's plot, there is really no way to separate the various elements that make up any good piece of drama. It is equally difficult to separate the characters and situation in your story from the social, emotional and historical context they exist in—their own individual plots (historical in this case doesn't necessarily mean we are dealing with real-life personalities, just the history of the characters and their world). For this reason, it is critical to have a clear understanding of all dramatic elements before embarking on the difficult task of constructing a plot. The clearer your understanding of these elements the easier it will be for you to make plot decisions for your characters, and those decisions will then be motivated thorough characters' knowledge, not momentary whims or wild guesses. This vast, complete knowledge of the world in which you are working will help you to avoid making poor decisions or untenable leaps of logic. By developing a clear understanding of the universe of your story, you will be able to immerse yourself and your audience in it. You will also improve your instincts for knowing what is important in that universe, and you will be able to paint a more complete picture of it for your audience.

Characters

Start by getting to know the people who inhabit your story's universe. I recommend writing complete, in-depth character descriptions for all the major players in your story. That means especially the protagonist, but other supporting characters as well. These character descriptions will act as a road map when you begin constructing the plot outline and composing the actual text. Each character description should function as a "virtual person," that is, a verbal blueprint of the character that will tell you everything you would ever need to know about this person.

It's really impossible to do too much at this stage of the writing process, and you should spend plenty of time on it. I'd suggest spending a couple of days or several different writing sessions on each character. This may seem like a waste of time, especially if you are anxious to get started on writing your piece, but you will find that the time you spend on this process will be tremendously rewarding and will save you lots of time in that these character descriptions will make later decisions intuitive. This part of the process is also an important element in the conception of your story, and you will come up with a lot of the raw material that will give your story depth and personality. So allow plenty of time for this process and try to relax with it. Don't force the ideas to come out, but do give your brain a gentle squeeze and challenge yourself to think deeply about the characters.

As you write your character descriptions, you'll also have the opportunity to note connections between characters in your story. This will come in handy later when you are constructing the plot or particular subplots. These connections will provide you with material around which to build plot points and also provide you with character development information that you will be able to work into your story later. During this early planning stage, it will be much easier for you to see these connections between characters. In this pure, unadulterated state you will be able to easily recognize common character traits, contrasting character traits, similarities and differences in personal history. From this cross-referencing, you should be able to gain a clearer understanding of who these people are and what their relationships are to one another.

If a character is a certain type of person, either professionally, ethnically or in some other way, try to spend time with real people of that type to get ideas for your character. While you don't want to write characters who are mere stereotypes, there are characteristics common to certain people that you may want to work into your character. As you think about these types and spend time with them, look for ways your character might be unique from them or complementary.

Take your time and try to enjoy the process of getting to know your character. See what unique things you can discover about him. These revelations can be the raw material that will later become elements of your plot. Actually, working on your characters is just another way of brainstorming for ideas for your plot.

Physical. You will be tempted to move quickly over the physical traits of your character to dig into the potentially juicier area of the character's psychological makeup, but don't overlook the physical as a source of rich character information and plot motivation. Be sure that any physical traits you discover are reinforced in nonphysical descriptions. You may also want to go back to the physical description after you've worked on the others to create physical manifestations of traits you discovered there.

 QUICK QUIZ

PHYSICAL DESCRIPTION

Decribe your character's physicality in detail.

What does his face look like?

What sort of build does the character have? Describe his height, weight and stature.

How does the character move?

How does the character dress?

What sort of social or psychological traits are manifested in the character's physicality? How do they appear?

What sort of energy or aura does the character give off? Happy? Carefree? Dour?

Social background. Do not overlook the character's social background in creating your character descriptions. The characters' sociology will have as much to do with who they are as any other element and will do a lot to influence their physical and emotional makeups. Think about each character's social standing in her society. This will be important no matter what period you are writing about, but if you are doing a story set in the past, it may well be critical to the character's life. If you are writing an eighteenth- or nineteenth-century piece, you should know that a young woman's reluctance to marry an older man, which the lead character in Jane Austen's *Pride and Prejudice* feels, will greatly compromise her social standing.

QUICK QUIZ
CHARACTER'S SOCIAL STATUS

Look closely at your character's economic stature and how this effects her life.

Consider also how the character feels about that stature—is she eager to leave it behind or content with it?

How does the character's financial status limit or enable the character?

Examine whether or not the character's social standing limits her ability to achieve her goals.

Think about what kind of home life the character had with his family.

Were there brothers and/or sisters? Ages? Factors like birth order will have a profound effect on a person, so look closely at that.

Extended families, particularly grandparents, often influence people's lives. Are there family traditions that impact the character?

Other relatives often have a profound impact on people. Does your character have a favorite uncle or other influential person in her life?

It's sometimes helpful to draw your character's family tree. Make comments on it about the various members and imbue them with interesting qualities. Then think about how that family, that tradition and that history affected the character.

History. Once you've gained a good understanding of the character's sociology, take a look at the specifics of her history. This entails looking at the character's past and either writing it or outlining it in detail so that you will have a clear understanding of events in the character's life.

This history will help in two major ways:

1. First, it will help you to understand the influences that shaped the character. If the sociology and psychology are the interior factors that shape the character, the history is the external facts and events that make up that character's life experience. These experiences, whether they be victories, defeats or wounds, will give that character a unique outlook on life. As the character evaluates the decisions she makes in the context of the story, those historic events will inform that decision. As the writer you will make better choices with a clear understanding of the character's history.

2. Second, it will help you to understand the facts of the character's

history so it will be easy to get those facts straight in the course of your writing. This knowledge will be useful at several points. Initially, when you are creating the major plot points and shaping the arc of the story, it will be helpful to know what happened before so these plot events make sense. It will give you a running start at the action of your story and the characters will appear to have actually existed earlier, outside the confines of your story. Later, as you shape character delineation and back story, it will be useful to refer to the history to avoid conflicting facts. You may even find that the character history you write becomes an actual part of the text, probably not the whole thing and probably not exactly as written, but you could certainly use parts of the text in your story.

QUICK QUIZ
HISTORY

What sort of social background did your character come from?

What sort of ethnic background influenced the character's history?

What events in the character's past have influenced her personality and behavior?

What events that may have occurred before the character was born influenced the character's personality or behavior?

What event in the past had the most profound effect on your character?

Psychology. The most important element in determining how your character will behave throughout your story is his emotional and psychological profile. You'll probably spend the most time on this element and you'll probably want to tackle it last. I suggest you do it last because all the other parts of the description will impact it. The character's physicality, sociology and history will all influence who that character is psychologically. The thing to do at this point is to examine all those influences and then decide how they've impacted the character and how the character has responded to them. Think of yourself as a psychologist who is treating the character. Dig into the depths of what makes the character tick and decide which influences have had what effect.

The psychological profile will help you find the root of the character's motivation.

While the character's goal in your story may be something simple

QUICK QUIZ
MOTIVATION

What deep desire is she looking to fulfill?

Does it come from a loss suffered earlier in life or from some missing element in her childhood?

Is there someone to whom she has something to prove?

Is this a long held desire or a newly discovered one?

What pain is the character willing to suffer in pursuit of the goal?

---

and tangible, think deeply about what it is that drives her toward it. It may sound like a cliché—the vain actor asking the director, "What's my motivation?"—but this is probably the single most important piece of knowledge you will need about your character, for it is the engine for the entire story.

Once you've spent plenty of time ginning up material about your character, you'll want to refine it into a more cohesive piece. What you'll have at this point is pages (hopefully) of material about your characters. Not all of it will be useful, and some of it may even be contradictory. The job now is to make sense of it all. Go back and begin to shape it. Look for contradictions and decide which quality is most suitable. Go through everything in your character description and work it into a manageable, readable shape. The end product should be something you could give to someone (in the case of a screenplay, an actor, perhaps) who could read it and have a strong, thorough understanding of your character.

Back Story

Once you have your characters delineated, turn your attention to the lives they've lived. Your story will have a much better flow and a stronger sense of reality if you are able to create your story's universe beyond the borders of the actual story. This means developing a well-conceived, detailed back story. You can approach this exercise just as you did the character descriptions. Take an adequate amount of time and begin to write in a stream of consciousness fashion. Think about where the characters began their journey toward the events of your story. It may not be necessary for you to go all the way back to their childhoods. Decide which portions of the characters' earlier lives are

EXERCISE

Write as much as possible about your characters. Divide your thinking into four main areas of consideration:

- physical description
- social background
- emotional/psychological description
- history

---

meaningful to the story you're writing and write about that.

- In some stories, say a romance, it may be necessary to go back just to the days or weeks before the story's inciting incident. In these cases, it's only necessary to learn about your characters' mental states and what changes they may have recently gone through that lead them to the events in your story.
- In other stories, you may need to go back several generations.
- If your story is about a blood feud between two families or gangs, you will want to think about the origins of that feud. If you are writing a historical epic, you'll want to know all there is to know about the time leading up to your story.

It is virtually impossible to do too much of this type of work, and the work rarely goes to waste. While some of this back story will certainly find its way into your story, even the portion that doesn't will inform your every decision. It will allow you to make decisions that have a historical basis for your characters. Rather than making sudden, uninformed decisions, you will be influenced by the characters' actual past history. You will have a record and a deeper knowledge of their previous tendencies.

If the back story isn't an important element in your plot, you will still want to know about the period immediately before your story began. Think of this exercise as getting a running start at your plot. If you have a good sense of the events leading up to the inciting incident in your story, your writing and, hopefully, your story will have instant momentum. By writing this back story, you may also decide to start your story with less lead-in to the inciting incident. Often, writers include a lot of rather dull lead-in to their plots because they, themselves, need the time and space to get the plot's momentum going. If you've written the back story, this won't be necessary.

Prewriting the back story will also help to keep the facts straight in your story. If you plan to sprinkle bits of the back story into your plot, you'll probably want to write out the whole thing in advance. If you attempt to write it as you go, you may find that it's hard to keep the facts clear and accurate. It will also be difficult to make it smooth and seamless. Even if your goal is to cut up the back story and tell it out of chronological order (and perhaps especially if this is your aim) you'll find it easier to create and the results will probably be better if you write it first as the events happened. This prewritten back story will give you all the material you need, which can be a big boost during the long, sometimes grueling, process of writing a first draft.

EXERCISE
PREWRITING THE BACK STORY

1. Spend time writing in stream of consciousness mode.
2. Filter out the bad ideas and bring structure and cohesiveness to the stream of consciousness work.
3. Overlay a time line on the events.
4. Find and highlight connections you want to make in the text.
5. Find and highlight exposition that you'll need to insert into the story.

After spending some time doing stream of consciousness writing, go back to the material you've generated and put some order to it. Filter out ideas that aren't compatible, and organize your work into coherent events. Ultimately, you'll want to put a time line on it, organizing the events in chronological order so that you have a cohesive history of events leading up to your story. This history of events is the finished back story and should give you everything you will need to know to begin putting together the elements that will make up your plot.

As you put together this history of events, you should be careful to note points of exposition that will need to be made later in the story. Mark these points with a highlighter or Post-it note so that you can come back to them later. If you know where a piece of exposition will be required, make a note of that too, so that you'll be able to transfer that note to the outline later and it won't be forgotten during the depths of the writing process. You'll know these points of exposition because they will contain bits of information crucial to the understanding of the plot and its characters. Comb your back story for this kind of information, and begin thinking about interesting ways to reveal it, either through conversation, a subplot, a flashback or even a dream.

You've now done all the homework necessary to begin the outlining process. You have a reference source that you can refer to for answers if you ever have questions about what you are writing. You may even already have some of the text written in the form of character descriptions and back story.

Review this information. Digest it and make it a part of your consciousness. What you should do next may surprise you: Forget it! That's right, let it recede from the conscious part of your brain for the time being. If you need details or facts, you can always refer to it, but try to put it in the back of your brain where things like memory live. Since this history is essentially memories for the characters, you'll want to have a similar perspective on it as you tell the story. Take a day or so away from your project to let all that you've created settle and set in your brain. Give yourself some time to replenish your creative juices, for you are about to embark on the most difficult and the most creatively demanding part of your project—creating the outline.

CHAPTER EIGHT

Constructing an Outline

There are as many approaches to writing as there are writers, but here are some tried-and-true methods for constructing your story from the ground up. Throughout this book we've approached the task of building a plot like an architect designing a building. We've gone step-by-step, dissecting each decision and testing it for structural integrity. With this firm understanding of the mechanics of how plots work, let's undertake the design or, if you will, blueprinting process. Much of this process may seem strange to you if you've always written your stories intuitively, starting at the beginning and working to the end. By no means should you abandon your intuition about your work. What's being presented here is simply a deeper, more organized approach to writing, one that will serve you in several ways:

- help you avoid dead ends
- help you plan for subplots and subtexts that will enrich your story
- help you more smoothly and effectively incorporate new plot or thematic elements you discover during the writing process
- free your mind and your intuition to work on the writing of your story, the characters, the dialogue, the language, etc., unconcerned about whether the construction is sound

A good blueprint will not restrict your writing; rather, it will liberate your writing by giving you a map, allowing you to focus on other elements of the writing and helping you avoid frustration.

Begin at the End

Once you've done all your homework on your characters and back story, you will be faced with the task of creating your outline. When they approach this part of the process, many writers begin to feel overwhelmed. They get that old writers' ailment "white page fever." "Where to begin?" they ask. The best way to get to where you want to go when writing is like finding your way on any other journey. The outline you're going to be constructing in the next section of this book will be like a road map for the writing of your story.

The way most people plot any journey on a road map isn't by starting where they are—it's by finding where they want to end up. Chances are, you didn't begin your writing project from nowhere, with only characters and some back story, saying, "Gee, I'd like to write a story." You probably have some idea of the point you'd like to make, and hopefully, you have a good idea of where you'd like your story to end up—the destination. So begin there. Begin at the end.

So, how does it end? The climax is the part you should think about first. Think of it as the tent pole that holds up the rest of the story, and once you've conceived it, you'll find that the other scenes will come to you much more easily. Since this scene is the crystallization of every element in your story, you'll want to be sure that it is soundly conceived. Begin with a list of all the elements that need to converge in that moment. That should include which characters need to be there and what points will need to be cemented in that scene. Once you've compiled the elements that will make up the climax, you'll want to look for creative ways of bringing them together. Think about:

- *Metaphors.* What sort of metaphor can you create in this scene that will help to illuminate the themes and ideas you have for your work as a whole? Even in the most realistic plots, the audience will tolerate a higher degree of artistic license in the climax. So be bold about devising the climax. Give it a dash of poetry (maybe not literally), and allow the drama in the scene to rise to a heightened level. If you've been developing a metaphor throughout the course of your story, now is the time for it to culminate, and you must be sure that it isn't left out at this most pivotal moment in the story.

In the book and movie *Being There* the entire story has been laced with religious metaphors and symbolism. In the climactic scene at the funeral, the protagonist Chauncy actually walks on water across a pond.

- *Motifs.* If there are visual or language motifs that you've been developing throughout your story, the climax is a good time to crystallize those elements for maximum impact. The climax is the perfect time to imbue those motifs with all the meaning you've been developing throughout the story. Throughout the "Star Wars" trilogy, there was much use of medieval-looking visuals. From costumes to architecture, many visual elements had a knight-in-shining-armor feel. So in the climactic scene in *Return of the Jedi*, Luke and Vader fight—not with blasters, but with the swordlike light sabers.

- *Location.* The choice of a location for your climax isn't one you should address casually. The location of your climax can say so much and provides the rich environment that will allow you to draw together all the elements of your story into this single moment. Try to choose a location that has meaning to the characters. It may be the destination in a journey plot, or some new unfamiliar ground that exposes the nuances of the characters and their situation. If you choose to set it in a familiar location, try to give the location a different spin. If you've always shown a family home in the light of day, set the climax at night. Or, try to use the site's familiarity as an element in the scene, drawing out its history and its meaning. The climax of *Psycho* couldn't take place anywhere else but in that creepy old house.

- *Characters.* All the crucial players should be present. Not only should the protagonist and antagonist face off, but think about surrounding them with the supporting players they've been interacting with all along. Be sure the characters are physically present in that moment—avoid climactic phone calls or other "virtual" interactions. The flesh and bone presence of the characters will heighten the drama. No story does this better than *Hamlet*. The play's climactic battle scene brings everyone together into a single room—of course they all end up dead, but that's Shakespeare!

- *Themes.* Express your major themes in the climax. The climax should act as the final exclamation point to these issues. If the themes have been subtle to this point, the climax is the place to make them more explicit (if that is your goal). In *Field of Dreams*, a story about fathers, sons, baseball and faith, the climax takes place between the father and son on the fantastical baseball field.

Don't feel pressured. The concept of the climax doesn't have to be planned exactly as the final scene will end up in the finished work. The process of writing is one of continual change—writing is rewriting—and you'll make discoveries as you write that will alter the climax of your story. Nevertheless, having a clear idea of what your climax will be is a good place to start the construction of your outline.

EXERCISE
BRINGING IT ALL TOGETHER FOR THE CLIMAX

Fill in the table below to be sure that all the crucial elements are present at your climax.

Metaphors	
Motifs	
Location	
Characters	
Themes	

Just as when planning a journey, you need to know your point of origin as well as your destination, so you should also have a good idea of what the inciting incident in your story is to be. Be sure that whatever you choose as your inciting incident is a strong scene that occurs at the precise moment the story begins to take off. As we discussed in section two, inciting incidents that occur too early or don't lead directly into the rising action are counterproductive to building tension in your plot. Once you've found your point of origin and your journey's destination, the next step is to plot the route.

Referring again to our map analogy, you will want to break up the trip into different legs. That means finding the major plot points and figuring out the route from one to the next. If you have several major plot points already in mind, describe them briefly on 3 × 5 cards (more on that in the next section) and put them in the order you think they will end up in the story. From there, begin working your way backward from the climax, conceiving each major plot point in reverse, finding your way back toward the inciting incident. Sometimes you may have an idea of what scenes you want to have immediately after the inciting incident. If you do, definitely put them in. It's not mandatory to work your way entirely backward. It just tends to be easier to figure out the story's arc this way. Starting at the highest point of the drama, it's easier to create the story "down hill." Think of it as building a bridge—you'd never build a bridge from the middle toward either shore. Start at the ends of the arc and work your way to the middle.

What about the resolution, the part of the story that occurs after the climax? When do you create that part? Using our map analogy, think of the resolution as finding a place to park! You want to know how your story actually ends, but it's hard to know that until very near the end of the process—until you arrive at the destination. Without a clear understanding of everything that happens in the story, writing or even conceiving the resolution is a difficult, if not impossible, exercise. As mentioned in section one, it's best to leave the resolution for the very end of the process.

Interpolation and Extrapolation

The map analogy may make it sound easy to plot the route between inciting incident and climax, but you may look at that vast desert between those two points and wonder how you can possibly make such a leap. The key, like solving most problems, is breaking the distance down into smaller pieces. There are two ways to do this, interpolation and extrapolation.

- *Interpolation* is predicting the location of something by knowing two points, one on either side of it. This allows you to make an educated guess about where the desired scene will occur.
- *Extrapolation* is predicting the location of something by knowing two points on one side of the desired point. By projecting the trajectory, you can make an educated guess about where the desired scene will occur.

As you begin to conceive the scenes that will make up your plot, starting with the climax and inciting incident, use these two principles to create the scenes in between. Take any scenes you already have in mind and place them roughly where you think they should go in the order of things. This should give you at least a third point to work

Interpolation and Extrapolation

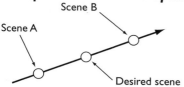

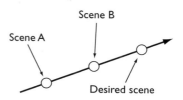

Interpolating Scenes

If you have scenes A and B, you can find the scene between them by projecting the dramatic line from A to B.

Extrapolating Scenes

If you have scenes A and B, you can find the scene following B by projecting the dramatic line forward.

---

with in plotting the story. The next step is to begin filling in the spaces between these scenes.

To do this, look at each scene as it sits in its place on the story's arc. Remember: These scenes may be roughly placed and may move around a lot later, but for now, just take your best guess and work from there. The process of plotting is all about making a guess and then refining it and refining it until it works just the way you want it to.

If you have two scenes that at this point are adjacent and are looking for the scene that you want to follow them, simply look at the arc that they are creating. How do dramatic elements like character development, subtext and tension grow from one to the next? If the dramatic change between them is on a steep curve, then it's likely that the next scene you conceive to follow them will also create a significant elevation in the drama.

While you will sometimes be dealing with a bend in the curve, you want that elevation of dramatic tension to be gradual so your audience doesn't get lost or confused. Look at the arc of the characters in that scene and the arc of the tension you are building and that should give you a good idea of what elements that scene will need to contain. You should also be able to figure out other elements like which characters need to be present or which story line or subplot needs development.

If you have two scenes and are trying to figure out what the scene between them should be like, the process is similar. Look at the arc between the two scenes and you'll be able to easily judge how the dramatic elements of the new scene should be balanced. The scene

DRAMATIC COMPARISON

In Alfred Hitchcock's *Psycho*, the story begins with a petty theft, what's known in literary terms as a McGuffin. The character takes the money and leaves town. She checks into a motel and goes for the infamous shower scene. She is murdered, and the story's arc takes a sharp upward turn, dramatically escalating events. If the change is more subtle, it's likely that this step will be subtler as well. In the book *Primary Colors*, there is a scene early on in which the candidate exchanges a smile and a kind word with a librarian. Innocent enough. In the next scene we see the candidate coming out of a hotel room with the librarian talking about "library funding" and "good work." It's also subtly obvious that a tryst has occurred. This behavior will become more problematic for the protagonist as the story progresses. The McGuffin is an event that seems to be a part of the main story but is actually just a device used as a catalyst for the central plot.

you are creating should build a smooth, logical bridge between the other two scenes. Avoid jarring changes in tension or pacing between the scenes. Ideally, the scene you are creating will draw the audience up the arc of the story from the previous scene to the next scene.

The more you go through this process of interpolation and extrapolation, the easier it will become as the leaps between scenes grow shorter. Remember, as you go through this process, keep in mind the various arcs that you will be constructing (central arc, character arcs, subplots). Be sure that each subsequent scene you write adequately delivers on those objectives. If you find it hard to match up the many objectives of each single scene, consider adding another scene or rearranging things so that the arcs work together.

The 3 × 5 Card Method

With all this talk of conceiving scenes and arranging and rearranging them, you may be wondering how best to manage all of this. The act of constructing good plots means breaking everything down to its essential, elemental parts, dealing in components that can be manipulated easily. One way of accomplishing this is by using ordinary 3 × 5 cards. The cards are small enough to work with and shuffle about easily. They can also be laid out on a table, allowing you to see your entire plot in one complete view. The cards are also large enough to write a considerable amount of information on, so you can include information like the basic action, the characters present, themes to be explored and other reminders that we'll discuss later.

By creating all your scenes on the cards, you will be able to manipulate them easily and try out multiple plot structures quickly. While the process is hopelessly analog in a digital world of computers, I've yet to find a software program that enables me to construct an outline as detailed and manipulate it as easily. The biggest shortcoming I've found in computer outlining programs is that it is usually impossible to see the entire story on a single screen. It is this big-picture view of the plot that is most important in constructing the plot and arranging the scenes.

This method has many, many advantages and makes the process of outlining your plot and, later, the process of writing your story quite manageable. Also, feel free to modify the method so that it works best for you. It is a method that was taught to me by a screenwriting teacher, and I've made many modifications to the system myself. The key to all the tools taught in this or any other book or writing course is to adapt them so that they work best for you.

Collecting Ideas for Major and Minor Plot Points

One of the best things about the 3×5 card method is how easy it is to gather your thoughts and ideas for the elements that will make up your plot. Each time you get an idea, just jot it down onto a card. It doesn't have to be a fully conceived scene or even a scene at all.

Elements to collect on cards:
- a location
- a thematic element
- a reminder about mood or style
- a line of dialogue

Because the cards can be arranged any way you want, you can simply collect the cards until you are ready to begin enforcing some order on them. Cards that don't contain scene information can be clipped to cards that contain scene ideas to remind you of an element

The McGuffin is an event that seems to be a part of the main story but is actually just a device used as a catalyst for the central plot.

you wish to include. You can also add stuff to each card as new ideas occur to you.

The portability of the cards is nice if you are the type of writer who is always thinking and always coming up with new ideas. A few blank records in a purse or pocket will assure that you'll always be prepared whenever the muse strikes. You can also carry the cards you've already written (just don't lose them!) for review and to stimulate other ideas. The ease of this method will make it possible for you to spend your idle time working on or at least thinking about your project.

The 3 × 5 Method: The Raw Material

Step 1: You should start the process of collecting scenes by just writing down all the ideas you have for your project. During the initial phase of conceiving your story, you probably had a number of ideas for scenes or chapters you wanted to write. Transfer those ideas to the cards. If you're thinking in terms of chapters of a book, you will probably want to break down each chapter into smaller units.

I use the term "scene" to describe any dramatic beat in a story. It is not meant to refer specifically to the scenes one would use in writing a play or screenplay. The idea is that the scene—a dramatic unit that takes place in a single location at a single, continuous moment in time—is the smallest unit in constructing a plot, and that is the level at which the construction of the outline should be approached.

Collect the ideas randomly and without judgment. Write them all down and put them aside, whether they are scenes or other notes. Don't concern yourself at this time with how they fit together or how well each is constructed. The goal now is just to get all of your notes, whether written on various pieces of paper, in notebooks, on napkins or in your head into one place and in a common format (the 3 × 5 card).

Step 2: Once you've collected these random, basic pieces, you can begin working with them. Start by pulling out all the scene cards you've got. Try to put them in the order in which you think they'll end up in the finished product. Your decisions on this probably won't be final, just make your best guess. Since the major plot points are the most crucial in the overall constructing of your story, begin figuring them out, using the processes of interpolation and extrapolation. You'll find that once you have them well worked out, you'll also be able to figure out the minor plot points, subplots and other elements much more easily.

Step 3: Start with the plot points that come easiest. Don't feel like you have to tackle the toughest problems first. The ones that come easily will help you figure out the tougher ones. In the process of writing a story, the more pieces of it you have, the easier the remaining pieces will come. You may also find that figuring out one part of your plot will trigger ideas for other parts. Don't wait to include those. Immediately jot down the new ideas that come into your head. Once you've worked out the major plot points that came easily, go back and start trying to crack the tougher problems.

At this phase of the writing process try not to get overly concerned with how everything fits together. Just collect as many ideas as you have, because the main goal of this part of the process is to collect the ideas—the raw material—of your story. Later you will focus your efforts on distilling it all down to the best and most compelling parts. For now, just try to mine as much raw dramatic ore as possible. You may find later that an idea doesn't work, but that it sparks another, more useful idea. You may even find that the note or scene doesn't even belong in this plot but makes perfect sense in something else you are working on.

As your collection of 3×5 cards grows, begin reviewing it regularly. Make it the first thing you do each time you sit down to work on the outline. This way you will refresh your memory of what you're working on and give yourself a running start at coming up with more. As you see connections between different scenes or have ideas that will work in a given scene, make note of it. If you want to, clip the cards together. This will help you to begin refining your ideas, which is the next part of the process.

Putting in Blanks

By using 3×5 cards to create and lay out your plot, you will find it easy to work in a natural, nonlinear fashion, creating scenes as they come to you rather than in some prescribed order. You may find that you will create a major plot point and several of the scenes or beats surrounding it, then skip forward or backward to another plot point.

You may also find yourself jotting down simple ideas that have yet to form themselves into fully developed scenes. What you should notice is that your own organic process is taking over, filling in the pieces of the plot in whatever order they occur to you.

As you collect a significant number of cards, you may have the urge to lay them out and look at them all together in one space where you can assess the progress of your work. As you do this, invariably, some pieces of the plot will be missing. These may be areas you've yet to consider, pieces of the story not yet formed or pieces that aren't working for you. Nevertheless, you will be left with a number of "blank" spaces in your plot. This is nothing to worry about. As the process of interpolation takes over, you will eventually fill them in. In the meantime, however, I recommend that you fill in the blanks with blank 3×5 cards.

These blanks will act as spacers, reminding you that, indeed, something is missing, that the two scenes you've created are not intended to occur back to back and that there is a beat or beats missing from the construction of your plot. Use blank cards freely, toss them into the sequence of cards wherever you think you might need a scene or a beat. It's just as easy to pull them out later if you don't need the scene.

The blank cards will help you begin to see the arc of your story. If there are large parts missing from your plot, and nothing is tangible to hold that space, it will be difficult to see how the whole plot functions on the arc. The cards will help you to know where on the arc a certain scene occurs, how far it is from the nearest major plot point, or how far it is from the inciting incident or the climax. Then you will be able to judge how it fits into the overall drama.

Knowing when to throw in a blank card will take a little practice; that's why I encourage you to follow this simple maxim: When in doubt, put in a blank. If you think for any reason you may need a scene in a given place, or if you just aren't comfortable with two scenes living side by side, simply throw in a blank. You can always take it out later.

As you create more and more scenes, the blank cards will begin to hold discrete places in the arc, between major plot points, beats, or even individual scenes. These cards will help you in the interpolation process discussed earlier. As you look at the various sequences that

QUICK QUIZ
FILLING OUT THE ARC WITH BLANKS, PART I

Ask yourself the following questions to determine if there are missing elements that you need to hold a place for with blank cards.

- Is the level of tension adequate?
- Has the character developed sufficiently?
- Is the arc of a subplot in sync with the overall scene?
- How is the pacing developing?
- Are my major plot points too far apart?

QUICK QUIZ
FILLING OUT THE ARC WITH BLANKS, PART II

Some things to look for when deciding whether or not to add blank cards are:

- Does the protagonist or other character need an additional scene to further develop his character?
- Is an element needed in order to preserve or improve the pacing of the overall story?
- Is this a good place for a subplot?
- Is this a good place for a major plot point?

make up your plot, you will find that certain scenes are well formed and in the right place on the arc. As you create more and more of these scenes, you will see spaces developing indicated by the blank cards. These blank cards will notify you that an element is missing. By looking at the scenes on either side of the blank (or blanks), you will be able to create the scene or scenes necessary to connect the two. The more you work this process of interpolation by filling in the blank cards, the shorter and shorter the distances between well-developed scenes will become and the fewer blank cards you will have.

Using Blanks for Transitions, Subplots, Character Development and Exposition

Some blank cards will fall in places where an action- or information-oriented scene isn't needed. Sometimes you insert a blank card just to give your audience a little breathing space between scenes. These blanks can be filled by other types of scenes, possibly ones having to do with subplots, character development, exposition or back story. By working from the blank cards between other scenes, you will be able to create these scenes so that they not only fulfill their objective, but so that they can provide smooth transition naturally into or out of the scenes adjacent to them. Thus, you can not only preserve the flow of your plot, but even discover opportunities to draw in or reinforce dramatic points from the previous scene or foreshadow something to come in the following scene.

Using Blanks for Pacing

Another good use of blank cards is to control the pacing of your plot. As you collect the scenes that will make up the major plot points in your story, you will begin to get a feel for the rhythm of your work. The major plot points, working their way toward the climax, will develop a pace, and you will notice a certain upward movement of the drama and the tension. The rate of this upward movement is the pacing. As the pacing becomes clear to you, you will notice a need for certain scenes to occur at certain points in the drama. Spacing these scenes in relation to other scenes can be done by dropping blank 3×5 cards into the sequence. These blanks will help you to position the major plot points and control the pacing. You can fill in the blanks with other elements later, but you will at least be able to establish some basic pacing for your plot.

Using the Cards to Map the Plot on the Arc

As mentioned previously, a time will come in the process of creating the 3×5 cards when you'll want to lay them all out so that you can see the progression of your story. I recommend doing this once you've got your inciting incident, climax and at least three of your major plot points. Once you've reached this critical mass of elements in your story, find a large flat surface—a large desktop table—and clear a space where you can lay out all your cards. You'll quickly be able to see what's missing and where you've made the most progress. If you haven't yet inserted blank cards to hold the places where you need to add plot elements, now would be a good time to do that.

This overall view of your plot will give you a good idea of how the structure is shaping up. Like viewing the skeleton of a building, you'll be able to see weaknesses and areas that need further work or refining and you'll be able to examine the flow of the scenes and get a feel for how the story's arc is shaping up. As you lay out the cards, you might find it useful to mark certain events like the inciting incident, the centerpiece scene of each major plot point, the climax, etc., with a small Post-it note. This will help you to overlay the arc of your story onto the array of cards you've laid out.

Once you've laid everything out, "read" your story through a couple of times. That is, read each card in order and see how the story feels. You should be able to read your entire story in just a minute or two. This will give you a high-level view of your planning, and the ability to determine how the following elements are shaping up:

- tension
- character development
- exposition
- the overall progress toward the climax

After a few readings, you'll probably notice some trouble spots: A couple of major plot points may be too close together or too far apart, or a main character disappears from the narrative for an uncomfortably long time. Based on these assessments, you can then go back to the cards and move them around to try to correct the problem.

Making Notes on the Cards

Before you move any cards, I suggest numbering them with a pencil in their original order. This will allow you to easily return your story to its original sequence if the changes you make don't solve the problem. There are other notations you may want to make on the cards:

- the act in which this scene occurs
- scenes that are part of a distinct sequence and, therefore, will most likely be kept together
- major plot points
- subplots—you may want to give each subplot in your story a different form of coding
- character development scenes
- exposition or back story scenes
- names of the characters appearing in the scene (highlighted)

- which scenes go together in time or location if your story takes place in multiple time frames, or contains other sorts of parallel action

These notations will track the many threads that make up your story. You can make these notations in a number of ways:

- penciled numbers or letters
- hatch-marks with different colored pencils
- different colored highlighters (remember, these are permanent)
- removable colored stickers

Whatever system you decide to use, be sure you make up a card with a legend on it, so you will know what each notation means. Don't rely on memory; you may return to these cards weeks or months in the future while you are in the process of writing your story and by then you may have forgotten what your notes meant! Put the legend on a separate card and keep it with the others. Also, put some thought into your system so that it is as intuitive as possible, and then stick with that system for all your future stories.

These notations only have to serve as guides as you begin to shuffle the elements in your story to make up a solid plot. You'll notice that most of the techniques described above for marking your cards are easily erasable or removable (highlighting being the exception), so if you change your mind about the function of a scene, which act it belongs in or even which sequence of scenes it goes with, all you have to do is change the notation. As you begin to construct your plot in earnest, you'll find these notations very helpful as a quick, at-a-glance way of seeing how certain pieces of the plot are working, and more importantly, how the various pieces are working together.

This process of "reading" and assessing the status of your story is an intuitive one. Each story is different, so you will have to judge for yourself how well your story is coming together. As you make this judgment, refer back to section one of this book to evaluate how each piece of your plot is functioning. You should begin to see the skeleton of your story emerging. As you create new scenes (cards) and as you rearrange the ones you have to improve the flow of the story, the outline of your story will become clear to you, and your vision of the story you want to write will become more specific and concrete.

Common Plotting Problems

As you go through this process, there are a number of pitfalls you'll want to avoid. By seeing your story as a whole in one glance, rather than having to page through an outline or notes on paper, you'll be able to easily recognize and easily remedy some common difficulties. And, it's far more efficient to iron out these issues at this stage of the process than it is when you are far into the actual writing process.

Jumping Around in Time or Location Too Much

As you look at the pieces of your story plotted out before you, you may notice that the story doesn't stay in one place long enough. This plot problem will make it difficult for your audience to get into the flow of your story. If readers are picked up in one place and plopped down in another in every other scene or chapter, they will find it difficult to immerse themselves in the world of the story. Frequent changes in time or location will create much work and frustration for your audience. This problem, however, is easily recognized if you look at your cards and see that practically each card happens in a different space and time. If you find this problem, there are a couple of solutions. First, if it is not your intention to tell an episodic story or one that moves from place to place quickly, think about these possible solutions:

- Rearrange your scenes wherever possible, grouping ones that occur in the same location to provide better story flow.
- Lengthen the sequences so that more action takes place in one location and at one time. Possibly restructure expository or character development scenes so that they occur in that location.

If you are trying to create an episodic feel or if your story needs to move from place to place frequently, try these solutions to smooth out the transitions:

- Create a framing device that will let the audience know that you are moving from one place to another.
- Add elements (narrative, linguistic, environmental, etc.) that are exclusive to the various times or locations you're moving between.
- Keep the movement from one time or place to another as consistent as possible. Try to keep sequences even in length and try to maintain a consistent sequence (e.g., New York, LA, Chicago, New York, LA, Chicago, etc.).

By simply rearranging the cards, you can retain your scene ideas while giving your plot a stronger flow and a better, more taut progression toward the climax.

Poor Transitions or Flow of Scenes

Creating transition and scene flow can be maddeningly difficult once you have begun the actual writing of your work. While you'll have to create the actual transitions when you're writing, you can set them up properly well in advance while planning your outline. Go through the cards you've laid out sequence by sequence. The cards that make up the same sequence should have natural, logical transitions between them. The cards at the end of the sequence are the ones to concern yourself with. How do these cards that make up the beginnings and endings of sequences flow into one another? If the story makes a major jump in time or location, you may need to build in some sort of transition device, such as a date or location stamp, or if you are dividing separate times or places with some other stylistic device, make a note of it.

Remember that each plot point in your work will have a smaller arc of its own in addition to the role the sequence plays in the overall plot arc. Be sure that the mini-arc of each sequence you finish comes to some sort of resolution. This arc should come to a natural ending as the final scene in the sequence plays out. By the same token, the first scene in the following sequence should commence its own arc. Also, make sure that these transitions preserve any tension you've built up and that they keep advancing the story toward the climax, keeping the story's rising action intact.

Poor Growth of Tension and Raising of Stakes Toward the Climax

The 3×5 cards can be very helpful in monitoring the growth of the tension in your story. Examine each plot point in order to determine if the story keeps moving at a good pace, and if each successive plot point raises the level of tension. In mysteries or thrillers, make sure that any digressions or tangents aren't sapping the story's tension. Your audience's sense of tension will only last a short time once they are taken away from the main story and the main source of that tension. If you've got a long subplot that doesn't feed the tension, you may want to move it or break it up into several pieces so that you keep coming back to the main story, the source of your suspense. You'll also be able to tell by reading the cards (tarot cards?!) if your protagonist's stake in the action is rising steadily.

- Is he becoming more and more heavily invested in his situation?
- Does he have more to lose in this scene than the last?
- Is the protagonist's gamble approaching resolution?

If the answer to any of these is no, you will need to rearrange your cards to keep the plot moving upward toward the climax.

Confusing Back Story

The way the back story unfolds can be crucial to the success of your plot, and when you've written pages and pages of a screenplay or manuscript, it can be difficult to extract how that unfolding is working. When your story is written on just a few dozen cards, it's easy to look at how you've managed the back story. Simply trace its progress from one card to the next. Be sure to mark your cards somehow to indicate that a particular scene contains back story information. If you do so, it will be easy to find those back story cards and examine what information is being revealed, and whether it is being revealed in a way that best suits your story. If you rearrange any part of your plot, review back story to determine if you have made inadvertent changes in it.

Logic

The logical progression of the narrative in most stories takes care of itself. However, if you begin to tinker with your plot, rearranging scenes with the 3×5 cards, you may find that certain facts and the revelation of certain information become scrambled. After making any significant changes to the order of your cards, it's always advisable to go back to the cards and reread them to make sure that all the facts of your drama are still straight. If you are telling a story that moves around a lot in time (using flashbacks, for instance) or changes location, or if you are telling two or more stories in parallel, you'll want to review your work to make sure that all the many pieces fit together, that there are no leaps in logic or discontinuities. These elements are easy to catch and fix at this early stage when your work is still in the form of a bunch of index cards. Also, if there are issues of logic, the order in which events happen, or what information is revealed when, you can sort these out clearly now, avoiding the need to wrestle with them later. Then as you write your story, you'll always have a clear understanding of how those elements are intended to work.

Overly Long Sequences or Too Brief Sequences

As you divide your cards into different sequences, you'll notice that the major plot points vary in length. This is natural. However, if your sequences vary too much in length, it may warp the dramatic balance of your story, creating a sort of bulge where the story may bog down. An overly long sequence may take on a weight in the story disproportionate to its intended role. A sequence may be overly long simply because you've worked on it more or it formed itself in more detail in your mind. This is fine, and the more detailed your outline, the easier it will be to write those sequences, but make sure that the other major plot points are equally well developed.

An equally serious problem is sequences that are too brief. A major plot point that is too short or underdeveloped will go by the reader too quickly and may not have the intended impact. If a character is at a major turning point and the sequence is too short, the audience may not realize the change that has taken place. Look at these sequences in depth; spend some time with them and develop them further. If they are truly major plot points, there are surely additional nuances to be explored, and possibly more setup time is required for them to have the desired impact. Let me emphasize that each sequence will be a little bit different, but you want to look at them all and assess whether or not they are sufficiently developed and whether or not their "size" accurately reflects their importance in the drama.

Major Plot Points That Come out of the Blue

In constructing your plot, you are essentially climbing a mountain from the beginning of the story to the climax. This progression should be gradual, although the degree of incline should vary somewhat along the way. The major plot points are like the major ascents, places in the drama where the story takes a quantum leap to the next level. While these major plot points, by nature, are a heightened portion of the drama, it's important not to disorient your audience by having them come out of nowhere. Be sure that each major plot point is part of a sequence that contains its own distinct arc.

Syncing Multiple Arcs for Maximum Dramatic Effect

The 3×5 card method can make complex plots and intricate narratives easy to manage. The cards will always allow you to break your story into the simplest pieces necessary for planning. With these individual components in an easily manipulated form, you can keep track of all the threads operating in your story, and you can coordinate those threads, weaving them into a rich tapestry so that each one will build on the others to create maximum dramatic impact.

As you are creating your scenes, writing each on an individual card, make notations as to how the scene should function in the overall plot. If you begin to develop a subplot in your story, mark all the scenes that make up that subplot with some notation of your own choosing. That way you will be able to recognize them quickly without having to read all the cards. As you structure your story, you can keep an eye on how that subplot is developing and determine whether its pacing is working.

An occasional problem with subplots is that, being subservient to the main plot, the elements in them can get pushed around until the subplot is no longer working optimally. For instance, if you have a subplot to be woven in and out of the main narrative for the length of the story, the cards will make it easy to tell if the subplot is disappearing from the narrative for a very long time. You may need to rearrange the cards in the subplot to compensate for this, or, if there is no way to work the scenes more closely together, you will know that your audience may require a little reminding of what is going on.

If you have subplots or parallel stories that will ultimately have a direct impact on the main thrust of the narrative, you can use the cards to make sure that these disparate threads come together at just the right moment, syncing up the arcs so that they all converge at the climax or some other desired moment in the story. By color coding the cards, you will be able to see how each separate subplot is developing, making it easier for you to draw parallels and smooth the transitions between them.

Using the cards will allow you to function like an air traffic controller who has dozens of jets in the air, all converging on the airport. From this high-altitude view of the story, you will be able to monitor all the dramatic aspects of your story, keeping them in tune with each other and avoiding difficult midair collisions. Using the cards, you'll be able to control and manipulate your story in ways that aren't possible with regular outlines, and certainly not within the full text of the story. By organizing all these pieces during the planning stage, you'll give yourself a clear, concise and detailed blueprint of your story, which will ensure the security of your story's integrity and enable you to devote all your energy to creating the best possible prose.

Other Uses of the Card System

The 3×5 card system can be used to monitor other elements of your story as well. While designed as a means to construct and refine the plot of your story, it can also help you to control and monitor the other elements of your story that have a profound impact on the plot as well as the overall quality of the work.

Character Development

Though this book isn't about character development, this element is critical to the success of your plot. The card system can be a great tool in working on your characters. Just as the plot has an arc, so do the characters who participate in it. Look at your character descriptions and examine closely the journeys (physical, emotional or spiritual) the characters will take through the plot. You will certainly recognize certain character development milestones, which might include:

- decisions they make
- changes in attitude
- the uncovering of emotions

Write each of these milestones on a separate card, and note which cards correspond to which characters. Now, insert these cards into the sequence. I suggest paper clipping or stapling these cards to the card that corresponds to the scene where the character will reach that milestone. Using these cards, you will be able to make sure that you match the scene to the point at which your characters pass these different milestones in their development. Once all the character development cards have been matched up with scenes in the plot outline, you can gauge the effectiveness of your characters' arcs and make any necessary adjustments, either to where the characters reach their milestones or to the plot itself.

By putting the character arcs on the cards, you will also be able to view the arcs of several characters, perhaps protagonist and antagonist, determine if they are developing together the way you want and avoid leaving out important pieces of each character's development. This will also allow you to use character-focused scenes to fill in some of the text between the major plot points and avoid the unpleasant task of having to go back later to correct any gaps between scenes.

Stylistic Choices

At some point during the conception of your story, you may decide to incorporate some unique stylistic element into your story. This could be a changing point of view, a different narrative voice, a visual motif or a distinct style. If this is a stylistic choice that will change occasionally throughout your story, you may want to use the cards to keep track of it. For instance, if you decide to tell certain portions of your story in a first person voice, you can note these portions on the cards either with a colored mark or sticker or some other notation, which will remind you to begin writing each scene with the stylistic element.

Managing nonlinear storytelling and nonlinear time. These elements can make for some fascinating stories, and nonlinear elements really show off the tremendous possibilities of different types of drama. However, nonlinear storytelling and the use of nonlinear time can be tremendously difficult to work with. The 3×5 card method greatly simplifies the implementation of these techniques by allowing you to conceive of them in a more natural, simpler linear fashion; then you can carve them up later to serve your nonlinear dramatic needs.

If all or some portion of your story is going to involve fracturing time in a nonlinear way, I suggest that at some point in the conception of the story you write out the scenes on cards in the order in which they occur in real time. Once you have done this, you can assure yourself that the events of your story work and that their logic is sound. You may also want to number the scenes in temporal order before breaking them up and shuffling their order as you work them into the story. You can easily see which scene "happened" first and thus keep track of the events. You may even want to write the first draft of these scenes in linear order so that the story flows well and the facts are all kept straight. Later, it will be easy to cut and paste the scenes into the desired nonlinear order in the narrative. A second draft of the manuscript will allow you to smooth the nonlinear scenes into the overall flow of the work.

CHAPTER NINE

Subplots

While it's possible to write an entire story without using any subplots, if you're doing anything longer than a short story, it will probably be rather dull. The subplot is an integral part of building the drama of your story. Among the many functions of the subplot:

- character development
- comic or other relief from main narrative
- back story
- exposition
- development of themes and extended metaphors

Like most things in writing, the definition of a subplot is open to interpretation. For the purposes of this discussion, however, let's define a subplot as a piece of action that takes place in a story that is separate or different from the main action of the story and subordinate to that main action. It can be a bit of exposition or back story, but it must be more than simple information conveyed to an audience. It should be a unique set of events that contains its own arc and its own plot points. It might take place in a separate location or in a separate time frame from the main story. The key elements that constitute a subplot are an arc, action and different location, characters or time. Think of subplots as another tool to deepen and broaden your story. Use them to illuminate critical information and to deepen your story's resonance with the audience.

Creating subplots that enhance and expand the main narrative takes a great deal of planning. You may conceive of your subplot in a couple of different ways, depending on the nature of the story you are telling. If your story is heavily plot driven, you may not initially be thinking about subplots at all. This is okay; spend the first phase of the development of your story concentrating on the two central concerns of any story: plot and character. Develop your character profiles and begin to look at the major plot points. As you develop these plot points, it's likely that you will come upon issues, possibly to do with exposition or back story or illuminating some theme of your work, that will require more in-depth exploration. This is a good opportunity to consider a subplot that will give you the time and space to look closely at that issue. Once you've discovered an issue that requires a subplot, you'll want to develop the subplot just as you would the main plot. Consider what the "minor-major" plot points will be, and try to discover and develop the dramatic arc of the subplot. Remember, though, that you are only doing a *subplot* and avoid getting carried away with it. While the key to major plot points in your main plot is illuminating the big issues, the intention in the subplot is to shine the spotlight on crucial details. Think on a smaller, more intimate scale and be sure to keep the subplot's main objectives clearly in mind. You'll find it very easy to get carried away on subplots, developing them into full stories. While these may be fascinating stories, you don't want them to draw too much attention away from the central story you are trying to tell. You also don't want a large subplot to warp the shape of your main plot and compromise your story's central arc.

Nonplot-driven stories will use subplots in a different way. If the major thrust of your story isn't the action in it, then you will probably find yourself conceiving of subplots from the earliest stages of your writing. It is even possible that in more episodic or character-driven pieces you may have an entire story made up of nothing but subplots. In these cases, create each subplot with a very specific objective. Develop the subplot just as you would any other plot, constructing an arc and several mini-major plot points.

As you begin to collect these subplots for either type of story, commit their pieces to 3×5 cards. Before you attempt to integrate them into the story, lay them out individually and make sure that they are sound units on their own. Do they make sense? Are the objectives of the subplot met? Once you've done this, make a notation on each card so that you know which ones go together. This will make it easier to keep track of them once they are integrated into the rest of your outline. When integrating the subplots into your outline, you will have to determine if they work best as complete, uninterrupted pieces, or whether they are more effective mixed into the main plot or with other subplots. Keep in mind the issues of rhythm and pacing and how the subplots effect the overall progression of the story toward the climax.

Subplots as a Diversion or Relief

Previously in this book we've discussed the pitfalls of overly linear storytelling. The story that progresses relentlessly from major plot point to major plot point until it reaches the climax can be terrifically dull. Even though the events that make up the story may be clearly compelling, their unyielding quality gives them a sameness that is counterproductive. Think about driving in a car through a spectacular desert. At first, the tumbleweeds and the cacti and the dunes are dramatic and interesting, but after several hundred miles of such scenery, even the tallest cacti or most beautifully wind-sculpted dune is boring. What makes any journey, physical or literary, interesting is the variances in scenery. In writing, as in life, everything is relative. And, to make your story interesting, you need to provide the audience with contrasts. There are numerous ways to do this and one is to provide a diversionary story element like a subplot.

A subplot can provide an audience a break from the forward progress of the main plot in many ways and can accomplish a number of goals. The first is to simply provide some variance from the main story. Particularly if your story is heavily plot-driven, like a thriller or mystery, or if the plot is highly emotional, a subplot will give your audience a chance to rest. While we all want our writing to be interesting and thrilling and while audiences require this from us, don't wear out your audience with too much all at once. A subplot can give the audience a welcome diversion, a chance to immerse themselves in a smaller, more focused aspect of your story. If the action has been nonstop, it will provide them an opportunity to rest their brains with something lighter and of less pressing consequence. You'll also allow the audience a chance to reflect on what they've just experienced and digest what has happened.

Subplots as Context or Background

A second and probably more important role of the subplot in breaking up the linear narrative is to provide context for the main plot of the story. In most stories the plot occurs over a relatively short span of time and the events in it may not seem extraordinary in and of themselves. A well-placed, well-constructed subplot can allow the author to place the events of the plot into the larger context of a character's life, a town or country's culture or a historical period. For instance, the outspoken matron of Edith Wharton's *The Age of Innocence* is refreshing among the other repressed, socially bound characters in the drama. However, seeing how it's marginalized her in that society helps us to understand the Countess's reluctance to divorce her husband. This subplot helps the author put the other characters' socially restricted behavior into the context of New York society in the nineteenth century. In the film *Chinatown*, Gittes investigates a crime against the backdrop of the battle for water rights in southern California. The antagonists' wranglings over control of the water don't form the central plot, but they provide the audience with context and an understanding of the larger issues of power, money, even racism in 1940s Los Angeles.

A subplot might also provide information for the audience that will give resonance to other elements in the story. In *Hoosiers*, Dennis Hopper's drunken assistant coach is emblematic of the creeping despair that is typical in the film's small town. He offers an example of the type of future that could be awaiting the boys on the team, which makes their eventual victory that much more important by providing hope for something better for themselves and the town. A subplot can help to show an audience just how important the protagonist's goal is to her, even if the actual accomplishment seems ordinary. Subplots can even explain events or characters or situations in the main story. Often they are good for explaining an antagonist's motives or to illuminate the pain behind her evil ways. They can also be good ways to illuminate the supporting characters' motives and their own personal goals, giving your story a greater number of well-defined, deeply drawn characters.

Subplots to Tell Concurrent or Parallel Stories

Another function of subplots is to tell multiple stories within the same narrative. Some stories have one or more highly developed subplots that are quite central to the main plot and in some cases on a par with it. In novels like *Fried Green Tomatoes* or films like *Pulp Fiction*, it is sometimes difficult to say which plot is the central plot and which is the subplot. Take *Fried Green Tomatoes* as an example. Is the main story the present-day tale of the two older women, or is it the story set in the past about the two young women in the diner? The two plots are each integral to the overall themes and messages of the book, and each one helps to expound on the other. The story of the elderly woman in the nursing home provides a forum for the telling of the story of the diner. She adds her perspective to events and leads into each episode then steps aside to let the other plot take its course. At the end of the episode the events then move to some action in the present-day plot as the Evelyn character continues her process of liberation, indirectly inspired by the two strong women in the diner. The author uses the two plots side by side to express her themes of feminine empowerment. Each plot has its own arc and its own major plot points. Those plot points skillfully build on one another, making the author's point all the more convincingly.

Episodic stories often use multiple plots to tell a single story. The story jumps from place to place in time or location, telling a completely different story in each place. The characters in the stories may or may not overlap, and the events may or may not build on one another. However, it is entirely possible to build the main plot arc on the backs of the subplots' individual arcs. As long as the subplots build on one another, they can provide the engine for the main story. Episodic subplots may also exist alongside a more traditional plot arc. Stephen King's short story "The Body" contains three subplots that have nothing to do with the main story (except that they are written by the story's adult narrator who is one of the kids in the central story). The stories provide humorous and poignant commentary on the way kids treat one another, expanding the story's theme of youthful comradeship.

Some plots are made up of a group of convergent plots. These are stories where several smaller plots, featuring overlapping but somewhat different groups of characters, converge to play out the story's central plot. The subplots may initially seem like they have little to do with one another, but as the story progresses, the overlapping elements become clearer, and the audience is gradually able to assemble the pieces. This is often done with mystery stories or stories that use nonlinear time. An example of this is the Quentin Tarrantino film *Pulp Fiction*. The first scene of the film actually happens much later in the film temporally. Then there are a series of seemingly unrelated and sometimes altogether unrelated subplots. Each basically has its own cast of characters, with a few characters overlapping. Eventually, all the stories begin to converge and the audience is gradually able to make sense of what's been going on. The fun of the film is twofold: enjoying the individual subplots for their own intrinsic value and trying to figure out how they all fit together. The film's central plot is loose, at best, but the film is no less enjoyable and makes its points well, without the benefit of a central, driving plotline.

These examples are the work of accomplished writers and constructing such stories takes not only a fantastic imagination, it also takes a firm, experienced grasp of the craft of storytelling. You probably won't want to attempt anything so ambitious when you start writing. However, if you've been practicing your craft for some time and feel ready for a new challenge, then these types of stories can test your command of writing and can push your work in new and interesting ways.

For the most part, however, when starting to write stories, you'll use subplots as tangential story lines. These will be adjuncts that will closely relate to the main plot. Use them to enhance the impact of your main plot, and keep them relatively short and simple. There's nothing wrong with this. Remember that the subplot is just another weapon in your writer's arsenal, another means of making your point and telling your story. The tangent can be a valuable and interesting detour in your story, a digression, taking its cue from a particular event in the story, probably a major plot point. You can also use it as an opportunity to "take the road less traveled" and use one or more subplots to track the adventures of minor characters in your story, simultaneously giving your audience a broader perspective and a richer narrative.

Some subplots will start from the end of the tangent. That is to say, a subplot will start out seemingly unrelated to the events in the main plot, but as it progresses, its relationship to the main plot will become clear. These shorter, less narratively ambitious subplots are no less valuable to the main plot of your story. Keep in mind that what you are trying to accomplish with a subplot is to enhance and deepen the audience's understanding of the main plot, as well as the themes and ideas you are expressing in your work.

Subplots to Develop Characters

Subplots can also be an effective means to deepen your story's resonance and delineate its characters. Creating compelling, fully drawn characters is not always possible within the constraints of the story's main plot. If your story is particularly plot driven, you'll find that there is very little time to explore the personalities of your characters in depth. Subplots, however, can be very good at this, allowing you to take the character out of the stream of events happening in the main plot and place her in situations that can illuminate personality in new and interesting ways. It's also much easier to explore the depths of your character when your writing is less constrained by the demands of the plot and its mechanics.

Here are some ways to use subplots to grow your characters.

Put Character in a Reflective Place

Often the events of the central plot can rush ahead so quickly that the character, the author and the audience have little time to reflect on what has happened, what changes the protagonist has been through and what is waiting for her in the coming action. A subplot related to the main action only peripherally will give the audience a break from that action and a chance to look closely at what's happened. The events of that subplot should bring the character's personality, particularly any changes in her attitude, to the surface. If a character has discovered a gentler side of her personality, create a subplot in which this new trait is expressed thoroughly. Also, during the events of a subplot you can examine certain issues that arise in the main plot without having to resort to long passages of exposition. Let the less pressing nature of the events of the subplot express the ideas you've been exploring. Subplots can create opportunities for the protagonist to express attitudes about her discoveries with other characters in an environment that is less action oriented. In *The Empire Strikes Back*, Luke's visit to Yoda does all of these things. He considers his place in life, and we see him maturing. This takes place in this more relaxed atmosphere, free of Darth Vader's menace.

Put Your Character in a Circumstance That Shows Another Facet of Her Personality

Often as a protagonist faces the conflict in the story she isn't given an opportunity to exist in situations apart from that conflict. This can often lead to protagonists who are one-dimensional or not fully developed. If you are writing an action or adventure story, try putting your hero in a family setting. Show how she behaves at home with people she loves. Is she nurturing, or is the situation awkward for her? You will give your audience a new perspective on the character, which will make her behavior in the rest of the story more interesting.

Remember: Great characters and great drama grow out of contrasts.

If you are writing about a character, possibly an antagonist, whose behavior is normally ruthless, try putting the character in a situation where he acts compassionately. In Ayn Rand's *The Fountainhead*, Dominique Francon is a rather cruel, sophisticated ice princess, but when she retreats to her father's country estate, we see her loosen up, riding horseback and lusting after swarthy quarrymen. We glimpse the passion that lives beneath her dispassionate veneer.

Reveal a Strength or Weakness

Sometimes within the less-charged atmosphere of a subplot, you can quietly reveal a protagonist's or antagonist's Achilles' heel. It's possible that the audience may not even realize that what they are seeing is a weakness, but as it becomes clear later, they will remember the events of the subplot where it was revealed with a satisfying sense of "aha!" Conversely, sometimes it is within a subplot, perhaps at the protagonist's lowest moment, that the character finds a previously undiscovered strength. Maybe the protagonist doesn't even discover it herself, and only the audience sees it, planting the seed for its resurfacing later in the story. In Shakespeare's *Henry IV, Part II*, we learn of young Hal's penchant for drinking and wenching. It is this tendency

---

Remember that great characters and great drama grow out of contrasts.

---

and reputation that makes others question his worthiness to rule later when he is made king in *Henry V.*

Subplots as Diversions

Sometimes a subplot doesn't have to contribute much to the main plot at all; its only job is to provide comic or other relief. This may sound like a frivolous use of dramatic time and energy, but it can be surprisingly useful to the overall impact of your story. If you are writing a tense thriller or exciting action adventure, it's very easy for your audience to get worn out. With one thrilling event after another, it's very possible that your major plot points will become less and less effective as the audience becomes desensitized to them. This can severely hamper your efforts to bring about an exciting climax.

One way to resensitize your audience and revive their ability to be thrilled is to take a short detour from your plot for a little comic relief. Take the opportunity to give your audience a lighter view of your characters and their situation. While you may be writing a serious drama, consider how you could inject some humor into the plot. The subplot could consist of just a humorous detour that your character takes, or it could be an interaction with a comical character. Think of action films like *Lethal Weapon 2* or *True Lies.* Both movies were built around the exploits of action heroes Mel Gibson and Arnold Schwarzenegger, but both movies benefited tremendously from the presence of comic characters played by Joe Pesci and Tom Arnold, respectively.

This comic relief will give the audience a breather and a chance to recover their ability to be thrilled again. If your story's been particularly suspenseful, it will give them a chance to relax. It cannot be stressed enough how easy it is to overwork or wear out an audience. Once that fatigue begins to set in, no matter what you do, you won't be able to keep the same level of attention and suspense as you continue toward the climax. Contrast the highs and lows, the tension and frivolity. A good comic subplot will help your plot to keep its balance.

These comic relief subplots don't have to be utterly hilarious either; they may be simple observations about the characters or their situation. What's important is to take the characters out of their usual context. This will also contribute to enlarging the tone of your story.

Subplots to Enlarge Tone

If you are writing a drama, the overriding tone of your writing should complement that genre and, therefore, will probably be rather serious. While this may be entirely appropriate for the most part, it may also mean that you won't get to explore other aspects of the story. The use of a subplot will allow you to take a slightly different perspective or even try a slightly different stylistic approach to your work. There are certain aspects of a work that will just naturally lend themselves to different styles or attitudes; if your work is all of the same style or attitude, you may miss this opportunity to broaden your work by incorporating some different styles. That is why a subplot providing some comic relief or another tone different from the rest of your work will help to broaden and enrich the overall texture of the work.

In addition to providing comic relief, you may use subplots to supply other sorts of relief. If you're writing a comedy, you may create a subplot in order to introduce a more dramatic element, lending poignancy to the action that is missing in the comic tone. Whatever the overall tone of your work, think of the subplot as an opportunity to use something different, to create a contrast with the rest of your work that will make your story more enjoyable and resonant.

Placement of Subplots

Whatever their function, one of the keys to using your subplots well is to place them appropriately within the overall drama so they don't detract from the main plot. While you may become enamored of your subplots, it's likely that your audience will still be interested in the main story. So be careful that they remain in proportion to the rest of your story and aren't such wonderful diversions that they upstage the central drama. Here are a few things to consider and some pitfalls to avoid.

One Scene or Several?

One decision you'll have to make is whether or not your subplot is one that can occur in one uninterrupted sequence, or whether it is one that will recur throughout some portion of your overall story. Break up your subplot if it:

- provides dramatic contrast to the overall plot
- is significantly long

- concerns the ongoing actions of a secondary character
- in any way functions as a parallel to the main story

By coming back to it several times, you'll give the story time to develop and give yourself multiple points of contact with the main story where you can draw contrasts and comparisons between plot and subplot. If the subplot follows a secondary character, you may want the character arcs for the secondary player and the protagonist to sync up.

Keep your subplot together if it:

- is short
- provides a digression to explore back story
- focuses on exposition
- serves as comic or other relief

This will prevent you from interrupting the main story more than necessary. Also, small pieces of a subplot scattered over a large section of narrative may be difficult for your audience to follow.

Establish the Main Story First

You don't want to confuse your audience with a diversion before they are sufficiently involved in the main plot. If you go quickly to a subplot, your audience may be unsure of which plot is the main plot and which is the subplot. Also, remember that your main plot will have to have enough momentum built up to carry the audience through the subplot's digression. If the subplot is a minor one that will occur in one, uninterrupted piece, you should start it no earlier than after the first major plot point. This will allow the main plot's inciting incident and first major plot point to get the story rolling before the audience is faced with any interruption. On the other hand, if the subplot is one that will recur throughout the story and if it concerns some sort of parallel element in the drama, you will want to be sure to start it early. Parallel elements are difficult to establish once a story is rolling.

Choose Logical Entry Points

If there is a reference in the main story to some important element in the subplot, this may make a smooth transition point to the subplot. The less radical the transition, the less obtrusive it will be, and the more sense it will make to the audience. It's even possible that the transition from the main plot will give the subplot a running start. The most important thing is that the subplot makes sense and does not have a jarring effect. Remember that by taking the audience on this secondary journey, you are asking for their patience as well as their attention.

Don't Interrupt the Flow

Avoid interrupting a sequence of scenes or a major plot point with a subplot. Not only will the subplot distract the audience from what they are most interested in, it's less likely that the audience will absorb the information in the subplot. Be sure that your subplots come at the end of a sequence, when the natural arc of the drama is entering a lull. Once your subplot begins, make sure that you don't keep the audience away from the main plot for too long. The momentum that your main story carries will only last for so long. An overly long subplot will force you to work very hard to reestablish your story's forward motion.

Wrap Up All Subplots Before the Crisis Begins

A subplot that interrupts the final rush to the climax will greatly compromise your story's momentum and will diffuse the impact of your plot's biggest moment. Use the 3×5 cards to place the subplots and time them so that their impact and influence is played out well before the climax. The lead-up to the climax is one part of your story when the more linear it is, the more effective it will be.

Weaving the Threads Together

Once you've finished writing the bulk of your scenes on 3×5 cards, it will be time to begin weaving the parts together, making adjustments along the way, so that they form the strongest possible plot. As we've been reinforcing all along, it is during this outline stage that you want to dedicate your energy toward perfecting the mechanics of your plot. While there will probably be some fine-tuning during the actual writing of the first draft and more in subsequent drafts, you want to begin the process of writing the actual screenplay or manuscript with optimum confidence in the integrity of the structure of your plot. To use our architecture metaphor, you want the blueprint to be sound before you lay the first real brick.

Hopefully, you've been structuring the order of your cards along the way so that you've already got a fairly well-organized version of your plot. Now, go back over those cards and work out the kinks and smooth out the wrinkles. At this point your plot probably has an overall arc in place and plenty of other material that needs to be included. Take these other threads of your plot and work them into the overall structure so that they are woven seamlessly into the central events of the plot, making your story a single, unified, but richly textured work.

Taking Inventory

Begin this process by taking inventory of the elements you've conceived. Remember, there may be some elements that are still missing from the plot. However, you should think about those elements only after you've completed this part of the process. Feel free to leave blank cards in your card groups. Make a list of all the elements that you need to work into your plot. If you've marked each card with some notation as to what pieces belong together, this process should be easy. Simply take each piece and list it on another card or on a piece of paper, recording the notation beside it so you can easily find the cards later.

MARK ALL THE MAIN PLOT POINTS AND THE SCENES THAT GO WITH THEM LIKE THIS:

Main plot		
Plot point #1	3 scenes	blue sticker
Plot point #2	2 scenes	blue sticker
Plot point #3	4 scenes	blue sticker
Plot point #4	3 scenes	blue sticker
Climax	1 scene	blue sticker/red dot
Subplot #1	5 scenes (together)	red sticker
Subplot #2	3 scenes (broken up)	green sticker
Character development	5 scenes (scattered)	orange sticker
Back story	6 scenes (scattered)	purple sticker

Now that you've listed the scenes, you'll have a good understanding of which elements you are going to be working with. You'll probably have some preconceived ideas of how the various elements will fit together, but before you begin merging them all into your final outline, take a few moments to review each individual element and be sure it accomplishes its objective and is what you want dramatically and stylistically. If you have reservations about a particular piece of your plot or about some beat within that element, take time now to see if you can improve it. If you don't feel like you can make the improvement you want immediately, turn the card over and note on the back what your reservations are about that item. This will be a reminder when you come across the card again. Also, be sure to make some notation on the front of the card that you aren't totally happy with it. Reexamine each piece of the story and make sure that the desired arc exists.

As you review these elements, look for ways to economize. Are there scenes that can accomplish the same objectives elsewhere (without adding unnecessary scenes)? Sometimes elements of back story, exposition or character development can be incorporated into a major plot point or subplot so that they won't slow down the narrative. These economies will also help to meld the elements of your plot in a more seamless way. The last thing you want to happen is for your story to continually shift gears at every transition. If you can accomplish two things in the same scene, you will have blended the elements more effectively, giving your audience a smoother read.

This period of taking inventory is also good for examining the possible connections you might want to draw between different elements in your plot. If the protagonist and antagonist have similar experiences in their past, you may want to draw that connection. As you look at your ideas, you might find connections between things that you didn't realize were there. Maybe you've inadvertently created a recurring motif: characters returning home, superstitions or other recurring imagery or metaphors. Make note of these connections now and find ways, either in the structuring of the story or in the actual writing of it, to draw out these elements. While much of the writing process is conscious and driven by intention, there is a significant amount that happens subconsciously. Ideas and feelings that were hidden just below the surface often seep into the writing. Look over the cards you've created for any of these hidden ideas that you could emphasize.

Read the exercise on p. 172. The point of this exercise is to shake up your preconceived notions of what your story is about and to question your assumptions one more time before you begin the writing process. Challenge what you think you know, and try to look at your story from a new angle. This is not to say that you will necessarily reconceive your story based on this exercise. The point is merely to

---

EXERCISE

To help you in finding the hidden or undiscovered connections in your work, number the cards you've created in the order in which you think you want them to come in your outline. This can be just a rough outline. Then, take the cards and shuffle them just as you would any deck of cards until they are well mixed up. Then randomly lay out the cards one by one. Start with any two cards. Examine them to see if there's any connection between these two scenes.

- What sort of connections do you see between them?
- Could they happen sequentially?

Then add another card and ask the same questions again.

---

look for more layers, more elements, more ideas that might be lurking in your work, unexposed and unexploited.

Keep laying out cards two or three or more at a time, and continue to look for interesting connections. You may find new ideas or possibly new means to tell your story. If you are working on a story with a nonlinear plot, this exercise can be particularly helpful in finding creative ways to play with time. Once you've finished the exercise, refer to the numbers you put on your cards to reorder them, after making any changes you feel advantageous.

Finding the Central Arc

When you've taken inventory of all your elements and shaken them down for any interesting connections you might have missed, the next step is to recommit yourself to your central arc. Take the scenes you've written onto the cards and begin arranging them into the arc of your plot. Read the Story Starter on p. 173 for hints on arranging your cards.

Once you've worked all the cards into a comfortable sequence, I suggest you take a pencil and number the cards again, erasing any other numbering system you may have used with them. You have the basic elements of your plot laid out, and you should now be able to read them and get a very good sense of your story as a whole.

Making Adjustments

Having combined all the elements of your story into one continuous outline, you'll want to reread what you've written. Read each card and

STORY STARTER
LAYING OUT THE CARDS

1. Start with the scene or scenes that make up the inciting incident. If there are additional scenes, either leading up to or out of it, put those together in the order in which you want them.

2. Lay out the climactic scene and the scenes that make up the crisis leading to it.

3. Next, place the major plot points in order between the inciting incident and the climax. Be sure to keep together all of the scenes that make up each plot point. Other scenes may ultimately occur within the plot point, but keep the scenes together.

4. Choose one of your subplots that will need to be worked into several places in your plot and place each scene where you think it will work best. Keep in mind that your transitions will need to be smooth and be sure there is some way for the audience to keep track of the subplot as it weaves in and out of the plot.

At this point, you should have a pretty solid and complete plot. Reread each scene in the order you have arranged and try to get a feel for how these elements work together. Since these are the most important pieces of the plot, make sure that they all move well up the rising action of the plot arc.

5. Now begin working in the other subplots. Find natural breaks in the action of the main plot where a detour will be the least disruptive and will have the most positive effect on the rest of the plot. Some subplots will be very sensitive to timing and will need to happen at a particular juncture in the plot. These subplots will be easy to insert.

6. Finally, add the other elements you've worked up: comic relief, character development, exposition and back story. As you work these in, look carefully once more to see if there is a way that you can achieve these objectives within another scene in the drama. If this is possible, clip the character development or other element to the plot or subplot card so that as you are writing the actual scenes you'll know to work in those elements. Sometimes you'll elect not to work an element into another scene. These may be cases where you want the element to stand separately or your plot needs a break in its linear progression.

envision the final product in your head. As you do this, get a feel for the flow of the work.

- Are the characters developing the way you'd hoped?
- Is the drama escalating at a pace sufficient to keep the audience interested?
- Are the subplots and exposition deepening and broadening the story as you desire?
- A simple, but crucial question: Does it all make sense?
- Are there any lapses in logic?

During this rereading, you'll probably find adjustments that need to be made to your outline, and now is the time to make those changes. Be sure you've numbered your cards (in pencil) before you begin these changes so that you can always find your way back to your original outline if your adjustments aren't working. As you find changes that might potentially improve your outline, rearrange the cards accordingly. You might be reluctant to actually move things around, but that is the central benefit of the 3×5 card system—easy changes that can be quickly changed back. Once you've made these adjustments to the cards, reread the outline once again and see if it feels better. If you're not sure, walk away. While it may seem admirable and disciplined to work diligently with your outline for long periods, sometimes you need a break to let the creative energy settle a bit and to get a little distance from the work.

Here's what you should be looking for during this period of making adjustments.

How do the various arcs (character, story and subplot) compare? Are they the right lengths? Are they in the proper proportion to one another dramatically? Is there a subplot arc that overshadows the central arc? Are they all sufficiently developed? Does one or more seem weak or anemic?

Do the various arcs sync up? A well-constructed outline will have the protagonist's character development arc peaking at the climax of the plot. Similarly, if a story has multiple characters with their own arcs, those arcs should sync up so that the characters' personal journeys work together to raise the level of the drama. Also, if you have subplots developing in parallel to the main plot, they should reach their climax just before the main climax, adding momentum to the central plot. On the other hand, you want to be sure the different arcs, whether character arcs or subplots arcs, don't compete with one another or neutralize one another. Be careful about having too much going on at once. Based on these criteria, you should be able to make further adjustments to your outline.

Finally, look closely at how the various arcs are woven together. It is in weaving the components of your plot that your story will take on the rich texture and resonance that make for great film or literature. Be sure that the various elements are placed in relationship to one another in such a way that they make all the connections you have in mind. Also, review the pacing of the plot. Does it move efficiently from element to element? Do threads of the story get lost for long stretches, only to make confusing reappearances later? How do the transitions from element to element work? Are they smooth and seamless? Do they have the appropriate dramatic impact?

As you make these adjustments, you'll quickly find that every change you make affects some other element of the story. Like a Rubik's Cube, you'll get one piece just right, then mess it up by working on some other element. This is a natural, if sometimes frustrating, process. Try not to get dismayed; just let it happen. As you make the changes, you'll find yourself homing in on certain areas, adjusting them over and over again to fit each different set of criteria. You should find that as the process works itself out, the changes you need to make get smaller and smaller. This means that you are perfecting the outline and that the process is working.

You may come to points where two of your goals are in competition with one another and there is simply no way to accomplish both. These points require you to come to a compromise. You'll have to look at the two goals—say, a certain element of character development and an ironic parallel that two adjacent scenes draw out—and decide which one is more important to the overall goal of the plot. These will be tough decisions, but no outline is perfect.

Come to this process of making adjustments with an open mind and a good deal of patience. This is perhaps the single most important requirement in the entire process of creating your plot. If a solution to a problem doesn't present itself right away, move on. The best solutions to problems of adjusting your plot will come naturally and easily. Some will require a great deal of thought, but the solution, once realized, will be satisfying in its simplicity and grace. Don't be afraid to walk away for a while.

Final Steps Before the Writing Begins

As you make these adjustments to your outline, you should be satisfied to see the story you envisioned beginning to come to life. Once the kinks are worked out of the pieces that you've compiled, you'll want to begin filling in any areas that you still haven't conceived. There will likely be transitions that will need to be designed and maybe a dramatic hole or two to be plugged. Once this work is done and you have no more blank cards in your outline, lay out all the cards on a desk or table. Be sure that you can see them all. If possible, divide the different rows of cards so that they break at logical points, like act breaks or at the end of major plot points or sequences. Now you should have a good visual representation of your entire plot. Number the cards one more time, making sure you erase any old numbers. (Author's note: This step is more important than you can imagine. I once had an unnumbered stack of cards for a screenplay I was writing get knocked off a desk by my feline assistant. The cards weren't numbered and it took a couple of hours to get them back into proper sequence, and to this day, I'm certain that they never got put back in the way I originally had them.)

Once you've got the cards ordered and are ready to begin writing, take a couple of days off. Get away from the plot, work on something else or work on nothing at all. What's important is that you give yourself some time away from your work. Let it all soak in subconsciously and try to forget about it consciously. Having spent so much time with the mechanics of your plot, it's likely that if you started writing immediately, your work would absorb that mechanical feel. Let the mechanics soak in so that you can go back to focusing on the creative act of writing. It's often said of acting that a performer must learn the technique of acting so well that he forgets it. The technique becomes second nature and only the performance comes through. It is the same with writing. You need to let the mechanics of your plot become so well cemented that they are no longer visible. Just as you seldom see the foundation or the girders that hold up a building, your plot structure will submerge and what will be left will be the complete story.

When you are ready to return to your work, take it a piece at a time. If you want to start at the beginning, that's fine, but if you'd rather start with some other part and go from there, that's okay, too. Simply use the cards that make up that portion of the story. You should take a portion no smaller than a single sequence. If you are working on a major plot point or subplot, take all the cards that make up that section and review them. Then begin writing. Keep the cards nearby to remind you of your objective for each scene and any special elements that need to be incorporated therein. With the cards as a guideline to the mechanical workings of the scene or sequence, you should be able to concentrate fully on the language, the emotion and the atmosphere of the scene.

These are some tools that you can use to design your plot. Feel free to make modifications. There is no one right or wrong way to write. There are as many techniques as there are writers, and just as every writer's work is different, so are the means by which each creates that work. So use the tools freely and adapt them to your own special needs. You may also want to adapt them to new technologies that have become available. I work on 3×5 cards because I can't fit a universal view of my outline onto a single screen of a computer, but if you feel more comfortable working on a computer, I'm sure these techniques can be adapted for the digital world.

STORY STARTER

3×5 PROCESS REVIEW

- Collect ideas on cards.
- Put in blank cards where necessary.
- Map the plot on the arc.
- Make notes on the cards.
- Sync up multiple arcs.
- Take inventory.
- Fine-tune.

The important part is to make the tools yours, adapt them for your unique needs and recreate them to serve your writing, for in the end, that is the only thing that really matters.

CHAPTER TEN

Deepening the Story's Resonance

I t's entirely possible to tell a gripping, exciting story with a very straightforward plot. Tricky narrative techniques aren't a requirement for creating good drama. What's more important is a solid, well-constructed and compelling story. It's also dangerous to tackle complicated narratives before you are totally comfortable with the principles discussed throughout this book.

You may decide to use a special dramatic element very early in your creative process. It may, in fact, be a part of the whole conception of the story—the story will take place during a single summer at a resort. In this case, you will want to keep the element in mind throughout the construction of your plot, and the device will probably inspire many of the major plot points, as well as themes, subtexts or subplots. It's also possible, however, that you will conceive of your entire story and not come up with any useful device until you have already laid out most of your plot. This is okay, too, because it may be that the actual plot you've come up with will inspire that dramatic device. If this is the case, you'll have to work your way backwards, going through the story and working the dramatic device into the story scene by scene. Hopefully, the device will make obvious to you the scenes in which it will work. Either way, the addition of a dramatic device will give you a new element to work into your plot. Treat it like any other character or subplot and be sure that it is seamlessly woven into the overall story. Be careful not to approach the dramatic device halfheartedly. Devices like this must be worked fully into the story or else they will seem like odd appendages, which will be confusing and distracting. How the element fits in with the other ideas and themes should be fairly obvious to the reader, and its benefit to the story's impact should be clear as well.

Ticking Clock

We discussed this sort of device earlier when we were talking about adding suspense to your work. This concept is similar, except that instead of working just within one discrete period of the story and serving just to maximize tension, this sort of device will inform the entire story from beginning to end. The ticking clock sets the story instantly on a schedule and forces the author, the characters and the audience to keep to it. It will establish the story's arc from the beginning and can be very helpful in guiding the author through the story. It will also help to prevent you from straying into unnecessary tangents.

Setting the Clock

The first thing you must do (of course) is to set the ticking clock. In an early portion of your story, you must let the audience know the time period in which the story will unfold. This can be done as simply as saying, "It all happened one night," or, "It was during that weekend at the lake." While this straightforward announcing of the story's time frame can be effective, it is preferable if the information can be worked into the regular patterns of the story, either through dialogue or through some other circumstance. For instance, a character opens an envelope and reads a document that has a date on it or a character is given a terminal diagnosis. These sorts of elements will set the clock ticking toward the climax.

Defining the Climax

Defining the nature of the climax is the second thing you you must do. In some cases the climax will be decided for you to some extent by the setting of the clock. If a terrorist sets the clock on a bomb, it's easy enough to know that the climax will come when that bomb is due to go off, and the climax will involve either the bomb exploding or not exploding. Just as in creating any story, you need these two end points in order to begin your journey through the rising action.

In some stories, setting the clock itself will define the climax early on for the audience, as in the bomb scenario. The audience will know that when the clock reaches 00:00, they will have arrived at the climax. While it may seem like giving away the ending is always a bad idea, in some cases giving the audience this piece of information will help to raise the level of tension. After all, just because they know when the climax will arrive doesn't mean you have to give them any idea about how you're going to get there or what will necessarily happen when you arrive.

Frequent Updates

The key to the ticking clock device is keeping the audience informed about its status frequently. As you move through the major plot points of your story, refer often to the time or the day to keep the audience aware of the status of the story. Again, there's no need to be wooden or obvious about this, simply work the information into the ordinary course of the story, just as you would any other piece of exposition. In some stories, a time stamp—Thursday, 10:45 P.M.—might be appropriate, but in others you'll want to be more subtle. If you've set a clock that two lovers must part in the morning, the observation of a star in the sky or the sunset can be a powerful reminder that time is fleeting.

Time Flies

If you keep your reminders regular and spaced evenly apart, your writing can develop a rhythm almost like the actual ticking of a clock. At other times, you might find it useful to surprise your audience. For instance, a student is writing a term paper that is due at 5:00 P.M. He works diligently and is going to make his deadline, so he decides he needs a nap to refresh. However, his alarm doesn't go off, and he oversleeps. Suddenly it's 4:30 and he's still got work to do. Your audience may worry about his napping or they may be surprised to turn the page and find that several hours have ticked past. Either way, you are creating tension and driving the story forward.

One classic example of a story that uses a time device is the fairy tale "Cinderella." The delivery of the invitation announcing the ball sets the clock. The Fairy Godmother's admonishment to Cinderella to be home by midnight gives the story a definitive moment for the climax. While the story takes place in more than just a single day, it is the day of the ball that is the story's defining moment. And, it is an excellent example of a ticking time bomb.

Maintain the Rhythm

One pitfall to avoid is upsetting the rhythm of the story by making any one section overly long. If an audience is used to a ticking clock with reminders spread evenly and time passing at a comfortable rate, an extended section of the plot that slows time down can be distracting and fatal to the building of suspense. If you need to extend a section of time, make sure that you don't lose track of the story's rhythm. Just as a ritard in music can be a dramatic device to build anticipation, slowing the rhythm in a story can accomplish the same thing, but be sure your audience understands what is happening. If the audience isn't aware that time is "slowing down," they may think they've lost track of the clock and your plot will be weakened. Simple information like "the afternoon dragged on" or "he looked at his watch over and over, but time seemed to have come to a standstill" will keep your audience aware of what you are doing.

A Day, a Night

Sometimes the most compelling stories can be told in a single day or night. The short time frame is perfect for short stories and will also make for a great screenplay. The compressed time will give the story an automatic sense of urgency, and the dramatic time bomb can be set quite easily. The compact time of a single day will make it necessary to pull out any unnecessary bits of time in the story, a technique known as telescoping.

Economic Use of Back Story and Exposition

The difficulty with ticking clock types of stories is that time is truly of the essence and makes elements like back story, exposition and character development challenging. Thus, writing a story with this sort of time constraint is, if nothing else, a great exercise in economy. If you undertake this type of story, you'll have to use every word wisely, working character development into every moment of each scene. Back story will need to be kept to a minimum. This doesn't mean you shouldn't exhaustively understand it; on the contrary, you should understand it completely since you will have to make very wise and careful choices about how you use it. The presentation of back story and exposition will be lessened, so you'll need to choose just the most critical information.

It's possible that you could use all the back story and exposition you want by simply interrupting the story's time line and going into detail about these elements. This could make for an interesting story, with the narrative being interrupted repeatedly by long subplots about various elements of back story. This, however, is really a different kind of story, an episodic story framed by the events of a single day. If you are looking for a story that has a time-driven engine, then you'll want to be careful about interrupting the flow of time with long digressions. The key to the success of the day-long or night-long story is the audience's awareness that time is fleeting. The more you can keep the audience within the flow of time, the more effective it will be in building tension.

In Martin Scorcese's film *After Hours*, the story is confined to the span of a single day. The film commences with the protagonist leaving his job for the day. He meets a strange woman to whom he is attracted (against his better judgment). She invites him to a party, and on the way to seeing her, his money is blown out of the window of a taxicab. The driver throws him out onto the street in a foreboding neighborhood in Manhattan. The rest of the story involves the protagonist's attempts to get first to the party to see the woman, and then just to get home. Along the way he encounters the woman's strange friends and is mistaken for a murderer and pursued by angry residents of the neighborhood.

What compels the action forward is the fact that there is no rest nor respite for the protagonist. His person and his senses are constantly under siege, and while the night is only a few hours long, it seems, to him, interminable. The audience is pulled through this plot by the twin forces of their desire to see the poor, hapless protagonist get home and their desire for the unrelenting night to turn into daytime. Once it does, the protagonist finds himself in an unusual situation, but he has, nevertheless, survived the night.

By setting a story over the course of a single day, and letting your audience know up front what the time frame is, you will automatically set the pacing for the story. The simple passage of hours, a description of a morning dawning or the fading of the afternoon sun will set the mood for the audience, providing the writer with a useful shorthand. The approaching darkness can raise the level of tension because the audience knows the end of the day is at hand.

If you elect to use a temporal device, it is important to allow it to guide the rhythm and pacing of the story. If you attempt to stretch or distort time too much by adding large pieces of exposition or back story, your work will no longer retain structure. Try to conform your story to the inherent rhythm of passing time, rather than trying to force time to fit your own. If you do this, the passage of time can help you make decisions about the structure of your plot and can help keep you focused on your story's most important issues.

Season

The use of a single season will give your plot a considerably different rhythm than the ticking clock. Unlike the ticking clock, structuring your story around a seasonal element will create a longer, less-compressed time frame. But it will set a definitive time frame for the story. It will also create a natural arc that your story will follow, providing you with a natural source of pacing that you can draw on. However, unlike the day-long or night-long story, with seasonally driven stories you won't be able to rely on the temporal device as much for creating tension.

The tension that can be created by a season will vary depending on which season you are using. The different seasons have different rhythms, depending on the mood of the season.

Summer

Summer's tension will begin to kick in only very near the end, as summer begins to wane and autumn encroaches. If you remember back when you were a kid, you didn't begin to feel the tension of summer vacation until the middle of August, when you could sense that the summer was winding down and you'd soon be back in school.

The story of *On Golden Pond* spans a summer in the life of one couple when they return to their summer cabin—perhaps for the last time. The elderly couple are well into the autumn of their lives and are struggling with the problems of old age. As Norman celebrates his eightieth birthday, he encounters the crisis of diminished capacity. The warm summer weather and his energetic grandson only exacerbate his feelings of helplessness. As the story resolves itself, the leaves are turning gold and red and the air is becoming crisp. The season makes the audience acutely aware that something is ending. It is certainly the summer, but it may also be the lives of this lovely couple. The season and its end are the perfect metaphors for the struggle the protagonists are going through.

Fitzgerald's *The Great Gatsby* tells most of its tale of love and loss during the passage of a summer, too. Fitzgerald uses the carefree climate of summer as a perfect metaphor for Gatsby's outward personality. Just as it is easy to hide decay beneath the leafy vegetation of summer, so, too, the wealthy New Yorkers who spend the season on West Egg disguise their own inner rot. The summer acts as a metaphor for the facade that all the characters in the story cling to.

Autumn

Autumn has a similar rhythm to summer, only autumn's rhythm is more urgent. The early days of autumn aren't much different than summer, leisurely and warm. Yet as the days pass, the changing season quickly becomes apparent. Days grow shorter and colder and the life that clung to the trees begins to surrender. The pace toward winter is short and quick.

In Ernest Hemingway's short story "Big Two-Hearted River," the reader can almost feel the leaves crunching underfoot. Ex-soldier Nick (a hero of a number of Hemingway's stories) feels dead inside because of his experiences in the war. His late season camping trip has the tangible feeling of something coming to an end. In his beautiful description of the scene, Hemingway conveys the sadness of summer's end that is autumn. One can almost feel the approach of winter's dead season.

Winter

Wintertime is like summer in that there is a long period of changelessness. The days are short and cold and the world is frozen. Time itself can seem to stand still. There is hardship and discomfort until the late days of winter when the world begins to thaw. Then the pace picks up as people and nature anticipate spring. This season is good for stories that involve long struggle and eventual triumph, for this is the metaphor of winter.

John Gardner's *October Light* covers a winter in a small house with an elderly brother and sister. The weather closes them in their house and eventually snows them in and the tension between them grows into hatred as their lives are laid bare just as the trees around them are. The story ends as the winter begins to thaw and the two siblings reach a tense, but manageable truce.

Spring

Springtime has a quickness to it. It is all about transformation and rebirth, so consider this device when writing this sort of thematic story. Spring is filled with hope, with relief and with joy. It is a time of relative ease between two seasons of extremes. The end of spring will convey a mood of either long-hoped-for summer or the prospect of long hot days ahead.

In the film *Bull Durham*, the minor league groupie, Annie, picks out a rookie with whom to have an affair. The affair is brief and light-hearted and has a freshness and fervor of springtime. By the end of the film, however, Annie has turned her attention to the aging catcher. While the rookie will be on his way to the major leagues, the catcher will be around for the whole long, hot summer to come.

Mood and Rhythm

This is how the element of tension works in seasonally driven stories. It has a latent quality that sets a mood and subtly drives the pace of the story. Seasonally based stories will give your plot a different natural rhythm. The mood at the beginning of the story will be set by the season, and the climax and resolution will be influenced by the season, as well as by the season to come.

In both *The Great Gatsby* and *October Light*, the season that defines the time frame also acts as a metaphor for what is going on within the characters. It provides structure, but it also provides context and many different creative jumping off points for the authors to make their points.

It's possible that a single season won't be enough to tell the story. It's very easy to use other, longer term temporal devices to give your story a framework to work within. Try using a whole year or setting a well-known, well-understood date toward which you will work. If you choose an entire year, think about how the various seasons can help you to mark the progress of the story and how they can provide you with metaphorical and structural landmarks.

It's also possible to set a "drop dead" date for your protagonist. A young person may be trying to accomplish his goal before the school term ends. A romantic young man may be trying to win his love in time for Christmas or Valentine's Day. These devices simply give you a skeletal structure in which to confine your drama. They will set the clock ticking and give you a built-in engine to help drive the tension.

Generations

Sometimes a story will not fit within a given time frame, but rather needs to spread over years or even decades. Some stories will even go so far as to invoke generations to create dividsions. Needless to say, a generation isn't short enough nor definitive enough to set a ticking clock. However, it can help to divide the sections of a story and lend epic scope to a plot. *Absalom, Absalom* by William Faulkner uses this approach, blending the stories of different generations to tell the story of one family. This story is so interesting because the stories of the different generations are broken up and told out of chronological order, making the narration into something of a puzzle, but this device affords Faulkner the chance to make many interesting comparisons and contrasts, highlighting the strange evolution that the family experienced.

The generational device can be helpful in stories where the changes and challenges the protagonists face are the kinds of slow, evolutionary changes that are prevalent in life. If you plan on using such a device, you'll need to be extremely detailed in your preparation. Preparing the back story will include more than just what happened before the story. It will have to include anything that happens between the different time frames in the story. You'll also have to do more character profiles since your story may have more than one protagonist. Generational stories with this sort of epic scope show the 3×5 card system at its best. You'll find that you can easily control all the various elements in the story with relative ease and keep track of the story's progression from generation to generation.

Other Unifying Elements

Time isn't the only unifying element that you can use to add depth and resonance to your plot. Sometimes you can find other threads that will tie your story together and give you something unique on which to hang your themes and ideas, giving them sharp relief and deep meaning. To find these elements, look at the pieces of the plot that you've conceived at any given point. Search through them for connections between various items.

STORY STARTER

UNIFYING ELEMENTS

Do the characters share certain jobs or professions that have a distinctive environment around which you could build the location for your story?

Is there a characteristic of the town or city in which the story takes place that could unify the elements in your plot? Certain cities or regions have distinct characteristics that make them unique. Texas, Alaska, the Rust Belt, the French Riviera all have qualities that make them unique.

Is there an ethnic or immigrant sensibility that defines the characters and their world?

What traditions do the characters come out of that might provide an interesting backdrop for your story?

Think about the location in which your story takes place. Often locations can lend a unique slant and contribute elements around which the characters and plot can orbit. These environments will allow you to present your story through the unique prism of that environment, and the environment will loan you numerous metaphors and dramatic devices.

Hemingway was a master at using the environments in his stories as more than mere backdrops. They became virtual players in the drama—sometimes, as in the case of *The Old Man and the Sea*, literally. Think of stories like "The Snows of Kilimanjaro" and *The Sun Also Rises* in which the environments informed everything about the story, from the plot to the characters to the themes. Hemingway had a unique ability to immerse himself, his characters and, ultimately, his audience in the environment of the story. By creating these unifying elements, he caused his stories to rise above being mere tales (as outstanding as those tales may be) to the level of visual and thematic poetry.

The novel *A Thousand Acres* uses the device of the family farm to unify the story. The farm, the family home, becomes the embodiment of the family and, in particular, its patriarch. The farm is both the source of wealth for the family and a cruel master whom everyone in the family, including the patriarch, must serve. While it represents warmth and family and security to the three daughters, it is also the place where the family's secrets are buried. As the daughters physically leave the farm and later return to it, the physical journey mirrors their emotional journey. When the farm is ultimately divided up, that division is a metaphor for what has happened to the family and the legacy the daughters have been left.

Challenge yourself with this task. Try to take your writing to the next level, where your ideas express themselves in such a way that they create visual and thematic poetry. This poetry will cause your ideas to set themselves indelibly on the memory of your audience.

The River in Huckleberry Finn

Many of Mark Twain's stories use these sorts of dramatic elements to give an overall unity. Consider the story *Huckleberry Finn* and Twain's use of the river in it. The river functioned on multiple levels in the story. It was a vehicle for escape. It was a source of adventure yet provoked respect and some fear from the protagonist. It also represented the relentlessness of time and the timelessness of life. Its vastness kept the problems of the protagonist in perspective, while framing them as the problem of Everyman.

Besides its metaphorical power, the river also functioned as a pure dramatic device, moving the story forward relentlessly, carrying the characters with it. Floating down the river was the perfect transitional device for Twain, allowing him to move his characters whenever the story needed to move forward. It quite literally carried the characters from major plot point to major plot point. It allowed Twain to take his characters easily from scene to scene and place to place. The nature of time spent traveling, particularly on a raft adrift in the Mississippi, also gave Twain an easy way to control the passing of time. The changelessness of floating down the river made it possible for hours or even days to pass without much of anything happening. Finally, it came as no surprise to the audience when the story picked up a day or so later far away from where various characters were last seen.

Each practical dramatic role the river played was, of course, imbued with all the thematic weight behind it. So getting from point A to point B was more than a mere dramatic device; the characters were carried on by the power of the river and the power of time's passage. In this case, the river beautifully disguises the mechanical workings of the story and wraps them in richly meaningful imagery. This is a case of a unifying device serving multiple purposes and doing those jobs in a way that is remarkably complementary.

The Journey and the Road Story

Another classic unifying element is the journey. Some of the most memorable stories ever written were journeys. Homer's *The Odyssey* was one of the first and the theme of the heroic quest was born with this classic. In the cinema, the "road movie" is a genre unto itself.

There is something truly magical about putting a protagonist "on the road" and challenging him with surviving in an unknown, ever-changing and sometimes hostile environment. The voyage is also a perfect metaphor around which to build a conflict. In the journey plot, goal and obstacle are made manifest. The goal is the destination and the obstacle is everything the protagonist encounters on the way to that destination. The road itself can, like Twain's Mississippi River, also help to embody and guide the passage of dramatic time.

The journey can also act as a metaphor for the character's transformation. A character coming out of the snowy, frozen mountains into the springtime of the valley can make for a powerful metaphor of rebirth. By contrast, the adventurer who leaves the comfort and safety of home to journey to a distant, desolate and lonely place can be the perfect metaphor for a character's journey to the innermost place in his soul, where character is forged and tested before returning home. The road story provides numerous metaphors for the author. Simply choose your road and destination, and you'll find an ample supply of potential visuals to exploit.

The Road in Rain Man

In the film *Rain Man*, the protagonist returns to his childhood home after the death of his father to find out that he has an older brother who is autistic. Charlie Babbitt's trip home becomes the start of a trip through his past. As he and his brother venture west, they are, in effect, reliving the childhood they never spent together because of their father's decision to keep them separate.

All along the way, Charlie resolves questions and issues about his past. It isn't until he arrives back in Los Angeles that he is able to fully be an adult and concern himself with adult things. He refuses to have his girlfriend accompany him, insisting on it being just he and his brother. The two brothers even travel in their father's vintage car, a powerful symbol of their past childhood and their father.

One of the strongest metaphors in any road journey is the means of transportation. Covered wagons, stagecoaches and trains all have mythical qualities about them. No vehicle, however, has been as thoroughly mythologized in American culture as the automobile. Often in road stories, the car is as much a source of meaning and metaphor as the road itself. From the bus that Ken Kesey's Merry Pranksters traveled in to the Corvette that carried the protagonists in *Route 66*, automobiles are mythic creatures in the tradition of Pegasus himself.

The whole journey in *Rain Man* is like time travel, out of the past and into the present. The places the brothers stay in the early days of their journey are motor lodges that seem suspended in another time. Their decor and the manner of their inhabitants is like something out of the 1950s. When the brothers arrive in Las Vegas, they are like adolescent boys, dressing up and acting like big shots. It is in this environment that Charlie begins to feel comfortable and thrive. Raymond, however, is clearly in over his head. Once they pull into Charlie's hillside home at the end of the road in Los Angeles, the roles have completely reversed from their journey's beginning in Cincinnati. Charlie is now comfortable and at home, and Raymond is the fish out of water. The road comes to symbolize the tremendous distance between them.

Finally, when Raymond boards the train to take the road back to his institution, it is as if he is traveling back through time to the place in the past where his development stopped. The road in *Rain Man* symbolizes so many different things: escape, time, physical distance, emotional distance. Writer Ron Bass and director Barry Levinson exploit all these metaphors to their fullest and, in doing so, create a well-textured and intricately woven story.

Atmospheric Unifying Elements

Sometimes the unifying element is something that exists in the background—a place or an atmosphere that can help explain a somewhat heightened state of emotions. These atmospheric elements can often give a good jumping off point for elements like mood, or they can create a provocation for the protagonist's actions. Consider an element like the heat in almost any Tennessee Williams play. It makes the characters irritable and uncomfortable and forces their buried emotions closer to the surface where events can expose them. Consider the role that the city of Los Angeles plays in a film like *Chinatown*. In that film, the last line of dialogue after everything has spun out of Jake Gittes's hands is "Forget about it, Jake; it's Chinatown." The city, whose politics have been a consistent subtext and subplot, surfaces again to become the characters' excuse to write off the almost inexplicable events that have occurred around them. In *Touch of Evil*, the border town and its conflicts between Anglo and Hispanic are a powerful backdrop that draws the elements together.

Another type of unifying element can be the person who is telling the story. A third party narrator who has a strong, distinctive voice can provide a wonderful unifying element for a story. If the narrator, who isn't a direct participant in the story, has her own character, with fully drawn characteristics, the audience will see the story through that person's eyes, and that character becomes the eyewitness for all that happens. This sort of narrator can do a lot to modulate the tempo and pacing of the story. She can also guide the audience toward what is important, and her "view" of events will help to determine which events in the characters' lives become the major plot points.

Sometimes the unifying element is a single place. Like the road, it is a marker, an anchor that holds the story in place and gives context to everything that happens. In the case of a "road" story, the road brings events and people to characters, who, relative to one another, are stationary. In the story that happens in one place, the characters are brought to the place that remains unchanged. The historical novels of James Michener are a good example of this. Most of them revolve around a single place, and that place and its history become inextricably entwined in the fabric of the plot. Novels like *Texas* or *Alaska* or *Hawaii* suggest by their mere titles that the location is going to inform everything that happens in those stories. The environment in them becomes an actor. In some of Michener's novels the location is more limited. *The Covenant,* for example, focuses on the history of South Africa, but most of the action centers around one particular plantation.

The main thrust of all of Michener's epic stories is the nature of the place he is writing about. His characters are practically throwaways. They aren't what one remembers years later about the books. On the contrary, what one does remember is what those characters said about the location in which the books take place. That environment, that atmosphere is what makes those books memorable. It more than unifies the story, it becomes the story.

Michener's novel *The Source* takes place almost entirely on a hill—the Tell—in Israel. The story is built around an excavation of an archaeological site. As the characters dig, they discover the history of the place all the way back to prehistoric times. They find artifacts, and those artifacts become the unifying element. Each level of the dig becomes the jumping off point for a story. The artifact is presented to the reader, a drawing is even included of each artifact, and as the story progresses, the reader discovers the meaning of the artifact. Then the reader is taken back to the present day to discover the next artifact.

This device works marvelously to keep the reader interested by using each artifact to prick her curiosity. As the history of each artifact is revealed and the history of its time period is explored, the reader cannot help but be drawn deeper and deeper into a sense of place. The story is further unified by the fact that all its history took place mainly in that one location and the desert of Israel becomes an important actor in the drama. Michener masterfully uses this plexus of civilization and all its rich history to essentially tell the story of western civilization in a mere 1,200 pages!

As you begin the process of creating your plot, look for elements, either in the scenes or in the characters you've begun to create, that can help to unify your story. Look for common elements in the events and characters you are conceiving. How might these elements comment on the main themes of your story, and what connections are there between those elements? Usually a unifying device will grow out of the intersection of themes and events, so that is usually the best place to look.

Sometimes your unifying event will be one of the first things you conceive: a road trip, a monumental location. Other times your unifying event will grow out of your work on the plot. If this is the case, and you are beyond the outline stage of your writing, you should go back to your outline and work the unifying element in wherever possible. It's likely that you will want to reconceive whole plot points if they do not deliver to the goals of the unifying element. The good news is that the unifying element should provide you with more than enough fodder for creating better, more directed scenes for your plot.

The unifying element isn't a mandatory part of the plot. There are many wonderful classic stories that don't contain this element. However, you'll usually find that a unifying device will project your writing to a higher level. Your themes will express themselves more clearly and eloquently, and your story will contain at least a little bit of poetry.

 STORY STARTER

UNIFYING DEVICES

- Farm or other homestead
- River
- Road
- Mountain
- Journey
- City or town
- Narrator (first or third person)
- State or country

Common Plot Devices

A standard, linear plot structure is adequate for telling most stories, but sometimes you want to raise the level of your story a notch or two. Other times, you need to frame the events in your story in a different way. It's helpful to understand some potential plot structure devices and how they might work for your particular story. These devices consist of different structures that in some way manipulate, distort or otherwise alter the natural, linear flow of events as we experience them in life.

These devices can function in a couple of different ways. For some stories they will help to impose a stricter sense of order on events, making them easier to understand and more focused on the most important events in the characters' lives. Framing devices, flashbacks and episodic plots can help an author structure a story that might otherwise be difficult to understand, need to be put into clearer context, or meander over long stretches of time and distance. These devices can help to distill the story down to its essence or make clearer sense of it.

Other times, the plot device will allow the author more freedom to use abstract expression because the plot device will lend the story at least a basic structure. It can also free the author to cover more sweeping territory or to relate events or ideas that seem disparate. In these cases the plot device can be used to provide the underlying dramatic structure that the audience will need to understand events. This can be useful if the author wants to create a strange, nonlinear narrative or other abstractions. In these cases the plot device will work to hold the story's pieces together and assist the audience to make sense of them.

The Framing Device

This is a popular device in both movies and literature. It consists of a main plot that is bounded on either end by a few short scenes that introduce and then wrap up the action of the central plot—framing it. The framing device follows this pattern:

- Usually, the story starts out in the present.
- The narrator then takes the audience back to hear how things came to be.
- Once the tale is told, the time then shifts back to the present where the characters move on with their lives.

In the opening portion of the frame, things may not be quite clear. There may be characters, situations and relationships we don't understand, but they are introduced to pique our curiosity. The closing portion of the frame often presents those same characters, situations and relationships, but now the audience understands their origin and significance.

The framing device can essentially be a way of saying "once upon a time." The key to creating a good framing device is making sure that it somehow sets into context the events to come in the main section of the plot. Through the opening part of the frame, you give the audience a prism through which to view the story's events or possibly hints as to the meaning of what is to come. The best framing devices are able to hook the audience in just a couple of minutes or pages. They spark a level of intrigue that will hold the audience through to the end when the vaguer ideas in the opening frame become clear.

The closing portion of the frame becomes the payoff. Everything is explained by that point, and the audience is conveniently reminded of the ideas and context that were established at the beginning. The closing frame provides resolution for the story. Often, framed stories will end the main plot right after the climax, leaving the resolution for the closing piece of the frame. The closing of the frame then becomes the "they lived happily ever after" ending to the story.

Framing devices are often used to establish the story's narrative voice and the attitude of that narrator. Many stories that are told from the limited point of view of one of the characters use a framing device to begin and end that character's tale. In the context of the frame, the audience is introduced to the character and informed that what they are about to hear is that one person's opinion.

In the film *The Usual Suspects*, the story begins with a police interrogation of someone involved in a crime. That character tells the entire story, leading back to the moment the interrogation began. What doesn't become clear until the end is that the story may or may not be completely made up. This point is called into question because in the opening piece of the framing device, we are clued in that this character is telling the story. The story is so well told, however, that the audience forgets that what it is hearing is just one person's point of view, and it's a surprise at the end when they realize that they may have been told a completely phony story.

Often, framing devices work so that the opening framing piece happens in the present. Then the rest of the story, which starts in the past, leads progressively back to present so that the closing portion of the frame is almost a linear continuation of the main story. The final piece of the frame elegantly closes the continuous circle.

It's also possible to use framing devices on a smaller scale. You may not want to have your entire story bookended by such a dramatic device. In that case, you can use the framing device to set off a subplot or another part of the story. You'll also find that the opening piece of the framing device is a great place to drop a clue or a hint that pays off in the main story. The framing device is usually far enough removed from the rest of the story that the audience will not be able to figure out the clue until they get into the heart of the story.

You may be wondering how a framing device works in the context of our 3×5 card method of designing the plot. I recommend that you create the main piece of your plot first. This will provide you with lots of the information that you'll need in order to make your framing device most relevant and most tightly woven into the overall fabric of the story. Once you've nailed down the structure of your plot, go back and look at what elements will make the most effective frame.

The Episodic Plot

The episodic plot is one of the more difficult plot devices to use successfully and is often used poorly. One of the most common plotting problems is plots that are *too episodic*. What makes episodic plots difficult is that since the story jumps around a lot, it is hard to build plot momentum. The episodes are often weakly connected or are too remote from one another in either time, distance or context.

If you decide to use an episodic plot structure, you must be careful that the episodes in it work well together and that your rising action isn't compromised. To accomplish this, construct episodes that relate well to one another, and if you plan on connecting the events of one episode to another, make the connection obvious and logical, and let the episodes build tension from one to another.

Some stories will have episodes that are only loosely connected. A classic example of this is Chaucer's *Canterbury Tales*. The tales of the various characters aren't related to one another dramatically; each tale stands on its own. Chaucer has constructed the story so that the journey the characters are taking acts as a connecting device between them. Beyond this, the stories' only connection to one another is thematic. Together, they paint an interesting picture of the characters and the society that they were a part of, but dramatically, they are almost completely unrelated. This leaves Chaucer with a story that must survive on the strength of its individual pieces. There is no driving force carrying the characters toward a climax in the overall story. Each tale makes its own independent dramatic statement.

For most episodic plots to work, you'll need to have some sort of connecting device to keep the story's forward momentum going. This can be a narrator who operates between episodes to wrap up one and tie it to another. The spaces between the episodes may even serve to tell their own story. In the last section we discussed James Michener's novel *The Source*, in which the story of the archaeological dig functions as a bridge between the mostly unconnected stories from the past. The spaces between the episodes are filled with a consistent story line, one about the archaeologists, but it isn't the main thrust of the novel.

The Flashback

One of the most popular plot devices is the flashback. This device has been used practically since the beginning of drama, probably due to the fact that storytelling in its purest, most primitive form works much like a flashback. The storyteller, in present time, tells the story of something that happened in the past—a flashback. Though it can be an incredibly effective means of telling a story, it is also a method that is fraught with problems. The primary problem is that the flashback has been used so frequently that it can easily become a cliché.

When a television show's picture goes wavy and a harp glissando sounds, the viewer instantly knows that he is traveling back in time in a flashback. You'll probably want to avoid that sort of camp quality in your writing, so try to find unique, interesting ways to move your story in and out of the flashback. If you elect to use a flashback, try to create a device for moving back and forth in time that fits in contextually with what you are writing. A writing style change or a verbal or visual cue can move the story smoothly (or jarringly, depending on the desired effect) between time frames.

Filmmaker John Sayles used flashbacks extensively in his film *Lone Star*. The film about two generations of Anglos and Mexicans on the Texas-Mexico border told its story through the eyes of the present-day sheriff of the small border town. The man had recently returned to his hometown and was on a kind of quest for an understanding of his own family history, in particular his enigmatic father who had been the sheriff before him. As the sheriff uncovers clues and speculates about his past, we are guided back to that past where we see events as they actually happened.

The transitions between these two time frames are handled beautifully by Sayles. He doesn't use tricky visual effects since he knew they would only provoke every cliché flashback ever done. Instead his camera casually pans away from the subjects of the scene, and when it finds another person, that person is from the different time frame. He is able to do this because things in and around the town have changed so little. And, in this simple camera move, he makes a comment about the town's unchanging physical characteristics, even though its human makeup has changed tremendously.

The flashback in this case enables Sayles to tell two stories simultaneously—the story of the past and the story of the present. If we knew the outcome of the drama that occurred in the past, the story of the present wouldn't be very interesting. Sayles weaves an intriguing tale, while creating greater audience sympathy for the protagonist because we learn the truth of his past just as he does. By the time the story reveals its final twist, we are as devastated at the fate of the sheriff as he is.

One of the greatest films ever made used extended flashbacks as a structuring device. Orson Welles's *Citizen Kane* told the story of Charles Foster Kane through the eyes of a journalist charged with finding out about the strange life of the tycoon after his mysterious death. One of cinema's most famous spoken lines, "Rosebud," sets both journalist and audience off on a search for the man's past. Through a series of interviews, each from a slightly different perspective, we learn of Kane's history.

The scenes with the journalist are short framing pieces that lead into and out of the body of the story, which covers decades of the protagonist's life. This is a case where the flashbacks make up the bulk of the story. In some instances, you'll want to use a flashback just for a certain scene or sequence. Even in these cases, you'll find that the flashback can be a useful device for breaking up the linear narrative and adding depth and a different perspective to your story.

Parallel Stories

If you are working on a story that seems to call for two plots, you may want to build your plots as parallels. This is a difficult type of story to construct but can create some most interesting opportunities for the use of contrasts and comparisons. The key to creating good parallel stories is balance and timing. This is a tricky combination and you'll

STORY STARTER
PARALLEL STORIES

Are the story beats too short, and does the drama jump back and forth between the two stories too rapidly or too frequently?

Are the stories equally well developed, or is one clearly stronger and more compelling than the other?

Are transitions between the two stories smooth, or do they sap momentum from each other at every shift?

Are the stories adequately different?

Are the connections between the stories clearly drawn? Does it ever become apparent how the two stories relate?

---

find that the 3×5 card method can help you simplify it greatly.

In parallel stories the two stories are kept separate, each having its own story arc and plot points. If you choose to use this device, there are a number of issues with which you'll want to be concerned.

Some parallel stories start out parallel but as they approach the climax, the two separate plots converge to become one. In order to make this type of device work, you'll have to plot your story so that the connections between the two plots gradually become stronger and stronger. If properly planned, the audience will realize at the precise moment you have planned how the two seemingly separate, unrelated or remotely connected stories will come together. This realization will be a powerful force toward the climax of your story.

In order to make parallel plots work, first construct each one individually. Put the plot points that make up each plot onto 3×5 cards. Before you try to work them together, be sure that each works on its own. Is each arc strong enough, and does the story move with an adequate pace? Remember that whatever pacing the story has on its own will be cut in half when it is integrated with the other story. This will force you to concentrate your work more and focus it more clearly.

Once you're confident that both plots work on their own, begin the process of integrating them. Do everything possible to sync up the stories' arcs so that they reach the various landmarks (inciting incident, rising action, climax) at roughly the same point. Ideally, each plot will increase the other's momentum, creating a slingshot effect, propelling the drama forward.

Once you've worked the two plots roughly together, go back over them and work on the individual transitions. These transitions are the most important part of this plot device. They will allow you to make the comparisons and contrasts and to move the story effectively back and forth, creating a strong rhythm and pace.

Combining Structuring Devices

Often you'll find these plot devices used in combination. Flashbacks and episodic plots almost by definition include some sort of framing device. Earlier we talked about *Fried Green Tomatoes* as an example of an unusual plot. That story combines a couple of plot devices. Certainly the story can be looked at as a series of flashbacks. The present-day interaction between Idgie and Evelyn is the perfect framing device for the flashbacks to the story of Idgie as a young woman and her friend Ruth. The drama in the two stories develops in parallel, and though more time is spent in the past, the present-day story has its own major plot points (though they are more modest) and its own arc. It's easy to look at this story as combining several of the plot devices we've discussed: parallel, flashbacks and framing devices.

Another good example of combining structuring devices is the classic Akira Kurasawa film *Rashomon*, in which the story of a murder is told from the points of view of four different participants. What makes the story unique is how very different the four witnesses' tales are. The story is framed by the inquiry into the murder. Since the four stories are so different, the film also has an episodic quality to it. Each story can also be looked at as a flashback.

As you can see, these devices can accomplish a great deal in making your story more interesting and compelling. They are a great means to highlighting the themes of your story and to giving it a consistent, strong skeleton. While they can do wonders for a story, they cannot replace a strong plot. Avoid forcing a plot device onto your story if it is a poor fit. The best plot devices work simply and easily. If your story can benefit by one, it will become obvious to you and working it in will be delicate, but the fit will seem natural.

Nontraditional Plots

The main thrust of this book has been to help you build plots in the traditional vein. This means captivating storytelling that follows a time-tested and well-worn formula of the story arc. The assumption has been that a story would start out at a relatively low energy level, and a fuse would be lit by the inciting incident, sending the story on an interesting, but inexorable rise toward the climax. That climax usually occurs in the last one third or one quarter of the story's length and is the high point of the story's drama. It is followed by a quick, meaningful resolution.

While this formula is one that allows for infinite variation and capitalizes on many of life's natural rhythms, there have been many writers in the past who have successfully and unsuccessfully challenged it. Writing is all about experimentation, and many authors have created compelling, involving stories by turning conventions upside down and inside out. While you may or may not aspire to this sort of nontraditional work, you should nevertheless understand it. I would even recommend that you do some experimentation of your own. By taking a story and constructing it outside the confines of the traditional arc, you'll have the opportunity to not only free your own creative process, but to actually learn more about the traditional story arc. By experimenting like this, you will at least have a chance to learn a few new tricks that can be used in your normal writing. Very often, authors have successfully incorporated nontraditional elements into a traditional story, greatly expanding the story's range.

The Epistolary Novel

In the eighteenth and nineteenth centuries writers began experimenting with a new type of story. This story was constructed as a series of letters from one character to another. Some novels used the exchange of letters between two characters to create the dramatic structure. This technique was remarkably well suited to romantic novels for it was easy for two characters, whether they were lovers or one lover reporting on the romance to a friend, to report the goings-on of the affair.

The difficulty with this sort of novel is that the story will, by definition, be episodic. It will also have a limited point of view, for every word in it will be reported by one or more characters from within the story. Constructing such a story on a traditional story arc is possible, but it will be much more challenging. Such stories will also be heavily reliant on the expressive powers of the character who is doing the writing. While this presents enormous challenges, it can also give your story a very distinctive quality since the character's voice will infuse itself into every word of your story.

A novel that did this remarkably well was Alice Walker's *The Color Purple* in which the novel's protagonist, Celie, relates the story to the audience through her letters. Initially, they are a part of a diary that she is addressing to God, but as the story progresses, she begins to receive letters from her sister, Nettie. Eventually, the two sisters are exchanging letters telling one another of their lives and adventures. When the sisters are reunited, Celie continues telling the story through her letters to God. What is most remarkable about the structure of this novel is how Walker takes the reader inside the heads of her characters.

When one begins reading the novel, just understanding Celie's unusual syntax and her heavy Southern accent is a challenge. However, this strange language that she speaks gives us volumes of information about her character and her naive view of the world. As the letters progress, we experience Celie's growing maturity. The letters also illustrate Celie's faith in God, which is central to her character. When the two sisters begin to trade letters, the contrast in their experiences and their writing styles is remarkable. It speaks volumes about the way the two sisters' experiences diverge when Nettie goes to Africa and, in spite of their distance, how strongly bonded the two siblings remain.

Walker uses nothing but the letters to tell the story. Every word is filtered through the prism of Celie's and Nettie's experiences. They define the action of the novel by what they choose to write and they give the novel their souls. As one reads the novel, one begins to share the sensation that the sisters must've felt in the anxious awaiting and then the satisfying rush of reading the communications. Since Nettie's letters are withheld from Celie for a long time, she gets to live her sister's entire experience rapidly, catching up with her sister's adventures with a ravenous hunger. When she writes to Nettie, there is so much to tell. This sensation makes the women's relationship much more intimate and the audience gets to share that intimacy.

The epistolary novel is an interesting form and one that requires a little something extra. In these novels, the *way* the story is told becomes almost more important, and certainly more central, than the actual story. The author must find a way to communicate the characters' inner thoughts as they themselves would express them, not from the removed, third person perspective normally used. The letters become more than just a means of telling the tale—they become an artifact that the reader sifts for clues about the characters and their experiences.

One author who took this form to its limit was Nick Bantok. Author of the Griffin and Sabine series, he wrote three whole novels about two characters (two lovers, no less) who never meet. Their letters take life, as the book is filled with real postcards and envelopes actually stuffed with unusual stationery. The reader gets to enjoy Bantok's mysterious, ethereal drawings and experience the actual tactile sensations that the characters experience. One can almost feel the tropical breezes of Sabine's home island and the cold, damp chill of Griffin's London.

Bantok makes excellent use of another feature of epistolary novels: Letters are usually written by people who are far apart. As the Griffin and Sabine books progress, the desire between the two characters becomes palpable, and though they never consummate their passion, the books are as passionate and romantic as any. They are truly remarkable books that immerse the reader in a complete experience.

One attraction of epistolary novels is that people are naturally voyeuristic and infinitely curious about others, and epistolary novels give the audience a chance to snoop, to peek at the intimate, private thoughts of the characters. These novels are immensely personal and tremendously titillating for the reader.

What makes them difficult to write successfully is that the rhythms, the pacing and the rise of the tension of the story are completely dependent upon the flow of the letters. The author needs to make sure that the transition between letters flows naturally, that one letter answers the questions of the one before it, and that the tension in the writing reflects the rising stakes of the story. Most importantly, the characters have to express their innermost psychology through what they say and what they don't say, but there is no other element in these books to comment on the characters' emotions or the events that they experience.

Another interesting nontraditional plot is found in the Jim Jarmusch film *Mystery Train*. The film actually examines the same period of time, a single evening, four separate times with four almost completely unrelated stories. Each of the four stories is played out start to finish without interruption. It isn't until about midway through the second of the four story lines that the audience really becomes aware of what is happening. Jarmusch cleverly inserts some distinctive visual clues to let the audience in on how his story is structured.

The most important element, however, is a cleverly placed sound effect: a gunshot. The shot is heard in each of the four story lines, but it isn't until the final story line plays out that we learn the origin and significance of the gunshot. The effect of the gunshot is to give each story a point of orientation. Once you've heard the gunshot in all four sequences, it is easy to mark a common moment in time and figure out where all the stories intersect. Jarmusch also uses another clever device: Background action from one story line shows up as foreground action in another story line. Frequently, the audience sees action in the background that makes no sense and seems irrelevant to the story they are watching, but later in subsequent story lines that action is seen as the main action in the scene. Other times we witness background action that we've already seen in an earlier story line. All these devices work together to cleverly weave the four story lines together.

What is most interesting is that all four story lines could function as interesting little vignettes by themselves. Each has its own protagonists and its own arc. They are fully self-sufficient, even if they're rather lightweight little confections. The film, however, really becomes interesting when Jarmusch ties them together. The gunshot and the overlapping action make it easy for the audience to follow the story and enjoy this rare opportunity to watch multiple points of view unfold.

Mystery Train is an excellent example of an author playing around with temporal conventions to explore an idea about how we interact in the world. The film makes a point about how there are many stories happening in the world at any given time. Each of those stories has its own actors and its own conflicts. It also comments on how those actors usually feel as if their own drama is the center of the universe and the only thing of consequence happening in it. Jarmusch's film also makes a point about how the random and unpredictable intersection of those little dramas can make for even more interesting dramas.

Using Time

In constructing your own story, take time to think about time. How does time play a role in your plot, and how might you make your plot more interesting by manipulating your use of time? Sometimes the most logical way to tell a story isn't chronological. Often stories make more sense and are more compelling when the events are told in an order other than that in which they occurred. While I don't recommend messing with the time line in your plot just for the heck of it, you may want to consider some other criteria in arranging the events of your story. For instance, you may want to arrange the events in your story by dramatic weight—building toward the most important events even if those events occurred first in time.

The important thing isn't to find clever ways of manipulating time in your story; what matters is exploring every possible way to tell your story in a more interesting fashion. Jim Jarmusch and Alice Walker didn't manipulate time just as an experiment; it was a conscious decision. They did it to increase the dramatic and emotional impact of their work and to comment on the nature of time and the role it plays in our lives.

One of America's greatest novelists, William Faulkner, was certainly no slave to time when he wrote. Faulkner's stories often unfold in a manner that is much like human memory—some would say like a dream. Memories are rarely linear, and the novels *The Sound and the Fury* and its companion *Absalom, Absalom* are structured with a fractured, often confusing style that challenges the reader to understand what is going on.

In his novel *The Sound and the Fury*, which, incidentally, he never completely finished, Faulkner told of the same event, the rape of a young woman by her brother, from multiple viewpoints. Each chapter focused on a different point of view of the rape, much like the film we discussed earlier, Akira Kurasawa's *Rashomon*. This book is even more interesting because the first chapter of the book is told by Benji, a retarded boy (who is the inspiration for the title, taken from Shakespeare's *Macbeth*: "It is a tale told by an idiot, full of *sound and fury* signifying nothing."). The reader is faced with the daunting task of reading the boy's "thoughts" about the event, which are often confusing and disjointed. The characters each take their turn at telling their perception of events, which makes it difficult for Faulkner to generate the kind of forward momentum found in more traditional plots. Since the story keeps cycling back, the engine that drives the story is the way the puzzle of the story itself is revealed a bit at a time. The audience is given pieces of information that don't make sense until combined with another piece of information that may not be revealed for fifty or one hundred pages. As the story progresses, things gradually, though never fully, come into focus. The story's arc is more akin to a spiral, circling back upon itself, but moving steadily upward.

Faulkner's novel *Absalom, Absalom* focuses on the same family and contains many of the same characters. It was written after *The Sound and the Fury* but actually concerns events that happened before those of the earlier novel. As mentioned earlier, the story concerns several generations of the same family and attempts to unravel the mysteries of that family, exposing many skeletons in the family closet. It even hints at why Benji was born retarded. The story unfolds in the way a grandparent might tell a family history. Have you ever told a story in which you reached points in the plot where you had to make a tangent from a particular point in order to explain the background of that point? That is how *Absalom, Absalom* seems to progress. It jumps around in time and location, giving the reader pieces of information in a seemingly random, but ultimately well-planned way. Again, Faulkner gives his reader a puzzle to figure out, leaving connections, comparisons and contrasts inexplicit, trusting the reader to figure them out. The result is a pair of novels that are good for multiple readings and multiple interpretations. The layering of detail that Faulkner uses makes them like looking at a finely detailed painting. The painting, and the novels, look different depending on where you are standing.

STORY STARTER
TEMPORAL ORGANIZATION

Is your tale most compelling when told chronologically?

Which moment in the plot is most important—where will it be most effective dramatically?

Is there a temporal element that can act as a structuring device?

Using the 3 × 5 cards, rearrange the sequences of your plot randomly and see if anything useful reveals itself.

While Faulkner certainly experimented with various techniques for manipulating time to serve his uses, he didn't challenge the boundaries of dramatic structure in nearly as radical a way as a group of writers did in the mid-1900s. The Oulipians were a group of writers who agreed with James Joyce's proclamation that the novel had been mastered. They sought a new way of expressing themselves and played with the conventions of drama in a number of radical ways. One thing they were famous for was putting constraints on their writing. Often they used mathematical formulas to dictate the number of paragraphs they'd write, or they would use numbers in other odd ways to give themselves a set of constraints within which they had to write.

One well-known Oulipian was the French writer Georges Perec. Perec was famous for a number of things, including writing the world's longest palindrome. The piece (which reads the same way forwards as backwards) was over 3,000 characters long! He also wrote an entire novel (in French) that never used the letter "e"! And, that novel was all about a character who was missing.

In his book *Life, an Owner's Manual*, Perec wrote a complicated piece about an eccentric character and his travels, but much of the book revolves around the character's apartment building. Frequently throughout the novel Perec's story goes off on tangential pieces about other characters living in the building. These tangents were formed completely independent of the main story.

These Oulipian authors challenged every convention that thousands of years of drama had produced. The result was some incredibly interesting work. While the books could be dismissed as the literary equivalent of a parlor trick, the stories in them hold up to the most important criterion of all—they are gripping, interesting, challenging stories to read. These experimental writers didn't forsake the basic goal of all drama, which is to produce a compelling tale. They accomplished this and added an enormous depth to their work by constraining their writing and using those constraints (which were always included with the text of the book) to comment upon the work as well.

The point of examining these different ways of breaking the conventions of traditional storytelling is to give you some ideas of how, once learned and mastered, the conventions of drama can be manipulated to create even more compelling stories. As I've mentioned before, the idea of learning any technique is to put it to work for you as a tool.

The principles of drama aren't meant to be constraining, merely to provide structure and guidance in your work. They are the accumulated knowledge of several thousand years of drama, and they provide the modern writer with certain verities that he can rely on in creating new drama.

Once you've mastered these techniques and developed a thorough understanding of how they work and how to use them, you are free to toss them aside or to challenge those principles with ideas of your own. Only your reader will be able to judge whether or not you've challenged them successfully or unsuccessfully. In either case, be bold about challenging the principles laid out in this book. You may not ever have the influence of a Faulkner or a Perec, but you will have challenged yourself to do your best writing, and even if you fall back on more established dramatic principles, you will almost certainly have gained new knowledge from attempting to take your story in a new, more experimental direction.

CHAPTER ELEVEN

Tutorial

This section brings together the exercises, quizzes and story starters from the rest of the book to offer you a place you can refer to whenever you are starting a new project. These exercises have been put into an order that will take you through the process of creating your outline.

Step 1: Pre-outlining Process

Understand Your Narrative
To better understand the concept of narrative and how it is different than just the simple events of a book, try the exercise on p. 210.

Choose Your Subject Matter
The quiz on p. 211 is designed to help you figure out what you want to write about, or what elements in your story idea will be highlighted in your project.

The next step in choosing your subject matter is deciding how you will approach it. What unique story are you going to be telling? To answer this, you must ask the "What if?" question (see p. 212).

 **EXERCISE**

Take a favorite book or movie and arrange the information in it (including back story and exposition—see glossary) in chronological order. See how this affects the dramatic impact of the story.

I have used the Stanley Donen film *Two for the Road* as an example. You can see how the author used the geographical journey as his basis for the narrative, jumping about in time. The left column shows the rather dull chronological series of events in a disintegrating marriage.

Use the two columns on the right to try this exercise with your own story.

Story: *Two for the Road*		Your Story	
CHRONOLOGICAL ORDER	**ORDER STORY IS TOLD**	**CHRONOLOGICAL ORDER**	**ORDER STORY IS TOLD**
Two single people take a trip from London to the south of France	Two single people cross English Channel		
Newlywed couple takes trip to France	Newlyweds cross English Channel		
Couple married several years takes trip to France	Couple married several years crosses English Channel		
Couple having marital difficulties travels to France	Couple having marital difficulties crosses English Channel		
Couple on verge of divorce travels to France	Couple on verge of divorce crosses English Channel		
	Two single people travel toward Paris		
	Newlyweds travel toward Paris		
	Couple married several years travels toward Paris		
	Couple having marital difficulties travels to Paris		
	Couple on verge of divorce travels toward Paris		

QUICK QUIZ
SUBJECT MATTER

Does my concept create obstacles that effectively challenge the characters?
☐ **YES**   ☐ **NO**
If so, which specific elements will be the source of that challenge?

_____

_____

_____

Does my concept provide a strong backdrop for exploring the strengths,
limitations and psychology of my characters?   ☐ **YES**   ☐ **NO**
What specific elements does the plot have that provide vivid comparisons
and contrasts that will delineate my character in intriguing ways?

_____

_____

_____

Does my concept provide a strong environment for the messages and
themes I want to explore?   ☐ **YES**   ☐ **NO**
What metaphors and motifs grown naturally out of that environment will
illuminate those themes and messages?

_____

_____

_____

Does my concept provide any realistic hooks that will make it easy for the
audience to relate to?   ☐ **YES**   ☐ **NO**
What elements will they relate to? Even if you are writing fantasy or science
fiction, you will want to give your audience some element to which they
can connect their sympathy.

_____

_____

_____

Does my concept provide enough tension to hold the audience's interest?
☐ **YES**   ☐ **NO**
What are those sources of tension?

_____

_____

_____

211

EXERCISE

Take the topic of your story, the central idea, and try to improve it or put a special twist to it by asking, "What if?" Simply think of your story, ask "What if?" and then fill in the blank with the most outrageous, unusual thing you can think of. See if this starts you toward a new perspective on your story.

STORY STARTER
"WHAT IF?"

What if the protagonist has an unexpected personal connection to the antagonist?

What if the protagonist's dilemma has consequences for his family, his community or the whole world?

What if the protagonist is forced into an unfamiliar environment?

What if a reticent protagonist is suddenly forced into an active leadership position?

What if the protagonist is faced with a physical challenge (adventure or illness)?

Know Your Perspective on the Story

Once you've chosen your subject matter, it is important to know what your unique perspective on it is. Try this exercise.

EXERCISE
WHAT'S YOUR PERSPECTIVE?

1. Think about what makes your approach to your subject matter unique.
2. If the narrator of your story is a player in the story, what makes that character the one who is most appropriate as storyteller?
3. What elements make up the prism of your perspective?
   - Narrator's voice?
   - Temporal structure of the story?
   - Narrator or protagonist's attitude toward events?
   - Narrative style or structure?

Define Your Basic Idea

Once you've decided on narrative, subject matter and perspective you want to solidify your idea so you have a quick reference card that tells you *exactly* what your story is all about.

EXERCISE

Write your story idea on a single 3 × 5 card, paring it down to its most basic elements. Write only the words or phrases that are absolutely critical to your story. This will help you find the essential pieces and make choices about what to tell, what not to tell, when and how to recount those events.

Use the result of this exercise as a starting place. You may feel a bit underqualified to answer those questions—that's probably why you're reading this book. But this exercise is a good one to give yourself an understanding of your starting point. The exercise is a good way to take an accounting of your knowledge of building plots. You probably came to your decisions using a combination of your existing knowledge of storytelling and plain old instinct. Do not underestimate the power of instinct.

Get to Know Your Characters

Before you can construct a compelling story, you'll need to know about the people who will populate it. Write in-depth character outlines about all your major characters. Use the following exercises to help in your discovery process.

QUICK QUIZ
PHYSICAL DESCRIPTION

Decribe your character's physicality in detail.

What does his face look like?

What sort of build does the character have? Describe his height, weight and stature.

How does the character move?

How does the character dress?

What sort of social or psychological traits are manifested in the character's physicality? How do they appear?

What sort of energy or aura does the character give off? Happy? Carefree? Dour?

QUICK QUIZ
CHARACTER'S SOCIAL STATUS

Look closely at your character's economic stature and how this effects her life.

Consider also how the character feels about that stature—is she eager to leave it behind or content with it?

How does the character's financial status limit or enable the character?

Examine whether or not the character's social standing limits her ability to achieve her goals.

Think about what kind of home life the character had with his family.

Were there brothers and/or sisters? Ages? Factors like birth order will have a profound effect on a person, so look closely at that.

Extended families, particularly grandparents, often influence people's lives. Are there family traditions that impact the character?

Other relatives often have a profound impact on people. Does your character have a favorite uncle or other influential person in her life?

QUICK QUIZ
HISTORY

What sort of social background did your character come from?

What sort of ethnic background influenced the character's history?

What events in the character's past have influenced her personality and behavior?

What events that may have occurred before the character was born influenced the character's personality or behavior?

What event in the past had the most profound effect on your character?

QUICK QUIZ
MOTIVATION

What deep desire is she looking to fulfill?

Does it come from a loss suffered earlier in life or from some missing element in her childhood?

Is there someone to whom she has something to prove?

Is this a long held desire or a newly discovered one?

What pain is the character willing to suffer in pursuit of the goal?

EXERCISE

Write as much as possible about your characters. Divide your thinking into four main areas of consideration:

- physical description
- social background
- emotional/psychological description
- history

EXERCISE

PREWRITING THE BACK STORY

1. Spend time writing in stream of consciousness mode.
2. Filter out the bad ideas and bring structure and cohesiveness to the stream of consciousness work.
3. Overlay a time-line on the events.
4. Find and highlight connections you want to make in the text.
5. Find and highlight exposition that you'll need to insert into the story.

EXERCISE

BRINGING IT ALL TOGETHER FOR THE CLIMAX

Fill in the table below to be sure that all the crucial elements are present at your climax.

Metaphors	
Motifs	
Location	
Characters	
Themes	

Step 2: The Outlining Process

Begin Constructing Your Story Arc

The first step in constructing your outline is defining and laying out the arc. On the following page are several questions you should ask yourself as you do this.

QUICK QUIZ
TESTING THE ARC

What is your protagonist's goal?

What obstacles keep him from that goal?

Who is the antagonist?

What does the protagonist have at stake?

What sacrifices must he make?

If the answers to these questions are unclear or not compelling, you need to reexamine your story.

Evaluate Your Scene Ideas

You've probably got several scene ideas for your story. Now is the time to test them to see if they accomplish your goals.

QUICK QUIZ
SCENE EVALUATION

Is the scene absolutely necessary to the central plot line of the story?

If not, does it constitute a meaningful, necessary subplot or tangent?

If it is a worthwhile subplot or tangent, is this a good place to put it? Would it be more effective somewhere else?

Add Blank Cards as Placeholders for Scenes You Haven't Yet Conceived

Once you've written out all the scenes you've come up with, you can position them on the arc by adding blank cards wherever you feel there is a scene needed.

Evaluate the Pacing of Your Scenes and Your Arc

You want to make sure that the scenes you are constructing are driving your story upward through the rising action, so use these questions to evaluate the pace they are establishing.

QUICK QUIZ
FILLING OUT THE ARC WITH BLANKS, PART I

Ask yourself the following questions to determine if there are missing elements that you need to hold a place for with blank cards.

- Is the level of tension adequate?
- Has the character developed sufficiently?
- Is the arc of a subplot in sync with the overall scene?
- How is the pacing developing?
- Are my major plot points too far apart?

 # QUICK QUIZ
FILLING OUT THE ARC WITH BLANKS, PART II

Some things to look for when deciding whether or not to add blank cards are:

- Does the protagonist or other character need an additional scene to further develop his character?
- Is an element needed in order to preserve or improve the pacing of the overall story?
- Is this a good place for a subplot?
- Is this a good place for a major plot point?

 # QUICK QUIZ
SCENES AND PACING

By following the story arc, you will also be able to judge the pacing of your story. Ask yourself the following questions after plotting your scenes against the story arc:

- Are you moving toward the climax at a pace to keep your audience's attention? Are you saving too many crucial scenes for the end?
- Are there long gaps between the significant events that move your story forward?
- Are you building (enough) tension into your story?

Evaluate Your Conflict

Crucial to a successful story is being confident that your story contains the three main parts of the arc and that they are soundly developed.

QUICK QUIZ
CONFLICT, CRISIS AND RESOLUTION

Is the story's conflict clear to you as the author?

Is the conflict communicated clearly to the audience?

Does the conflict challenge the protagonist?

Does the conflict engender enough sympathy for the protagonist?

Does the conflict lead to a crisis?

Will the crisis have a strong impact on the characters and the audience?

Does the crisis put the protagonist in an all-or-nothing situation?

Does the resolution provide a satisfying, meaningful end to your story?

Does the resolution answer the audience's questions about the protagonist and his journey?

Will the resolution leave your audience sated, but thoughtful?

Now that you've evaluated these three pieces of your arc, define them for yourself as concisely as possible.

EXERCISE
YOUR STORY

Conflict = _____

Crisis = _____

Resolution = _____

Deal with Conflict Weaknesses

If you feel that your conflict is weak or that it doesn't provide enough drama to create sufficient audience investment in your story, try working with some of these elements.

STORY STARTER

What if the protagonist's rival turns out to be his own best friend?

What if the hero is reluctant to confront his domineering father, but challenging his dad is the only way he can become his own man? Look for ways to make these two elements function on multiple levels.

What if the protagonist's goal is in opposition to his morals?

What if the achievement of his goal would result in the loss of something dear?

Define Your Protagonist's Obstacle

Critical to a strong conflict for your protagonist is giving him or her a significant obstacle to overcome and placing that obstacle in such a way that it challenges the character.

 QUICK QUIZ

PLACING THE OBSTACLE

"What would make the attainment of my character's goal the most difficult?" Once this has been identified, the central obstacle in the story will become much clearer.

In *Casablanca* seeing Ilsa safe means that Rick must let her go.

"What is my character's greatest weakness?" Exploiting this vulnerability will provide a rich source of drama.

Hamlet's course of action is clear—expose his uncle. His weakness is his indecisiveness.

"What is my character's greatest fear?" To draw the most depth from your protagonists, they must face their greatest fears.

In *Vertigo*, Scottie's greatest fear is high places, yet he must go into the bell tower to expose the murderer.

"What is my character's greatest strength?" This will give you a clue as to how your protagonist will eventually overcome the obstacle.

In *The Fountainhead*, Howard Roarke is able to succeed only through the tremendous force and conviction of his principles.

Answering these questions should point you right at the obstacle that will give your story the greatest drama and create the utmost tension.

The next step is to define for yourself the type of conflict you are dealing with (see p. 220).

QUICK QUIZ
TYPES OF CONFLICT

To determine the type of conflict in your story ask yourself these questions:

- Which person or people oppose your protagonist in pursuit of his goals?
- What natural forces (if any) does the protagonist confront?
- What societal forces (if any) does the protagonist confront?
- What personal obstacles does the protagonist confront?
- Which of these opposing forces is most primary in the protagonist's efforts to reach his goal?

The answer to this last question will give you the type of central conflict your are dealing with.

EXERCISE

Think about the elements of goal and obstacle in their raw state early in the writing process, before they are integrated into the story. Just as we did with conflict, crisis and resolution, try to sum up each of these two elements in one sentence. Just as a sporting event is billed as Wildcats vs. Spartans, try to boil down your protagonist's goal and obstacle to an X vs. Y equation. For example, "desire for independence vs. father's need for an heir."

Goal = _____

Obstacle = _____

My plot boils down to:

_____ vs. _____

Once again, after you've written this formula down, post it with your other reminders. Slowly, you should begin to see a preliminary sketch of your plot developing.

EXERCISE

Chart your own story's conflict below:

PROTAGONIST	ANTAGONIST	TYPE OF CONFLICT	FACILITATOR OR REPRESENTATIVE FOE

220

Create the Inciting Incident

Once the climax is determined, the next piece to define is the inciting incident.

STORY STARTER

INCITING INCIDENT

Here are some events around which you could build your inciting incident:
- a confrontation between two characters
- the delivery of some piece of news
- a diagnosis
- a natural disaster
- a coincidence

EXERCISE

IDENTIFY AND DEVELOP YOUR INCITING INCIDENT

Start by writing a short description of the inciting incident of your story on a 3 × 5 card.

Evaluate the timing of the incident.

How close to the beginning of the story is it?

_____

What information must you communicate to the audience before it occurs? _____

_____

_____

Evaluate the duration of the incident.

Does it occur in a single scene? _____

How many pages/minutes does it last? _____

Evaluate the magnitude of the incident.

Does it change the course of the story? _____

Does it change the protagonist's life? _____

How? _____

_____

Evaluate the conjunction of the incident.

Which themes are present? _____

Which characters are present? _____

Which motifs and metaphors are present? _____

Create Your Major Plot Points

Having defined your inciting incident and climax, you've got the beginning and ending points of your plot's rising action. Now begin building the pieces in between—the major plot points.

EXERCISE
IDENTIFYING MAJOR PLOT POINTS

Just as we've done with the other parts of the plot, identify each major plot point in your story. If you are writing a novel or screenplay, you should have in the neighborhood of six to ten major plot points. If you are writing a short story, you will probably only have two to five.

Once you've identified these major turning points, write each one onto a single 3 × 5 card. Describe the action of the plot point completely, but concisely, keeping just to the simple facts of the sequence.

We'll use these cards later to construct an in-depth outline of each plot point in your story.

QUICK QUIZ
OBJECTIVE OF MAJOR PLOT POINTS

Determine the objective of each major plot point by looking at several different criteria:

How does this event advance the story?

Does it lead the protagonist and the audience toward the climax?

How does this event increase the tension and suspense of the story?

How does this event affect the development of the characters?

Where does this event need to lead the protagonist emotionally/mentally for the plot point to be successful?

Try Spicing Up Your Plot with a Twist

You can raise the stakes and increase audience investment in your story by giving the plot a twist during the rising action. Try the exercise at the top of p. 223.

Lay Out the Story

At this point you are ready to lay out all the cards which make up your outline (see "Laying Out the Cards," pp. 223-224).

STORY STARTER
PLOT TWISTS

A few of the things a plot twist can do include:

- Raise the stakes for the protagonist
- Throw the audience off the trail
- Act as a catalyst for getting a reluctant protagonist to act
- Deepen the resonance of a character or relationship

STORY STARTER
LAYING OUT THE CARDS

1. Start with the scene or scenes that make up the inciting incident. If there are additional scenes, either leading up to or out of it, put those together in the order in which you want them.

2. Lay out the climactic scene and the scenes that make up the crisis leading to it.

3. Next, place the major plot points in order between the inciting incident and the climax. Be sure to keep together all of the scenes that make up each plot point. Other scenes may ultimately occur within the plot point, but keep the scenes together.

4. Choose one of your subplots that will need to be worked into several places in your plot and place each scene where you think it will work best. Keep in mind that your transitions will need to be smooth and be sure there is some way for the audience to keep track of the subplot as it weaves in and out of the plot.

At this point, you should have a pretty solid and complete plot. Reread each scene in the order you have arranged and try to get a feel for how these elements work together. Since these are the most important pieces of the plot, make sure that they all move well up the rising action of the plot arc.

5. Now begin working in the other subplots. Find natural breaks in the action of the main plot where a detour will be the least disruptive and will have the most positive effect on the rest of the plot. Some subplots will be very sensitive to timing and will need to happen at a particular juncture in the plot. These subplots will be easy to insert.

6. Finally, add the other elements you've worked up: comic relief, character development, exposition and back story. As you work these in, look carefully once more to see if there is a way that you can achieve these objectives within another scene in the drama. If this is possible, clip the character development or other element to the plot or subplot card so that as you are writing the actual scenes you'll know to work in those elements. Sometimes you'll elect not to work an element into another scene. These may be cases where you want the element to stand separately or your plot needs a break in its linear progression.

Find Your Story's Rhythm

The pacing of your story and its rhythm are critical in building a strong arc and an exciting rising action. This exercise asks you to start with stories written by others to get practice at tuning into a story's rhythm.

 EXERCISE
FINDING THE RHYTHM

Part one
Start with short stories. Read several and try to get in touch with the rhythm of the plot. Mark with sticky notes the key moment in each major plot point. Notice the distance between them and their relative intensity.

Part two
After doing this with a couple of short stories, try a play or novel. Mark the key moments in each major plot point, but before you reach the climax, try to predict where it will occur.

Part three
Later, take the same novel or play and try to tune in to its rhythm. Chart the major plot points and try to understand how the author is regulating the rhythm in order to lead his audience to the climax.

Refine the Climax

One way to refine and improve your climax is to have the protagonist make a crucial discovery during that time of heightened tension.

QUICK QUIZ

CLIMACTIC DISCOVERIES

If you make this sort of discovery while writing the climax to your plot, evaluate this new information and decide how it fits into the story.

Is it an interesting diversion, but one that defocuses the climax you've worked so diligently to deliver?

Are the issues your plot has been dealing with somehow different or have they changed from what you originally thought?

Review

Before moving on to step three, review the way you've constructed your story.

STORY STARTER

3 × 5 PROCESS REVIEW

- Collect ideas on cards.
- Put in blank cards where necessary.
- Map the plot on the arc.
- Make notes on the cards.
- Sync up multiple arcs.
- Take inventory.
- Fine-tune.

Step 3: Deepening Your Story's Meaning and Resonance

Find Connections in Your Plot that You May Have Overlooked

Often in the process of creating your plot, you may find great undiscovered connections between characters and events that may add to the subtext or themes of your work. Now is the time to draw them out. Try the exercise at the top of p. 226.

Techniques for Giving Your Story Greater Resonance through Motifs, Metaphors and Narrative Devices

To create the truly remarkable story, draw out certain elements to give your story a deeper thematic structure and resonance. Try the story starters on pp. 226-227 to see if any of them work in your plot.

EXERCISE

To help you in finding the hidden or undiscovered connections in your work, number the cards you've created in the order in which you think you want them to come in your outline. This can be just a rough outline. Then, take the cards and shuffle them just as you would any deck of cards until they are well mixed up. Then randomly lay out the cards one by one. Start with any two cards. Examine them to see if there's any connection between these two scenes.

- What sort of connections do you see between them?
- Could they happen sequentially?

Then add another card and ask the same questions again.

STORY STARTER
UNIFYING ELEMENTS

Do the characters share certain jobs or professions that have a distinctive environment around which you could build the location for your story?

Is there a characteristic of the town or city in which the story takes place that could unify the elements in your plot? Certain cities or regions have distinct characteristics that make them unique. Texas, Alaska, the Rust Belt, the French Riviera all have qualities that make them unique.

Is there an ethnic or immigrant sensibility that defines the characters and their world?

What traditions do the characters come out of that might provide an interesting backdrop for your story?

STORY STARTER
UNIFYING DEVICES

- Farm or other homestead
- River
- Road
- Mountain
- Journey
- City or town
- Narrator (first or third person)
- State or country

STORY STARTER
PARALLEL STORIES

Are the story beats too short, and does the drama jump back and forth between the two stories too rapidly or too frequently?

Are the stories equally well-developed, or is one clearly stronger and more compelling than the other?

Are transitions between the two stories smooth, or do they sap momentum from each other at every shift?

Are the stories adequately different?

Are the connections between the stories clearly drawn? Does it ever become apparent how the two stories relate?

STORY STARTER
TEMPORAL ORGANIZATION

Is your tale most compelling when told chronologically?

Which moment in the plot is most important—where will it be most effective dramatically?

Is there a temporal element that can act as a structuring device?

Using the 3×5 cards, rearrange the sequences of your plot randomly and see if anything useful reveals itself.

GLOSSARY

Allegory—A story or representation in which a person, event or idea stands for itself and for something else; a complex metaphor. Types of allegories include *parables*, which are religious in nature; *fables*, in which animals act out moral lessons; and some forms of *satire*.

Ambiguity—Uncertainty and/or doubtfulness in a story's intention or meaning. Refers to situation in which more than one interpretation of words or actions is possible. The word comes from a Latin root which means "to wander" or "to waver."

Antagonist—One who opposes another in a conflict. In literature it signifies the main character's principal opponent, often the villain. Any person in a story who comes in conflict with the hero (or protagonist) is an antagonist.

Arc—The trajectory of a plot from beginning to end. The use of the word relates to the shape of an arc, which is a gently curving segment of a circle. The ascending arc is analogous with the rising tension and drama of a story as it proceeds toward the climax and the descending arc after the climax as the story relaxes into its resolution.

Archetype—Inherited ideas or ways of thinking derived from the experiences of a culture and present in the collective subconscious of that group. It includes a collection of myths, icons and other symbols that have become recognizable in the literature of a culture.

Aristotle—A Greek philosopher who lived in the fourth century B.C. He was a student of Plato and teacher of Alexander the Great. His lectures, known as *Poetics*, had a profound effect on literature and served to codify many of the concepts of storytelling that endure to this day.

228

Back story—This refers to events that occurred in the characters' lives before the commencement of the story being told. This information is crucial to the writer's understanding of the characters and their situation. It is also frequently used within the text of the story as exposition or to add depth and resonance.

Beat—A single dramatic or emotional event in a story.

Catharsis—From a Greek work meaning "to clean or purify," this describes the effect of emotional purification that audiences often receive from experiencing drama. This emotional release purges the audience of feelings of anxiety or fear as they participate in the make-believe emotions evoked by the story. The audience thus experiences an emotional and spiritual rebirth as a result of interaction with the story.

Cause and effect—This concept is the essence of drama. It is also basic to universal order, and it can be argued that all action is the basis of cause. Everything that happens is a cause. Everything that results from that action is the effect. This effect creates another cause and so forth. The writer relies on this bedrock foundation to create the story, and the audience uses it to understand the events presented to them.

Climax—The point when a story's conflict comes to its moment of greatest intensity. In this moment the conflict is somehow resolved. It is also the apex of the story's arc.

Comic relief—A moment of humor occuring at some point in a serious or tragic story. The moment of comic relief is an intentional device used to relieve tension and inject a fresh perspective into the story.

Complication and denouement—According to Aristotle, these two elements make up the overall movement of drama. Complication is everything that happens leading up to the climax, and denouement is everything that happens after the climax.

Conflict—The characters or forces that are in opposition in any plot. Conflict is the issue out of which the entire drama grows; without conflict, there is no plot. All other elements of the plot grow out of this central issue.

Conflict, types of—Conflict can be broadly parsed into four basic types, described by the nature of the forces that stand in opposition to the protagonist: protagonist vs. antagonist, protagonist vs. society, protagonist vs. nature, protagonist vs. himself.

Conjunction—The place or time where various forces in the plot come together. These may be forces of circumstance, characters or conflicts. The synchronization of these elements so that they come together in a moment of conjunction is a reliable way to increase the dramatic tension of a plot.

Crisis—The turning point in a plot where the story is set on an irreversible course toward the climax.

Episodic plots—Stories made up of several loosely related, but thematically similar scenes, events or even complete stories.

Epistolary novel—A book composed of a series of letters. The epistolary novel gives the author an opportunity to present the points of view of different characters. The style was popular in eighteenth-century Europe.

Exposition—The part of the plot that explains or illuminates the story's events, characters and circumstances.

Extrapolation—The act of estimating or inferring the events to come based on the characteristics or tenor of the preceeding events.

First person—A story that is related by one of the participants in the drama and told exclusively from that character's perspective.

Flashback—A narrative device in which the main course of the drama is interrupted by a scene that took place in an earlier time frame, prior to the commencement of the plot.

Framing device—A narrative device in which the first and last scene in the plot occur in a different time frame from the scenes that make up the central action of the story.

Goal—The protagonist's objective in the course of the plot.

Inciting incident—The event that establishes the conflict and sets the protagonist upon the path toward the climax. This event is always the first major occurrence in the story and is the story's first major plot point.

Interpolation—The act of determining the characteristics of an event by evaluating the qualities of the events that will occur immediately before and immediately after it.

Limited narrator—A narrator who may or may not be a participant in the plot, but whose perspective on events is limited to his own personal knowledge and is therefore incomplete.

Major plot points—The central events that make up the story's rising action and during which the protagonist deals with the issues of the story's conflict. These plot points may occur over one or more scenes, but they comprise a distinct portion of the plot arc and a complete piece of the story's overall movement.

Metaphor—An analogy in which something is compared to another thing to which there is no literal relationship. It is a means of ascribing certain characteristics to something or someone in an imaginative, meaningful way.

Mood—A state of mind, a feeling or a prevailing emotion in a scene or story. It may also describe the atmosphere or tone of the story's subject or its language.

Motif—A recurring element in a story. It may be a visual icon, a characteristic of language or a persistent use of certain metaphors.

Nonlinear plot—Any plot in which the sequence of events is told out of chronological order.

Objective—The protagonist's goal or desire in the story. This objective is the motivating force for the protagonist and the primary source of forward momentum in the plot.

Obstacle—The elements in a plot that oppose the protagonist's quest for a goal. These can be the primary elements in the conflict or other hurdles injected into a story to raise the dramatic stakes.

Oral tradition—The way stories were told and preserved before they were written down. Early civilizations preserved their histories and legends through their oral repetition. Certain members of the community were charged with remembering and telling these stories. The unreliable nature of human memory often allowed the stories to grow and change as they were passed from storyteller to storyteller over time.

Oulipians—A group of radical European writers who wrote in the 1960s. Believing that the novel had been perfected, they experimented with the structure of drama and broke many of the Aristotelian conventions in the pursuit of new ideas and literary forms.

Parallel plots—Stories in which two or more plots are developed separately, but concurrently. The stories may or may not converge at some point. Often they explore similar issues, but in different time frames or locations and with different characters.

Plot—The arrangement of events in a story to elicit a desired effect on the audience. A series of events organized to progress from inciting incident through rising action to climax and finishing with the resolution.

Poetics—A collection of essays by the Greek philosopher Aristotle that codified the elements of drama and that has endured through more than two thousand years.

Point of view—The perspective of a story or a character, that expresses the character's or story's feelings or attitudes toward the subject. A point of view can be limited to the knowledge of one particular character or that of an omniscient narrator.

Protagonist—The leading character or hero (heroine) in a novel. From the Greek for "first combatant."

Raising the stakes—The introduction of an obstacle or a plot twist that increases the characters' emotional and physical obstacles and the audience's emotional investment in the story.

Recognition, reversal, suffering—According to Aristotle, these three elements must be present in a story in order for it to be considered a complex plot. These three elements signify the emotional change or evolution in the protagonist, which Aristotle felt was crucial for satisfying drama.

Red herring—A dramatic device through which the audience is given a false clue in order to throw them temporarily off the trail. Used most often in mystery stories. The red herring poses an obstacle for the audience that will ideally cause them to put more thought into the story and thus increase their emotional investment.

Resolution—The portion of the plot that occurs after the climax; also the downward curving portion of the plot arc. During this phase of the plot, the events and circumstances that have been examined in the plot are wrapped up and conclusions are reached.

Resonance—The deep and enduring impact of a story. The emotional aftertaste of a story caused by the story's connection with larger themes and ideas about life.

Reversal—An emotional turnabout in a character caused by the experience of some event or internal realization.

Rhythm—The emotional or physical pacing of a story. Also, the story's dramatic ebb and flow.

Rising action—The part of the plot between the inciting incident and the climax. During this phase of the plot, the conflict is addressed and complications and obstacles are overcome.

Setting—The place, location or environment, as well as the time period, in which a story takes place.

Subplot—A minor or ancillary sequence of events in a story. Frequently used to highlight or expand on elements of the primary plot.

Subtext—The underlying theme or message of a story. While inexplicit, the subtext is explored through use of metaphors and symbolism.

Suspense—A state of mental excitement, indecision or uncertainty in a story. The sense of tension and anticipation created in an audience by the characters and events in a story.

Suspension of disbelief—The audience's voluntary decision to accept the laws and tenets of the story's dramatic world. This forgiving attitude allows the author to create worlds and explore ideas that might not stand up to close scrutiny in the real world.

Tangent—A portion of a plot that veers off from the linear progression of events. Often used to explore themes, characters or expository elements of the story.

Three-act structure—A classic structure of modern plays and movies that involves three distinct sections of the plot and their corresponding dramatic movements. Act one is usually the setup, culminating in the inciting incident; act two encompasses the rising action of the story; and act three is the resolution.

Time bomb effect—The introduction of a piece of information that increases tension or creates concern in the audience. The consequences of the information are not played out until much later in the story, creating suspense.

Tragedy—A calamity or disastrous event. Also, a type of literary form in which a hero experiences a fall and gains recognition or wisdom through the experience of the ensuing events.

Twist—An unexpected dramatic event that alters the course of events or introduces a new complication, often raising the dramatic stakes for the characters and the audience.

Unifying element—A device that draws together the themes, ideas, motifs or metaphors of a story, coordinating and synchronizing them for greater dramatic effect. This can be a common setting like a road, a temporal device like a story encompassing a single day or another dramatic element.

INDEX

More Great Titles
for Storytelling Success!

1999 Novel & Short Story Writer's Market—Get the information you need to get your short stories and novels published. You'll discover listings on fiction publishers, plus original articles on fiction writing techniques; detailed subject categories to help you target appropriate publishers; and interviews with writers, publishers and editors! *#10581/$22.99/656 pages/paperback*

Writing in Flow—Learning how to write in flow is the key to enhancing your creativity. Also known as "the writer's high," it allows time, frustration and writer's block to melt away. Through clear, insightful instruction, author Susan K. Perry, Ph.D., shows you how to both achieve and maintain flow in your own work. *#10622/$19.99/272 pages/hardcover*

Writing Fiction Step by Step—Award winning teacher and writer Josip Novakovich provides more than 200 exercises that can be connected in a multitude of combinations. Each chapter of this ingenious book will push the writer to forge engrossing short stories and novels. *#49034/$17.99/288 pages/paperback*

You Can Write a Novel—Veteran novelist James V. Smith helps beginners make their writing dreams come true with his unique "writer's toolkit." He begins by breaking down the complex process of novel writing into simple pieces, showing writers how to create memorable characters, gripping plots and vivid settings. *#10573/$12.99/128 pages/paperback*

Conflict, Action & Suspense—Keep your stories spellbinding by using devices such as plot twists, description and pacing—all the way to a gripping and satisfying close. Instructor and lecturer William Noble can teach you how to create these stories full of drama, tension and surprise. *#10607/$12.00/185 pages/paperback*

20 Master Plots (And How to Build Them)—Presents 20 fundamental plots that recur through all fiction—with analysis and examples—outlining benefits and warnings, for you to adapt and elaborate in your own fiction. *#10366/$17.99/240 pages*